Jacob Harris Patton

Political Parties in the United States

Their History and Influence

Jacob Harris Patton

Political Parties in the United States
Their History and Influence

ISBN/EAN: 9783337143534

Printed in Europe, USA, Canada, Australia, Japan

Cover: Foto ©Suzi / pixelio.de

More available books at **www.hansebooks.com**

POLITICAL PARTIES

IN THE

UNITED STATES

THEIR

HISTORY AND INFLUENCE

BY

JACOB HARRIS PATTON, M.A., Ph.D.

AUTHOR OF

"FOUR HUNDRED YEARS OF AMERICAN HISTORY," "NATURAL
RESOURCES OF THE UNITED STATES," "POLITICAL
ECONOMY FOR AMERICAN YOUTH, WRITTEN
FROM AN AMERICAN STANDPOINT"

"Truth is not Partisan"

NEW YORK

NEW AMSTERDAM BOOK COMPANY

156 FIFTH AVENUE

1896

N DIRECTORY
PRINTING AND BOOK BINDING COMPANY
NEW YORK

PREFACE.

The Author of this monograph never held an office, nor excepting by his vote aided others to obtain one; and in writing it, his only motive has been to direct the attention of the intelligent and thoughtful to the different historical phases of our political life and National policy—Foreign and Domestic. He invites the attention more especially of comparatively young men who for years, perhaps, have exercised the privileges of citizenship, and also of those who are about to enter upon such duties; in addition he extends the invitation to a large and worthy class of intelligent citizens of foreign birth, who are presumed to be less informed on these subjects than the native-born. Thoughtful citizens, as well as true statesmen, are recognizing more and more the importance of our younger men being well informed on the political, the moral, the financial, and the industrial questions of the day.

In writing a "History of the American People" the Author has had occasion to study the principles held and put in practice, during the Nation's life, by our different political organizations. In the present work, which has grown out of that, his

attention has been directed to these parties—The
Democratic, the Federal, the Whig and the Republican. The democratic being the first to take
form and to remain till the present time. In order
to understand fully the phases of character pertaining
to any one political party, it is essential, likewise, to
have a knowledge of the antagonistic principles
actuating its rivals. By "politics," here so briefly
treated, is meant not only the influence and outgrowth of legislative measures, advocated or opposed, but likewise the manner in which political
power has often been attained and kept.

This monograph is not written in the interest
or spirit of partisanship—Truth is not partisan; its
nature forbids. Facts are immutable; prejudices,
even, cannot change them: of those here introduced, some are *historical,* some are *notorious;*—
the latter are equally true with the former, though
they may not be found in the books. In illustration of this remark may be adduced the summary
of results found in the last three pages of this
book. If statements or sentiments herein seem
harsh or severe, their severity consists in their
truthfulness.

For the facts derived from our Nation's history
references are made, that the reader may verify
them; those which have been called "notorious"
are so well known that intelligent citizens will not
challenge their accuracy.   J. H. P.

NEW YORK CITY, April, 1896.

CONTENTS.

INTRODUCTION.

POLITICAL PARTIES.

INTRODUCTION.

We give with that of its rivals a history of one of
the oldest existing political organizations in the
world, yet one which has passed its life within the
youngest of the family of nations. We design to
trace, concisely, the causes of its remarkable vitality,
what innate principle permeated its life and gave it
strength ; and also to note how, even on account of
the combination of dissimilar elements in its inner
life, it has in greater or less degree retained its hold
upon the American people.

For sixty years—from the inauguration of Thomas
Jefferson to that of Abraham Lincoln—it had a pre-
dominant influence in the councils of this nation,
and during that period largely moulded its destinies ;
either when in absolute control, or, negatively, as a
most determined opponent of the policy of its rival,
under whatever name, that for the time being
wielded the national authority. During these three-
score years its prominent political rival held national
rule, nominally for only *eight years,* and in truth

even then but partially. This was owing to the deaths, while in office, of the two Presidents belonging to that rival organization, as the Vice-Presidents who succeeded to the office carried out only in part the avowed policy of the party to which they owed their election. It is interesting to note, however, that this venerable organization, whose age is more than fourscore and ten years, often twits its stalwart rival of to-day, whose age is a score and a half, with having lived too long.

Differences of Opinion.—There were elements in existence, even in colonial times, that led to differences of opinions and customs among the colonists. These differences had their origin in the motherland, and in consequence the Puritan of New England retained his prejudices against the cavalier of Virginia, and the latter reciprocated them most cordially. In a modified form these disturbing elements passed over from the colonial period into that of the nation, wherein in numerous ways they have had influence.

The common people of the eastern colonies were far more intelligent than those of the same class in the southern. In the former, public schools, which were unknown in the latter, had been in existence about one hundred and thirty years when the Declaration of Independence was made. (See *Four Hundred Years of American History* pp. 124, 126, 127, 322, 857–859.) The intercourse, in business or otherwise, between the eastern colonies and the southern was quite limited during the colonial period. The former had much more intimate relations with the middle ones. To the latter, before the Revolution, great numbers of eastern people migrated from time to time, especially those who sympathized with the Presbyterians ; these settled principally in New Jersey and Pennsylvania. The non-interference by the magistrates with religious opinions or forms of worship in the middle colonies was in marked contrast with their interference as practised in both the eastern and southern. The liberality of the Dutch in New York was proverbial, while the demand for equal rights in religious affairs was one of the cardinal principles of the Presbyterians of New Jersey and Pennsylvania, in which demand the Quakers of the latter colony were in full sympathy.

Prejudices Partially Removed.—The prejudices mentioned above began to wear away when the leading men of the colonies became better known one to another. The oppressions of the mother country compelled the people to unite in their own defence, and for the first time their leading men met in council as delegates from their respective colonies. Thus was constituted the Congress of October 1, 1765, held in New York for the purpose of devising measures to vindicate their rights, which were about to be infringed by the famous Stamp act.

These prominent gentlemen were well informed,

and in the main had enjoyed similar courses of
study in their education, the influence of which became a solvent, to a certain extent, of the prejudices
cherished by both parties. Mutual interests produced a kindred feeling that was blended with a
growing love of country, which led to an enlightened patriotism. The latter, in becoming more and
more comprehensive, achieved success in vindicating
the independence of the colonies, and in establishing a nation that controls a continent.

It was not till the common soldiers from the various colonies came together as patriots, in Washington's army, that the prejudices of this less intelligent class began to manifest themselves. The
officers of the army labored hard to overcome these
evils, which cropped out when "the men of one
colony hesitated to serve with those of another, or
under officers not of their own choosing," or of their
own colony. Provincial distinctions that caused
dissatisfaction and sectional jealousies sprang up
between the troops of the different colonies, while
a disposition was common among the Southern
officers to disparage the Eastern soldiers. "The
Southern troops [from Virginia and Maryland],
comprising the regiments south of the Delaware,
looked with unkind feelings on those of New
England, . . . and made them the object of ill-
disguised derision among their fellows. . . .
Their scarlet and buff uniforms contrasted vividly
with the rustic attire of the yeoman battalions of
the East." (*Irving's Life of Washington.*)

Though these prejudices and bickerings had their origin in trifling causes, they were none the less annoying and had a bad influence.

The Need of Closer Union.—During the Revolution intercourse became more frequent than hitherto between the people of the several colonies, and after peace was concluded this element continued in business relations until it became evident to thinking minds that there should be a closer union between these independent States. Though there were many clashing interests (see *Four Hundred Years of American History*, pp. 563-565), the people of the respective States magnanimously agreed, for the good of the whole, to relinquish their special interests, and they chose delegates to the convention which framed the Constitution of the United States (1787). At this period, though there was much discussion as to the merits of the Constitution, it was adopted, and under it George Washington was inaugurated President (April 30, 1789). There appears also at this time to have been an unusual degree of sympathy between the different sections of the Union, but soon after the inauguration differences arose, which will be treated further on in this narrative.

Political Equality and Intelligence.—From the inauguration of Washington onward, the United States Government, in respect to the management of its internal affairs, holds a unique position among the nations of Christendom. It was the only one so far in advance of the times as to recognize the right of voting to be in the man himself, *as a man*, and not in a property qualification. This position placed all voters on a political equality, and endowed every citizen with a dignity never before so universal, and one which the intelligent were able to appreciate. The latter, under such circumstances, became conscious of their own responsibility in respect to the management of public affairs, which they themselves by means of their votes could indirectly influence. The thoughtful reader will infer from this inauguration of political equality the vast importance of American voters being intelligent and able to do their own thinking, and, if occasion requires, to detect the misrepresentations of unscrupulous partisans, who profess to be laboring only for the good of the dear people.

Classes Based on Intelligence.—One hundred years ago, as is the case to-day, two general classes were found among the American people— the intelligent and the unintelligent. On questions of public affairs, political or otherwise, the intelligent usually read and think for themselves, and though equally well-wishing, they often differ in their opinions as to the best mode of promoting the interests of the people at large. It is only among the citizens of superior general knowledge that political parties originate. The less informed, from the nature of the case, are unable to grasp the intricacies of

many of the public questions that often arise, and
consequently they are inclined to adopt as their
own the opinions of those superior to them in intelligence with whom they come in contact. They
are, moreover, liable to become the victims of designing partisans or demagogues, who often first
create prejudices in their minds and afterward foster
the same by misrepresentations, and in this manner
secure the votes of their dupes. It is sad to note
how often in American history unintelligent but
well-meaning citizens have been and are influenced
by plausible theorists to vote against their own interests. The latter class, because of their numbers,
unfortunately, holds the balance of power in elections between the two main parties into which the
more intelligent portion of the people are divided.

The Doctrinaires.—Intelligent readers who for
the last fifteen years have kept themselves in touch
with the policy of encouraging the various industries
of the Nation, have, no doubt, noticed the persistent
putting forth of certain financial and economical
theories by a class of writers, known in the literary
world as *doctrinaires.* They are defined as those
" who would apply to political or practical concerns,
the abstract doctrines or theories of their own philosophical systems." This class of writers, both
American and English, have had, for the most part,
no experience in practical business affairs. The fallacies of their theories, thus elaborately put forth,
have been pointed out again and again by competent writers and speakers, and who were familiar

with the conditions of our mechanical industries, while they have also been absolutely repudiated by practical, level-headed statesmen. Notwithstanding all this, the advocates of these theories, ignoring their perfect refutations, continued to press them upon the attention of the American people, as coolly as if the truths of their statements had not even been called into question.

The reader may ask, how can this fact be accounted for? The answer is : Funds were furnished to bear the expense of public speakers and publications, especially during presidential canvasses, by interested parties, some of whom were Democratic free-traders and others were foreign manufacturers and exporters of their products to the United States. In consequence, the whole land was flooded with pamphlets inculcating free-trade notions, and which incessantly proclaimed the great blessings that would accrue, especially to the "poor man ;" that is, to those who worked for wages, if the National Government would only put in practice their theories. It is not very strange, therefore, that the persistent reiteration for years, of these theories and promises should have influenced multitudes of American citizens—in other respects fairly intelligent—to entertain the impression, that perhaps, after all, there might be some truth in these free-trade notions. The result was that great numbers of wage-earners, thus influenced, voted the Democratic ticket in 1892, and thus gave the free-traders an opportunity to virtually put in practice their theories.

POLITICAL PARTIES.

I.

NEUTRALITY.

The Trying Period, 1789-1801.—It would seem, when the circumstances are taken into consideration, that the most trying period of our national existence was the first twelve years. We had just entered upon the experiment of a uniform and united government. The Constitution had been adopted by the requisite number of States, but in some of them by a very small majority; and in consequence there was a strong undercurrent of half-expressed opposition, while many were watching for defects in its application to the details of government, and others manifested a carping rather than a friendly spirit. In truth, the latter secretly expected it to fail, if they did not half wish it. These leaders were, perhaps, unconscious of the presumption in their own minds that, as their cherished theories had not been embodied in that instrument, it would fail in its adaptation to the wants of the people, which wants they professed to thoroughly understand. In addition to these difficulties were others growing out of the wars then carried on with but little intermission between the nations of Europe, during the greater portion of the eight years of Washington's administration, and also through that of his successor, John Adams.

The government was sorely perplexed in dealing with these complications; Washington himself, Vice-President Adams, Alexander Hamilton, Secretary of the Treasury, and General Henry Knox, Secretary of War, were decidedly in favor of the United States standing aloof from the quarrels and wars between other nations. This policy of neutrality, after careful deliberation, was formally adopted, and a proclamation to that effect was issued by the President. Time has shown the wisdom of that decision, and we have ever since remained strictly neutral under such circumstances. What could have been more ruinous to a nation only a few years old, and just beginning to recover from the evil effects of an exhausting war of eight years, and in addition weighed down by an enormous debt, than to have taken part in a general war among the nations of Europe? "Washington's administration had the hard task of maintaining statesman-like steadiness and wisdom in establishing sound precedents for the details of the government under the Constitution." (*Prof. Sumner's Life of Jackson*, p. 11.)

The Clubs.—Birth of Democratic Party.— During these troublous times there were numbers in the United States, among whom were a few prominent

statesmen, who were in sympathy with revolutionary
and republican France, and in favor of aiding that
power in its conflicts with England. To promote
that object a " Democratic Society " was formed in
Philadelphia—the seat of the national government
at that time. This "Society" was modeled after
the famous radical clubs in Paris, known as the
" Jacobins," whose object was to oppose the government by secret measures and intrigues; the extremists of the revolution, and the factious minority
of the later republic. Such was the origin of the
present Democratic Party.

This association was designed at the time to oppose Washington's administration in its policy of
neutrality in respect to the wars then raging in
Europe. In order to accomplish the object more
fully, affiliated societies were formed throughout
the State of Pennsylvania and also in other States,
(*Hildreth, U. S. IV.* pp. 424, 503; *Irving's Washington,* II. p. 708; *Patton's American People,* p.
583).

The formation of these associations—variously
called " Republican " or " Democratic "—attracted
the attention of the Parisian clubs, and "The Society
of Charleston, S. Carolina, on its own application,
was recognized by the Jacobin Club of Paris as an
affiliated branch."

Within these clubs the turbulent men of the time
found congenial quarters. At first many well meaning citizens sympathized with Republican France in
what was deemed her struggle for liberty; but her

terrible atrocities soon cost her many of these friends; yet for these excesses the extremists in the clubs found apologies. Says Prof. Sumner, (*Jackson*, p.11), — " The Republican (Democratic) party in 1796, was filled with ill-informed and ill-regulated sympathy for the French Revolutionists, and if it could have had its way, it would, under the lead of refugee editors, filled with rancor and ignorant zeal, have committed the United States to close relations with France, and by importing Jacobinism into this country, have overthrown constitutional liberty here." On this same point says Von Holst—(*Constitutional Hist.*, I. p. 107),—"The French Revolution introduced from abroad an element which kept up excitement during many years at the boiling point;" and "The farther France proceeded, by the adoption of brutal measures, the more rank was the growth in the United States of the most radical teaching; and the more attentively the legislators of France listened to the fierce cry for blood, the more boldly did demagogism, in its most repulsive form, rage in the United States."

Policy of Washington.—It is proper to notice here the difficulties of the situation at that time. Discussions arose in Congress in respect to our relations with foreign countries, especially on the complaints of our merchants that their ships were captured by the belligerents of Europe—by the cruisers of both France and England. The Democratic clubs, taking their cue from their patron, Jefferson, who had returned from France where he had been our Minister, and who was deeply imbued with French radicalism, were ardent partisans of "The Great Republic," and were inclined to connive at her harsh treatment of our merchant marine, and had equally strong prejudices against England, for whom they tolerated no excuse. While, on the other hand, President Washington and his cabinet, with the exception of Jefferson, desired to be strictly neutral in respect to the European belligerents; deeming it madness for our nation to join in an alliance with either of the parties, and thus expose still more to the hazards of war our merchant vessels, which, at the time, had much the greater share of the carrying trade of the world. Belonging to a neutral nation—though often interfered with by the cruisers of the belligerents—they managed not only to carry merchandise for the French and English, but to supply Germany and Russia with manufactured goods and raw material. It must not be inferred that Washington and the Federal party did not sympathize with France in a struggle for genuine liberty as they understood it; but she had passed far beyond that into anarchy and truculent bloodshed, the most terrible told in history— with that they did not sympathize. The turbulent portion of the clubs continued untiring in efforts to accomplish their ends, and sometimes adopted measures that the well-meaning deprecated; but still many of the latter remained members and were pointed out as leaders when they were only figure-heads; the turbulents being the ruling spirits.

The respectables mildly protested, but did not openly condemn, and thus virtually threw their influence in favor of these objectionable actions.

A Secret Influence.—Thomas Jefferson, though at the time a member of the cabinet as Secretary of State, exercised his influence against the policy of neutrality in an underhand and secret manner, characterizing it in his private letters as "sneaking neutrality." In virtue of his office, he held frequent intercourse with the French minister, "Citizen" Genet, but in a peculiar manner—a sort of diplomatic flirtation, leading the latter to believe, as he alleged, that Jefferson was in favor of giving France material aid in her contest with England. But when the policy of neutrality became popular, Jefferson changed his course, and treated the French Minister in a manner which caused the latter to charge him with double dealing; after pretending to be his friend, with "having an official language, and a language confidential." (*Hildreth*, IV. p. 435.) How different would have been the position of the United States, if the policy desired by Jefferson and his followers had been carried out ! We should have become embroiled in European wars and complications, and who can tell when or where these entanglements would have ended? Certainly, under such conditions, the damages to the nation would have been exceedingly great.

This decision in respect to neutrality was the first instance in which the newly organized government declared its policy as an independent and self-

respecting nation ; and George Washington stands
forth grandly, when he demands for the United
States an honored position among the nations of the
world—the spirit of colonial dependence now vanished forever.

Change of Front.—Some ten years afterward, on
becoming President, Jefferson in his inaugural approved the policy of neutrality, and in a neat for-
mula announced it as follows :   " Honest friendship
with all nations—entangling alliances with none."
(*Randall's Jefferson*, II., p. 632.)   Not a reference
was made to what Washington and Adams had
done in sustaining the dignity of the nation, but an
assumption of the policy as his own ; and his admirers have quoted these words ever since as one of
the fundamentals of their political faith, while they
as an organization opposed neutrality, until its manifest advantages overcame all opposition, and became popular.

It is very noticeable throughout American history,
in how many instances this political organization
has opposed measures which by their excellence
have since received the sanction of leading minds
among the people, and in consequence become the
fixed policy of the National government.

Another instance in which the same influences
were exerted against Washington's administration,
was in relation to Jay's, or the second treaty with
England; (*Patton's American People*, p. 587.)
space forbids our going into detail. Says Professor
Sumner :—" Jay's Treaty was a masterpiece of di-

plomacy, considering the time and the circumstances
of this country. Those who objected to it could
propose nothing but a policy of bluster, which the
country was not prepared to follow up, or the imbe-
cile device of a commercial war." Again, " Washington succeeded in maintaining neutrality by this
treaty, but at the cost of bitter hostility at home."
When, in consequence of these and other objectionable doings of the clubs, Washington thought proper
to refer to them because of their violence, Jefferson wrote that it was " wonderful indeed that the
President should have permitted himself to be the
organ of such attack on the freedom of discussion,
the freedom of writing, printing and publishing." He
continues, and fears lest the " honest and political
errors " of Washington might cause the people to
exclaim, " Curse on his virtues!—they have undone
the country." (*Morse's Jefferson.*) It is remarkable that the principles involved in these " political
errors " of George Washington have become the
political truisms of our land.

Thus during the first three Presidential terms
the machinery of the National government was
adjusted and put in motion, and for sixty years—
till the Rebellion—it moved on seemingly without
friction. The people, temperate, industrious and
economical, secured unprecedented material success, and that in spite of drawbacks, caused, often,
by injudicious legislation, which affected their
finances and their industrial interests.

II.

GOVERNMENT AND THE GOVERNED.

Democracy and Demagogism.—The aphorism, " The world is governed too much," had its origin in the theories of Thomas Jefferson. In his *Life* by Morse, he is quoted (pp. 90, 91), when writing of Shay's rebellion in Massachusetts in 1786. " A little rebellion now and then is a good thing : . . . An observation of this truth should render honest Republican governors so mild in their punishment of rebellions as not to discourage them too much."—"It is a medicine necessary for the sound health of government." Again, "God forbid we should ever be twenty years without such a rebellion. . . . What signify a few lives lost in a century or two ? The tree of liberty must be refreshed from time to time with the blood of patriots and tyrants. It is its natural manure." If the writer of this had had a prophet's vision of the terrible scenes enacted (in 1861–1865) in a rebellion, which was the legitimate, though extreme outgrowth of his own doctrine of State Sovereignty, and of the principles of the famous Resolutions of 1798 (p. 34), instead of rejoicing he would have recoiled from the sight in horror ; for he was a man, kind and humane.

Still further (1787), "The basis of our govern-

ments, being the opinion of the people, the very
first object should be to keep that right ; were it
left to me to decide whether we have a government
without newspapers, or newspapers without a government, I should not hesitate a moment to prefer
the latter." Intelligent people would repudiate
such sentiments, both on the ground of their absur-
dity, and of their innate evil to the community at
large. He illustrates still further, saying, "Societies exist under three forms : 1. Without government, as among our Indians. 2. Under governments, wherein the will of every one has a just influence. 3. Under governments of force. It is a
problem not clear in my mind, that the *first* condition is not the best." Is it strange that under such
teachings and influence the disorderly elements of
society gravitate toward a political organization
which reverences the author of such sentiments almost as a demigod, and whose leaders use his name
as a talisman? It may be said the rank and file of
the Democracy do not read these sentiments of Jefferson ; yet they are under the influence of leaders
who are imbued with his political theories, unless
they belie their professions, when they celebrate his
birthday, and extol him as preëminently the greatest statesman this nation has produced, and as such,
demand for him the homage of their followers.
Says Professor Von Holst, already quoted on this
period of our history : "The philosophical reveries
about the goodness of human nature in the abstract,
had developed in the concrete (or practice) in such

manner that nine-tenths of the worst elements of society were the promoters of that party who proclaim that the 'world is governed too much'; they dislike wholesome restraint." Again: "From the time that the blessings of the Constitution began to be felt, the lower strata of the population of the larger cities commenced to swell the ranks of the Anti-Federalists." "Sounding phrases and all the arts of the demagogue could here be made use of with the greatest success." (Vol. I. p. 124.)

Insurrection Encouraged.—The whiskey insurrection in Western Pennsylvania (1794), was for a time a great boon to the opponents of Washington's administration (*Patton's American People*, I., 585–587). The Democratic clubs by indirect means encouraged these insurgents; first they found fault with the government for taking measures to suppress the rebellion, though it had been in existence more than a year; then they proclaimed that it was too strong to be put down, meanwhile asserting that the insurgents numbered 16,000 men; this latter statement was designed to have influence with the militia, who were liable to be called out to quell the insurrection. But the government, notwithstanding, raised an army of 15,000 men. This was judicious, as thus the shedding of blood was prevented, for all hope of resisting so large a force vanished; and as soon as this army crossed the mountains the insurgent leaders fled the country, and their deluded followers at once submitted. Now the opposition raised the cry that all this was an unnecessary expense, and that the *poor people* would in consequence be burdened with taxes.

Jefferson's evident sympathy with the whiskey insurrectionists was consistent with what he wrote in relation to Shay's rebellion just quoted, and with his views of "too much government." In his private letters he chuckled over an absurd story "that one thousand men could have cut off their whole force in a thousand places in the Alleghenies;" and "that though the people let them pass quietly, they were objects of their laughter, not of their fear." (*Works*, IX., p. 112.) Washington himself expressed the opinion that the members of the clubs encouraged this outbreak. The more violent evidently favored the insurrection, though the more moderate deprecated extreme measures. The protests of the latter had, however, little influence, as the protestors remained in the societies, some even as officers, thus imparting a certain kind of respectability to the more turbulent.

From this time forth the term "Democratic," became prominently known in American politics. The ultras of the party assumed the name—they being the most bitter opponents of the general policy of Washington's administration—while the more moderate adopted the term "Democratic-Republican," which name they sometimes have since taken. Jefferson preferred the simple term "Republican," that being the designation used in France.

Aristocrat and Democrat.—In order to secure

more fully their ends, the leaders in these societies endeavored to array one portion of the community against another. Those who were in favor of neutrality they characterized as *Aristocrats;* every lover of order or supporter of the national government was denounced as such, and as an enemy of the "poor man," a favorer of the hated aristocratic England and not of democratic France. It has been the policy of the leaders of that political organization from that day to this, to proclaim themselves preëminently the friends of the "poor man," as they affectionately designate those who obtain a living by working in any form for wages, but more especially those engaged in manual labor or as employees in manufacturing establishments. They imply at the same time that the men of wealth or capitalists—in a word those who employ workpeople—are the enemies of the latter.

The epithets which they then used had a meaning and a purpose, as we shall see in respect to similar terms employed throughout this narrative. The term *aristocrat* in that day had a peculiarly unpopular significance, and was designed to excite prejudice against those who were in favor of Washington's policy. By this term they meant to imply that the advocates of neutrality were imitators of the English aristocracy, who had been the bitterest foes of the colonists in their recent struggle for independence, while France aided them. The offensive epithet was seized upon and used to rouse a prejudice against the more educated and well-to-do in the community.

The Poor **Man's Friend.**—While leaders of the Democracy from that time to this have never ceased to proclaim themselves the special friends of the " poor man " or of those employed by others, yet the influence of that party's measures—both negative and positive—shows it to have discriminated, let us hope unwittingly, *against* the interests of that portion of the people, if we are to judge by its acts and not by its words.   This statement is proved to be correct when history tells in what manner the interests of those who worked for wages have been affected *favorably* by the national measures which these leaders *opposed*, and *injuriously* by the measures which they themselves *introduced.* The class of persons whose only support is from their wages is the largest in the community—estimated by political economists at three-fourths of the adult population, and it will be ever so from the nature of the case. To secure the good will of this large class these leaders have labored incessantly. One of their most influential means has been to infuse distrust of employers among those employed. The result is one of the facts which we characterize as *notorious ;* it is well known that the unintelligent of those who live by wages, and the unskilled laborers, especially those of foreign extraction, are nearly all hostile in politics to their employers. This unfortunate antagonism between different classes of the community in our country—commencing shortly after our Revolution—is due to influences described above, exerted systematically from that time to this. The employed

are induced to believe that in some indefinable way
their own interests are not interwoven with those
of their employers. This feeling has been induced
by the continual reiteration that the poor or laboring man was the special protégé of the leaders of
the Democracy, and to befriend him was to it a labor of love, at the same time broadly intimating
that those who employed him had no friendly interest in his welfare. In testimony of this see numerous platforms of the party—both National and State
—put forth in years gone by.

Republican Simplicity.—In the early days of the
government, when customs and ceremonies were in
a state of transition from the courtly to the more
plain republican style, much was said and written
in deprecation of the forms or ceremonies practised
at the official receptions of the first and second
presidents. We of this day are certainly unable,
from our standpoint, to conceive of the violence of
the social tempest which is said to have been roused
at that time. The extremists among the Democracy
proclaimed that these receptions, conducted in this
formal manner, were aping similar ceremonies at
the English court, and broadly intimated that there
was perhaps in these things a lurking design upon
the liberties of the people! Eventually these ultra
notions on both sides neutralized each other, and as a
result of the agitation was brought about the common-sense custom among the people of leaving without much comment such ceremonies—plain or osten-
tatious—to regulate themselves in accordance with

the sense of propriety pervading the White House.

The pandering to the vulgar instincts of the ignorant, however, which was illustrated in the foregoing acts, was a deliberate policy from the outset, nor has it yet disappeared. Later, when Jefferson was about to assume the office of president, he intimated that he would have no special ceremony at his inauguration. He kept his own counsel; when the hour arrived, he quietly rode up to the Capitol, tied his horse to a post, went in, and took the oath of office at the hands of one of the judges of the Supreme Court of the United States. This phase of simplicity has never been imitated by any succeeding president.

In carrying out his assumed role, Jefferson went still further, and compromised himself as well as the nation over which he presided. The circumstances were these: according to the account given by Mr. Merry, the British minister, of an interview to which he was accompanied by the Secretary of State, James Madison, whose duty it was to introduce the minister to the newly inaugurated president, he says: "Mr. Jefferson's appearance soon explained to me that the general circumstances of my reception had not been accidental but studied." He was "not merely in undress, but actually standing in slippers down at the heels, and both pantaloons, coat, and under-clothes indicative of utter slovenliness and indifference to appearances, and in a state of negligence actually studied." This occurred at an hour which Jefferson himself had ap-

pointed for his first reception of the British minister,
who came in his " official costume." Such manifesta-
tion of discourtesy might have been for two reasons,
one to gratify the less intelligent members of his
political adherents, and the other to treat with
disrespect the minister of that country which he
personally disliked.   Jefferson's social training forbade his doing such things without a plan and a
motive.   The British minister said and believed
that the scene was prepared " as an insult to the sov-
ereign whom he represented."

III.

FINANCE AND COMMERCE.

The Second Mistake.—When the clubs and their promoters had failed to prevent neutrality being fully and fairly carried out, they next directed their opposition against the financial measures designed by the general government to liquidate the Nation's debt. This debt was originally in the form of "certificates or notes of obligation to pay for value received;" the latter had been issued both by the Continental Congress and the States during the war for independence, and in addition was a foreign debt for money borrowed from friendly nations in Europe. These various obligations were assumed by the United States Government when it went into operation. The Anti-Federalist or Democratic party bitterly opposed the National government's assuming and paying these debts, thus contracted for the benefit of the whole people. This opposition came mostly from the Southern States, and the reason given was that much of the debt was not in the hands of the original owners, the latter having, it was said, disposed of it at a large discount. This was true to a certain extent; but the debt was a debt, nevertheless.

Import Duties.—Alexander Hamilton, Secretary

the Treasury, made a report to the first Congress at its second session on the financial measures necessary to meet these demands. This report, because of its lasting influence, is the most important in our annals. He recommended an indirect tax by imposing duties on imported merchandise, in order that that class of property, as well as real estate, should bear its proportion of the public burdens. His design was also to equalize the expense in the production of manufactured goods, so that our own work‚people might be able to compete with the low wages paid in Europe, and with the acquired skill of centuries. The finances of the country at that time were in a deplorable condition. "From 1783 to 1789 the trade of the thirteen old States was *perfectly free* to the whole world. The result was that Great Britain filled every section of our country with her manufactures of wool, cotton, linen, leather, iron, glass, and all other articles used here; and in four years she swept from the country every dollar, and every piece of gold." (*Bolles's Financial Hist. of U. S.*, II. p. 437.) This was our first and only experiment in absolute Free Trade. It is easy therefore to divine the reason for the following explanatory statement in the preamble to our first National tariff, which was passed by Congress and signed by George Washington in 1789: "For the support of the Government, and for the encouragement and protection of domestic manufactures."

United States Bank.—Hamilton likewise recommended a National Bank to facilitate exchange, and to increase its usefulness, that it have branches in the States, should the people so desire. The first Congress thoroughly discussed these propositions, and in its second session passed laws in accordance with their main features. The bank had a charter for twenty years, thus giving for that length of time one assurance of stability in business ; its bills being payable in coin on demand, raised the credit of the government and inspired confidence in commercial circles. Industry received a new impulse and the whole country bounded forth as one man in energy and enterprise. Strange as it may seem, these measures, which proved so beneficial to the whole nation, were bitterly opposed by the then Democratic organization, thus affording, as in the case of neutrality, an instance in which they desperately fought against measures that have, from their own inherent excellence and adaptation, become the fixed policy of the land. (*Patton's American People*, pp. 577, 581.)

Jefferson's Chinese Policy.—The reason why Jefferson during his administration opposed the policy of defending the commerce of the country, was to be found in his contracted views of what constitutes a prosperous nation. He appeared to deem property owned in commerce, such as ships and the benefits derived from trade, as less valuable than that belonging to the planter or farmer. He wished the United States, as he expressed it, to engage in neither commerce nor navigation, but stand in respect to Europe as China did to the rest of the world ; that is, to be isolated from all other nations. He had but little sympathy with those who engaged in manufacturing, except of articles of the simplest forms, and that only for home consumption. In truth, this school of statesmen had very inadequate conceptions of the elements that constitute a nation, perfect in all its component parts, such as the diversities of industry —mechanical, commercial and agricultural—which are the outgrowth of differences of climate or arising from variety of location. It is certainly not the Divine order, that nations should be isolated from one another, if the world is to advance toward a complete Christianized civilization.

Disregard of Commerce.—Thus it was the practice of Jefferson and his school to give little protection on the ocean to the vast amount of property engaged in commerce, and owned in one portion of the Union, but to permit the foreign trade of the Nation to be virtually destroyed by belligerent cruisers, when it was as truly property, and ought to have been held as sacred, as either cotton or tobacco. In consequence of these limited views he was opposed to maintaining a navy or having foreign commerce, while his notions about our being separated from the rest of the world had influence upon his policy to diminish our intercourse with other nations. Presidents Jefferson and Madison being Southern country gentlemen, did not fully value the importance of commerce and the mechanical industries of the land, and while comprehensive in their abstract theories of government, they both

failed in practice ; either because of their lack of
interest or their disregard of the wants of those
who lived in a region less fertile, but having a more
dense and intelligent population, and other facilities
for manufacturing, and in addition nearer the seaboard, so that a large number could engage profit-
ably in commerce.

State Rights.—Jefferson's idea of isolation from
all the world, like the Chinese of that day, was analogous to his view of State Rights ; so different from
that of Madison, who held in substance that the
States under the United States government, were
great municipalities analogous to that of cities under State governments.   In the convention that
formed the United States Constitution, Madison
said : "The States never possessed the essential right
of sovereignty," and Washington said : "It is only
in our united character that we are known as an
empire ; that our independence is acknowledged."
We all believe in State Rights ; but not in State
Sovereignty,that extreme view which would disinteg-
rate the nation, and put the individual States above
the Union, or make them all entirely independent of
each other.   Statesmen holding such limited views
became narrow in their conceptions of the true
elements constituting a nation.   They are inclined
to become selfish in a State or sectional point of
view ; we see this cropping out all along our history.

IV.

ALIEN AND SEDITION ACTS.

Vice-President Jefferson.—We have already seen that refugees fleeing from anarchy and bloodshed in France came to this country, and in their opposition under the leadership of "Citizen" Genet much annoyed Washington in his endeavor to preserve neutrality. Later (1797) during the administration of John Adams, they became more bold and insolent in manifesting their contempt for the United States government. There were obvious reasons for these impertinent demonstrations—Jefferson was now vice-president, and hostile to the administration, though holding in it an official position. This anomaly occurred because at that time, of the candidates for the presidency, the one receiving the greatest number of votes was declared president, and the one receiving the next highest number, vice-president. John Adams was the "Federal" candidate, and Thomas Jefferson the "Republican or Democratic;" thus the vice-president became the virtual leader of the opposition. The mode of electing these two officers of the government has since been changed, [*Constitution of the United States*, Arts. II and XII.], and now the president and vice-president are members of the same political organization or party, as of course they should be.

Jefferson, because of his position, was the more influential in stimulating the malcontents by means of his private letters, while abuse, equally scurrilous with that heaped upon the first president, and by the same class of men, was meted out to John Adams and his administration by newspapers whose editors were foreigners, one of whom—Freneau, the slanderer of Washington—was a special protégé of the vice-president and others. " Time has not washed out the stain of his Mr. Jefferson's intimacy with William Duane, the editor of the infamous " Aurora "—so abusive of John Adams and his administration, (*Stevens's Gallatin*, p 296). The means thus used to influence and poison the minds of the people had to be counteracted. To-day, we are unable to appreciate fully to what extent the hospitality of the nation was abused by many of these refugees ; and yet they never would have dared insult the National authority, had they not been encouraged and aided by the *native* opponents of the policy of the administration with the connivance and secret aid of the vice-president.

The Plots of Aliens.—A brief summary of what these exiles or refugees attempted may afford a clue to the reasons which induced Congress to enact the two laws mentioned at the head of this section. The refugees had been increasing in numbers from year to year, so that at this time it was estimated there were more than 20,000 in the United States. They were all opposed to the policy of neutrality, and were emboldened to clamor for the govern-

ment's in some way aiding France in her struggle
with England. What they could not obtain by
open and direct means, they attempted by secret
and indirect. Some laid plans to seize Louisiana,
others to make an expedition against Florida ; both
of these belonged to Spain, and the object was to
embroil us in a war with that country, then an ally
of England. They even went so far as to tamper, by
means of agents, with the settlers of Kentucky, to
induce them to furnish men to capture Louisiana.
These settlers were for the most part from Virginia,
and their prominent men seem to have been imbued with the abstract theories of politics so prevalent in that State, and also with French notions of
democracy and infidelity.

The National government seemed thus compelled
in self-defence to take decisive measures, and it
passed the " Alien and Sedition laws" (July, 1798)
—the former to expire by limitation within two
years. The " Alien Act" authorized the president to
order out of the country foreigners who by their conspiracies might embroil the government in war. The
law was never enforced ; its effect was preventive,
since great numbers of these plotters, seeing their
occupation gone, left the country. The " Sedition
law" forbade conspiracies against the government,
and publications designed to bring it into disrepute.
This was also preventive. It might perhaps have
been better for the government to have borne the
misrepresentation and abuse of unscrupulous newspaper men, though foreigners, than to endeavor to

punish such offenses by restrictive legal enactments. The law was a welcome boon to the leaders of the Democracy; with sadness they lamented the loss of liberty and of freedom of speech, and in addition they proclaimed the act or law to be null and void, because unconstitutional. If that was the case, they might have spared themselves much anxiety, since on the very first trial under the law, that question would have been tested and settled, and, moreover, the law itself would expire within two years. But such sober thoughts seem to have been at a discount with these gentlemen, and the consequence was the most ludicrous and extravagant partisan furor that ever occurred in our political annals.

Resolutions of '98.—Jefferson hastened to the rescue, with a set of resolutions known as those of '98. (*American People*, pp. 709-712.) These he sent to be introduced into the legislatures of Virginia and Kentucky, having meanwhile carefully enjoined upon his friends to keep their authorship a secret —Why was that ?—which they did for twenty years. These resolutions advocated principles that have been a curse to the land. In them was the germ of Nullification, and of resistance to national authority, as exemplified in the late rebellion. Said Alexander Hamilton, when he learned their contents : "This is the first symptom of a spirit which must be killed, or it will kill the Constitution of the United States." (*Life of John Jay*, II., p. 89.) These resolutions were a standard theme of eulogy for certain orators and writers till their principles began to be tested in

1861. Were it not for the far-reaching influences that grew out of this political furor, the story of this episode—though it was the occasion of making Jefferson president—need not have been told; but it belongs legitimately to the history of the Democratic party, whose leaders for nearly half a century afterward harped on the enormities of the "Alien and Sedition laws," and continue still to eulogize the "Resolutions of '98."

The material prosperity of the country had been steadily advancing for twelve years, and at the close of John Adams's presidency, the revenue was amply sufficient for the current expenses of the government; while the assurance of the latter's stability had inspired confidence in industrial pursuits; and commerce too, both in the exportation of raw material and in the carrying trade, had advanced far beyond precedent. Strange to say, the ludicrous clamor just mentioned led the unintelligent among the Democracy to believe that the country was going to ruin; and when by their votes they put Thomas Jefferson in the presidential chair, they verily thought they had saved the country and their own precious liberties too. And why? Because a few foreign refugees in consequence of their abuse of the Nation's hospitality, and impertinent intermeddling in its affairs, were invited to leave the country or conduct themselves properly, and a few foreign-born editors were warned that their wholesale abuse of the government and its officers must cease. A little more than a quarter of a century afterward was enacted a similar scene, when the more radical of the same political organization proclaimed and thought that they too had saved the country.

During the first three administrations of the government the law required a residence of *fourteen years* before an alien could be admitted to citizenship. Toward the close of that period it was estimated there were in the United States between twenty and thirty thousand foreigners, principally French and Irish refugees. With scarcely an exception these aliens were in sympathy with Jefferson and the Democratic clubs in their opposition to the policy of neutrality adopted by the National government (pp. 12–16). Very few of those foreigners, in consequence of the above law, had become citizens and voters. The reader can understand why, in the *first* session of the *first* Congress in Jefferson's administration, that law was so changed as to reduce the time of such residence from fourteen years to five. This is *one* of the only *two* instances in which a law, primarily introduced and carried through Congress by the Democratic party alone, became the *policy* of the Nation. (*Johnston's American Politics,* p. 54.)

V.

STRICT CONSTITUTIONAL CONSTRUCTION.

Nature of the American Constitution.—The leaders of no political organization have been quite so inconsistent in the application of their theories, as the *Strict Constructionists* of the Constitution of the United States, as they styled themselves. On this subject we intend to notice only, and that very briefly, one or two salient points. Immediately after the inauguration of the government under President Washington, came the practical application of the principles of the Constitution, and of course the latter's interpretation. The departments of foreign affairs or of State and of War, had been, virtually, in existence from the beginning of the Revolutionary struggle, and their present secretaries could learn much from the experience of their predecessors; but that of the Treasury, as applied to the whole Nation, involved an entirely new financial system, which included the means of raising the funds necessary to carry on the national government, and likewise meet all its other pecuniary obligations.

Alexander Hamilton, the Secretary of the Treasury, contended that if the Constitution authorized the doing of a certain thing, it impliedly authorized,

also, the use of the proper means to accomplish
that object. He characterized this principle as the
" implied powers" of the Constitution. That interpretation was so much in accordance with the dic-
tates of common sense, that the national government
—though sometimes its prominent administrative
officers were strict constructionists—has ever since
virtually acted upon it. Thomas Jefferson, and the
school of which he was the most prominent exponent,
believed in the strict constructionist theory; but
his explanation lacks clearness, while his application
of it is inconsistent. These gentlemen must have
thought the Constitution, instead of being an instrument comprising general principles, and thus
affording room for the use of the knowledge and
wisdom acquired by experience in its application to
the necessities of the Nation, was a sort of governmental cast-iron frame that was ever to remain
inflexible. England's great statesman, W. E. Glad-
stone, thought differently when he said, "As the
British Constitution is the most subtile organism
which has proceeded from progressive history, so
the American Constitution is the most wonderful
work ever struck off at a given time by the brain
and purpose of man."

Application of Implied Powers.—The first
struggle of the strict constructionists was on the
policy of chartering a United States Bank. The
Constitution gives Congress the power "to regulate
commerce among the several States"; and the
second Congress at its first session chartered a "Na-

tional Bank for twenty years, with the privilege
to establish branches in any of the States"; this
was done at the suggestion of Hamilton. Congress
thought that it would "regulate commerce" by
facilitating financial exchanges among the States,
but the "strict constructionists" seemed to demand
the authority in explicit terms, or in so many words.
The Constitution authorizes Congress "to establish
post-offices and post-roads," and yet the statesmen of
the strict school, at this time in authority, were
much puzzled what to do, when it was proposed for
Congress to construct the famous national or Cumberland Road across the mountains, thus uniting the
Atlantic slope with the valley of the Ohio. But it
was a measure so important that they held in abeyance their "strict" scruples and authorized the work
and voted appropriations to carry it on toward completion. That road was at the time, in proportion
to the population and territory belonging to the
Nation, as important as in 1869 was the finished
Union Railway from the Mississippi to the Pacific.
On the same general principle, as well as in aid of
commerce, Congress still makes appropriations to
improve rivers and harbors, all under the implied
powers inherent in the Constitution.

Again, the Constitution says: "New States may
be admitted by Congress into the Union." There
is no intimation nor direction given as to what territory these States were to come from, nor by what
means they were to be obtained; there is the power
granted, and the wisdom of Congress was to devise

the means. Could anything be clearer by implication than that ?   Practical wisdom would say no;
but the speculating theorist would be in doubt.
Thus Jefferson, as a strict constructionist, was
greatly puzzled whether or not he had the constitutional power to purchase Louisiana.   Finally he
made the purchase—saying it was *extra*-constitu-
tional.   Alexander Hamilton was strongly in favor of
thus obtaining the territory of Louisiana, while numbers of the Federalists of the time were mistakenly
opposed, but not on constitutional grounds.   It is
remarkable that all the territory we ever acquired,
with the exception of Alaska, was obtained by professed strict constructionists, who, for the time being, adopted Hamilton's interpretation of the implied powers within the Constitution itself.   It is
worthy of notice that the people only in one instance,
that of the annexation of Texas, had an opportunity
by their votes to express their views on the subject ;
all the other territory being obtained by negotiations conducted by the different presidents without
consulting the people.

VI.

A COMPARISON.

Party Material.—"The Democrats were far inferior to the Federalists, in the numbers and the ability of their leaders; and, moreover, the great moneyed interests of the Northern States were the corner stone of the Federal party." (*Von Holst*, I., p. 179.) A similar comparison may be instituted in point of the general intelligence of that day, between the main supporters of the former—the planters and farmers—and the main adherents of the latter—the merchants, the manufacturers, the importers and bankers—and in contrast equally as striking as that made by Professor Von Holst. This is an important element that should be taken into account, when forming an estimate of the causes that modified the politics of that portion of our history. There were legitimate reasons for the differences existing between the rank and file of these two rival political organizations. The Federalists were mainly in the States where public schools had been in existence for generations, and where their influence had permeated the whole community, as well as in those States where education was cherished, but not through the medium so much of public as of private schools; while in the Slave-Labor States public schools were unknown. Where the latter existed the people became readers, newspapers were patronized, and flourished in consequence; and by means of these the readers informed themselves on the current topics of the time, rather than by the vehement harangues and *ex-parte* statements of stump orators. The earnest public speaker is often tempted to make assertions, while addressing an audience, that he would not dare write and publish. The extreme bitterness of party spirit that existed at the time of which we write, in certain portions of the Union, may be traced, more or less, to the fact that the populace caught the animus of the stump orators to whom they listened. On the contrary, had they read even the same sentiments in the quiet of their own homes, thus having more opportunity for reflection and for reading counter arguments, they would have been influenced more by reason than by the eloquence of political speakers.

Prejudices Instilled.—A curious phase of prejudice, as already noted, was instilled into the minds of the unintelligent Democracy of that day. They were often led, by the insinuation and hasty assertions of their leaders, to suspect the well-to-do and the educated portion of the community of being hostile to themselves. These leaders, at first, as we have seen, characterized those who sustained the policy of the government for the first twelve years of its existence as "*Aristocrats*," and that term of presumed reproach was used until superseded by that of the "*Moneyed Power*," meaning by the latter epithet those who continued to sustain the financial principles introduced by Alexander Hamilton and embodied in the policy of Washington's administration; the policy of Neutrality in the meantime having become popular, the epithet "Aristocrat," as originally used, was no longer available. But in relation to financial measures, taxes, tariffs, banks, etc., "moneyed power" suited their purpose admirably, and every "poor man" who worked for wages, was impliedly invited to look upon the well-to-do and the intelligent as having but little sympathy for him. The persons thus affected in that day—the planters and farmers—were of a lower grade of intelligence than those of the present time. Now the vast majority thus influenced are foreigners or their direct descendants, and a hostile feeling is fostered between the employers and the employed.

Financiering.—In respect to the management of the finances of the nation, the contrast between the two leading political organizations in our history has been always very marked. Those financial measures, which were comprehensive, and in their influence beneficial to the whole nation, are due not to the leaders of the Democracy, but to their opponents. It is true that individual members from the commercial and manufacturing centers often voted with the latter for such measures, but in doing so they, for the time being, severed their connection with the theory and spirit of their own party. This unwise legislation in respect to commercial interests and mechanical industries, originated in contracted views of states-

manship, which rendered such officials sectional in
their ideas—though it may have been unconsciously
—and unable to comprehend the wants of a well
organized nation. Hence there has been always a
crudeness of legislation on financial affairs, including
tariffs, whenever the Democracy have predominated
in the nation's councils. Jefferson, when president,
though opposed to the United States Bank, was
anxious to use the other banks as political machines,
and on the 12th of July, 1803, he wrote to his secretary of the treasury—Albert Gallatin—saying :
" I am decidedly in favor of making all the banks
Republican [Democratic] by sharing deposits among
them *in proportion to the disposition they show*. If
the law forbid it, we should not permit another
session of Congress to pass without amending it. It
is material to the safety of Republicanism [the De-
mocracy] to detach the mercantile interests from its
enemies, and incorporate them into the body of its
friends." (*Bolles's Financial Hist. of the U. S.*, p.
140.)

Internal Improvements.—Another element—
the dogma of extreme State Rights, or Sovereignty
—influenced the statesmen, both in relation to the
United States Bank and to internal improvements.
They seemed to have a horror of any policy that
would exert an influence in uniting the people in
closer bonds of union—especially those living in the
slave, with those dwelling in the Free-Labor States.
Hence they deprecated the United States Bank with
its branches in the several States. For a similar

reason — predicated on assumed constitutional grounds—they had their doubts as to internal improvements being made by the national government : such as canals, that might extend from one State to another. This was before the era of railways; which, being constructed by corporations using private capital, have made sad work with the retarding policy fostered by the extreme theory of State Rights.

Secretaries of the Treasury.—The Presidents from the South practically recognized the inferior skill in financial affairs of the public men of that section by selecting Northern men as Secretaries of the Treasury. George Washington set the example by appointing to that office that prince of financiers, Alexander Hamilton. Another Northern man, Albert Gallatin, was for fourteen years Secretary of the Treasury under Jefferson and Madison. With scarcely an exception, for seventy years Northern men were selected for that office. The only Secretary from the South who left his impress upon the financial and industrial interests of the country was Robert J. Walker, of Mississippi. The London *Times* characterized his first report to Congress as the only "properly Free-trade document ever made by an American minister of finance." Upon the theories contained in that report was based the principles of the tariff of 1846 (pp. 118–121). John G. Carlisle, of Kentucky, was appointed Secretary of the Treasury in 1893.

VII.

JEFFERSON'S EMBARGO.

Foreign War.—Toward the close of Jefferson's first administration, war broke out more fiercely than ever between France and England, and the cruisers of both belligerents, knowing its helpless condition, began to prey upon our commerce, under the pretext of searching our merchantmen for articles contraband of war. The peace policy of the President invited this kind of treatment from these unscrupulous cruisers. The merchants petitioned for licenses to arm and protect themselves, as they had done in the previous administration; but that petition was denied on the ground that, if granted, it would be virtually war. Yet the illegal seizure of our merchant vessels by these cruisers was looked upon in the light of the "Chinese Theory" —of non-intercourse with the rest of the world—as quite a venial offence.

Domestic Paralysis.—Now was the time to apply the potent remedy for these evils, and the president, whose political wisdom was deemed infallible by the great majority of his admirers, recommended, and Congress—without a moment's warning to the country—passed the Embargo Act (Dec. 1807); a law forbidding the American people to trade with the French and English. (*Patton's American People*, pp. 612-614.) This was done with the expectation that these two nations, for the want of our raw material and produce, would hasten to respect our flag, and no more board our merchantmen in search of articles contraband of war nor impress those of our seamen who happened to be born in the British Isles; or, if worse came to worst, we would have no ships on the ocean for them to board, at all. In consequence of this law, the commerce of the country was ruined; ships in hundreds lay rotting at the wharves, and thousands of sailors were thrown out of employment, while the surplus agricultural produce of the land was valueless for want of a market, and all this ruin brought about by the crude legislation of a Democratic Congress, held in hand by a president who was the idol of the party. If one doubts the accuracy of this statement, let him read the history of the period from Dec. 1807 to the end of Jefferson's administration. "The Alien and Sedition laws were not nearly so unjust and tyrannical as the laws for enforcing the embargo, and they did not touch one man, when the embargo laws touched hundreds." (*Sumner's Jackson*, p. 28.)

An Unforeseen Blessing.—These measures bore very hard upon the laboring men and mechanics of the time, nearly all of whom were deprived of employment. As the embargo lasted almost a year and a half, their misfortunes led to a large emigration of these workmen from the seaboard States to the west. The movement, which continued for some time, grew out of the circumstances, and was indirectly beneficial to the Nation in commencing settlements in several new States. This advantage to the country is not to be attributed, however, to the far-seeing policy of the political leaders of that day—for they planned no such movement. What a contrast to the laws enacted for the purpose (1863), under which States and Territories have since been, and are now being, settled in accordance with the comprehensive policy, as shown by the *Homestead Law*, and the opening up of new territories by means of railways.

Failure of the Embargo Policy.—Meanwhile, the complications in relation to the cruisers continued as the weakness of our defences, both by sea and land, was well understood by the belligerents of Europe, and when the English frigate *Leopard* wantonly fired upon and boarded the United States frigate *Chesapeake* (1807), and carried off four men, President Jefferson, in consequence, ordered the English war vessels out of American waters; but their officers, knowing he was unable to enforce the order, in the most contemptuous manner, took their own time. This unpleasant condition of affairs between England and the United States continued until Congress declared war (1812) in Madison's administration. Though, owing to the "penny wise" policy of Jefferson, which also was practised to nearly the same extent by his successor, the country was as unprepared to enter upon such a contest, as was Napoleon III to contend with

Prussia. The despised little navy came to the rescue, and afterward had the honor, by its victories, to raise the drooping spirits of the people, and save the nation from disgrace.

VIII.

SECOND WAR WITH ENGLAND.

War Preparations.—Though Presidents Washington and Adams used every honorable means to avoid collisions with the belligerents in Europe, yet they caused the power of the United States to be respected by putting our military forces, both land and naval, in such condition that in case of war the government should not be unprepared. At important ports along the coast our defences were strengthened, and three frigates—the *Constitution*, the *United States*, and the *Constellation* — commenced in Washington's administration, were finished in 1798, when the people themselves came forward, and, by their liberal subscriptions, aided in equipping them for active service. These National vessels soon had influence as convoys in protecting American commerce from the interference of French and British cruisers; in addition President Adams licensed more than three hundred American merchantmen to carry arms and protect themselves, which they did. Congress also authorized the building of six additional frigates, which were well under way when the administration of John Adams came to a close.

Jefferson's Peace Policy.—Mr. Adams was succeeded by Thomas Jefferson, who, on entering upon office, began to put in practice his peculiar theories. For illustration, he was not so much in favor of commerce as to protect it from the aggressions of belligerent cruisers by means of a navy; he rather preferred that the public ships should be hauled in out of harm's way. He also deemed the keeping up of harbor fortifications along the coast as a useless expense; if we should have difficulties with foreign governments, he would retaliate by cutting off our trade with them by means of embargoes; if the navy of an enemy attacked our seaboard cities, he would defend them by using gunboats in our harbors instead of men-of-war upon the ocean; and at his suggestion Congress authorized the frames of the six frigates already mentioned, and on which work had been stopped by order of the President, to be taken to pieces and the timber used in building gunboats. The latter were to be anchored in the harbors to defend the cities: but they proved to be absolutely worthless; the sailors were afraid of them; they said that if heavy guns were fired from their decks they would topple over. For six years not an ocean-going vessel of war was added to our navy. It is worthy of note that the Southern members of Congress, following Jefferson's lead, were specially hostile to our marine while there was abroad in that section an opinion that it was better to give up commerce altogether, than incur the expense of a navy to protect it; while as to the people living on the seaboard, if they were attacked, why, they could retire into the interior, as was recommended by Jefferson himself.

IX

OUR FIRST IMPORTANT TARIFF.

American Manufactures.—Our industrial progress had been very great, when it was interrupted, as we shall see, by the influence of the attempt at Nullification in South Carolina (1833). A brief notice of this progress will not be out of place here. At the close of the second war with Great Britain in 1815, American manufactures had increased beyond precedent. This was owing in a great measure to the suspension of commercial intercourse with England, which had hitherto furnished nearly all the foreign made articles used in the United States. Thus from necessity the American people began to manufacture those articles for themselves, while their genius for invention was brought into requisition in devising labor-saving machinery. (*American People*, p. 713.)

Lord Brougham's Advice.—England was then striving to hold the control of the ocean, and also to become the workshop of the world; and was determined to permit no interference with either of these assumed prerogatives. The spirit with which she was imbued may be inferred from what Lord Brougham said in Parliament in 1816, when he declared he was very far from placing the vast exports which tho peace with America had occasioned "upon the same footing with those to the European market the year before; both because ultimately the Americans will pay, which the exhausted state of the Continent renders unlikely, and because it was well worth while to incur a loss upon the first exportation, in order by the glut *to stifle in the cradle* those rising manufactures in the United States, which the war had forced into existence contrary to the natural course of things." (*Hansard's Parl. Debates*, 1*st. Series*, XXXIII. p. 1099.) The last phrase intimates that the " natural course of things " was for England to do the manufacturing for the world.

At the time of which we write (1816) England had been for a century or more training her people for this triumph of skill in various mechanical industries. In addition to *highly protective tariffs*, she forbade, by stringent laws and severe penalties, persons *taking from the kingdom any machine used in manufacturing*. Samuel Slater had brought to the United States in 1790 the drawings of the machinery used in England for spinning cotton. From these drawings was made the first " spinning jenny " in this country. It was set to work in Pawtucket, Rhode Island (*American People*, p. 578), 1793, thus becoming the pioneer of our extensive system of cotton manufacturing.

As soon as the treaty of Ghent (Dec. 3, 1814) was ratified, and a way opened to commerce between England and America, English merchants flooded the markets of the United States with their goods. These were put at very low rates, frequently below cost, with the avowed intention, as we have seen, of destroying our domestic manufactures, which had come into existence during the war. *This they did effectually.* Great multitudes of our working people were thrown out of employment, causing much distress; while the prospect was that henceforth our industries would be held in bondage at the will of the foreign manufacturer.

An Equalizing Measure.—The statesmen of that day, who followed the example of Alexander Hamilton, had a policy that was not merely theoretical, but based upon reason and common sense. They labored to introduce measures that would lay a firm foundation for the future progress of the country. In consequence, they imposed a tariff upon foreign-made articles, thought to be sufficiently high to *equalize the cost of their production,* or, in other words, *counterbalance* the low wages paid the operatives in Europe. They designed to promote the industries of the whole land; endeavoring, meanwhile, to make them as diversified as the wants of the people required. They wished, also, to develop the natural resources of the country, then thought to be great, and now known to be almost inexhaustible. In accordance with these principles Congress passed a tariff (1816) sufficiently high in its rate to produce revenue and protect our own industries, which, having had no foreign competition for the previous four years, had been carried on prosperously, until overwhelmed as we have just seen. The Slave-Labor States were then in favor of fostering domestic manufactures. John C. Calhoun, of South Carolina, took a prominent part in the movement, and so did Henry Clay, of Kentucky; the latter, however, continued to view protection against the skill and low wages paid in Europe, as necessary for the development of our national resources of every kind. The slave-owners seemed to have had reference to employing their slaves in manufacturing, especially coarse cottons, the material used mostly for clothing the negroes. The making of these cottons had been introduced successfully into American mills within the last few years.

The Results.—Years passed on and this tariff (1816), amended from time to time to make it more effective, encouraged the various mechanical industries of the Union so that they progressed with amazing rapidity; the whole country gained under the influence, as all classes, especially in the Free-Labor States, were busily employed, and the nation was never before so prosperous. In less than a score of years, it was found, however, that the slaves, because of their ignorance and lack of interest in their work, could not spin and weave cotton. They could only hoe and pick it. Senator Hayne of South Carolina put the case in this manner:— "The slaves are too incapable of minute, constant, delicate attention, and the persevering industry which is essential to the success of manufacturing establishments." Senator McDuffie, of the same

State, argued in opposition, saying he believed "that the slaves could work in factories" (*Debates in Congress*, Vol. X). Meanwhile, in New England, in New York, New Jersey and Pennsylvania, the people during this period had been acquiring skill which they applied very successfully in many kinds of manufacturing, such as textile fabrics and iron. It was owing to the intelligence of those who worked in the mills, and their zeal in their work, that these rapid strides were made in the Free-Labor States. Though they had not learned to make the finer kinds of textile fabrics—woolen or cotton—so as to compete with the much older establishments in France, in Belgium or in Great Britain, yet the New Englanders were able to compete in coarse cottons with the English in the far east, especially in the markets of China, and at the same time supply the slave-owners at home. England, before long, virtually gave up the greater portion of that trade in China, as she found it more profitable to manufacture the finer fabrics from cotton.

X.

LABOR AND INTELLIGENCE.

In the Slave States.—The South might have been at least fairly successful in manufacturing, if the slave-owners had wished. Had they taken measures to invest capital and establish cotton mills, even when they found that the slaves could not work to advantage in them, and employed native whites, male and female, as was done in the Free-Labor States, they might have succeeded, so far as to have changed the industrial condition of that section of the Union. The only probable drawback to success might have been found in the lack of intelligence among the " poor whites ; " for this, their misfortune, the slave-owners themselves were responsible, because for generations, as legislators, they had neglected to establish common schools in which the youth, male and female, could at least have been taught the rudiments of an education. Their water-power was abundant, and scarcely liable to freeze in the winter; in that respect the James was superior to the Merrimac. In the highlands of the Carolinas and Georgia were numerous streams and waterfalls, and abundance of white labor to be obtained from those who did not own slaves, for in that region the evil influence of the system of servitude in degrading labor was not so much felt as in other portions of these States. These mills might have made coarse cottons, and, in time, other manufacturing industries might have been intro duced.

The truth was, the slave-owners wanted the entire profits accruing from both raising the raw cotton and its manufacture by slave-labor. On the other hand they had no desire to elevate the laboring man, or " white trash," as they contemptuously termed those who did not own slaves, but who earned their living by manual labor, either on small farms or in workshops for wages. They preferred to abandon almost every attempt at manufacturing throughout the land, and compel Congress to enact laws which tended to free trade, regardless of the injury thus done to the industries of the Free-Labor States. In 1831 the latter's capital invested in cotton manufacture alone amounted to more than $40,000,000 (*Industrial Hist. of U. S.*, p. 413). The slave-owners expected to make this change in the existing tariff by using the votes of the Northern Democratic members of Congress whom they controlled; they themselves would, henceforth, raise cotton only, which the slaves could do. Cotton, at that time, was the most important export we had. We shall see how the union of these two wings of the Democracy brought ruin upon the industries of the country, and threw the laboring men and mechanics out of employment.

Ignorant Laborers.—Perhaps the greatest crime against the " poor whites" of the Slave-Labor States, was the indirect efforts made for generations to keep them in ignorance. "The mass of the small slaveholding land-owners and of the poor artisans, was the most sorrowful social product which the history of civilized nations had to show ; an aristocratic class of common people, which both from its lack of culture and its arrogance was terrible material in the hands of a self-seeking aristocracy and of politicians greedy for power" (*Von Holst*, I., p. 347). Aristocracies are, and always have been, tyrannical and selfish, treating with contempt those below them in the social scale. The slave-owners—the rulers and legislators—forbade, by laws sanctioned by cruel penalties, the negroes learning to read and write, and punished severely those who should teach them. They likewise neglected to provide public schools for their own children, and for those of the non-slaveholding portion of the people. This policy continued for more than one hundred and fifty years, the legitimate result of which was, at the end of that period, the most illiterate native white population in the entire Nation (*Census of the United States for* 1860).

A Change of Base.—When the tariff of 1816— characterized as "protective "—was passed, it was deemed *constitutional* by John C. Calhoun, and his compeers from the cotton-growing States. It is a singular coincidence that *thirteen* years later, when it was found that the slaves could not work in cotton or woolen mills, the views of these statesmen changed. The theory now advocated was that a tariff, in its effect protective to American industry, was *unconstitutional* (*Debates in Congress*, X., pp, 243, 245). This was *assuming* that the tariff then in existence was made with the intention to aid one portion of the community—the manufacturers—by virtually prohibiting the importation of certain classes of goods that could be made here; but that was never the intention of its framers, nor that the result produced. The protest issued by the South Carolina Convention (1829) pronounced protective duties "*unconstitutional, oppressive and unjust.*" These were the mutterings of Nullification. The ground taken was that the existing tariff must be modified, and, instead, one bordering on free trade established.

In the Free States.—During this period (1816–1828), so progressive compared with the past, great advances were made, showing the energy of the people. New York city was fast becoming the center of the foreign commerce of the United States, because of her position at the mouth of the Hudson, and now (1825) by means of the Erie Canal in connection with the great lakes and the northern portion of the valley of the Mississippi; being also further west and nearer the center of the States than Boston, which in commerce had, hitherto, taken the lead, and still was the money center of the Union. The two cities of Boston and Philadelphia gradually withdrew a large portion of their capital invested in shipping, because of its becoming less profitable. After the downfall of Napoleon (1815), and the closing of the wars known by his name, their immense carrying trade began to slip out of the hands of the Americans. The French, the Germans, the Hollanders, meanwhile, were recovering their commercial marine, which had been virtually ruined during the twenty-five years of these wars; while the English, owing to their supremacy upon the ocean, had kept theirs up to a high standard. These nations were now carrying on the greater part of their commerce in their own ships. In consequence, the American shippers of the Free-Labor States sought other outlets for their capital, and turned their attention to manufacturing industries, and were so much aided by the general intelligence of the workpeople employed, that they succeeded well in that field of enterprise.

Boston furnished the capital that established the mills of Lowell and Lawrence, and indeed, more or less, the mills up the Merrimac. In Rhode Island, the same process was going on, and Providence, where the first successful cotton mill in the Union was established in 1793, rapidly grew into a manufacturing city. Philadelphia was largely investing her capital in two branches of industry, textile fabrics and iron. Iron ore in connection with coal was found in the mountains of Pennsylvania, and in some of her valleys. These deposits were known to be rich in quality, and in vast quantities, indeed presumed to be inexhaustible for ages to come.

Slavery in Politics.—This period is remarkable, also, for the first prominent disagreement in Congress on the subject of slavery. The occasion of this discussion and action was the admission of Missouri as a Slave State, by the enactment of the famous bill known as the Missouri Compromise (1820), which guaranteed that all territory west of that State and north of its southern boundary line should be forever free. Slavery was henceforth recognized by the thoughtful as a future element of great influence and power in the nation's politics, but held in abeyance only for the time being. In the treatment of the question it was evident, even at this first issue, that the leaders of the Democracy in the Free-Labor States sympathized with the slave-owners.

Imported Laborers.—During this period began also a large immigration to this county, principally from Ireland. This fact was first noticed officially in a report of the Secretary of State in 1819. This class of immigrants were nearly all unskilled laborers; that is, they could handle the spade, and the mattock, or pickaxe, and were employed in digging our canals, somewhat in grading railways, and in carrrying bricks and mortar in building our cities. At that time, few of these were even so far skilled as to work in brick and stone, as masons, and unfortunately great numbers were illiterate, and unable to inform themselves in respect to the workings of our government and institutions. They were taken in hand as protégés by certain political leaders. To the Irishman the name "Democrat" seems to have a peculiar fascination.

The term is used in the British Isles and on the
Continent as the direct opposite of kingly or aristocratic rule ; and the people of their class looked
upon such rule as their political enemy, no matter
how kind and just the government might be.   This
led the Irishman, when he landed on our shores, to
sympathize with the political organization known
as Democratic without stopping to learn its principles or the history of its acts.   It is noticeable
that a much smaller proportion of the immigrants
from Germany or Northern Europe connect themselves with the same party, though they come from
countries where the governments are not so liberal
as that of Great Britain.   The solution of this fact
is in their greater intelligence.

  From this time (1820), onward, we find the Democratic organization, as such, abetting the slave-
holders in their every demand, and itself uniformly
sustained by the naturalized citizens of Irish birth.

XI.

TESTIMONY OF A DEMOCRAT.

Martin Van Buren, in his "History of Politics," seems to have been suspicious of the intelligent portion of the people, who happened not to be found in the ranks of the Democracy; in this he was in sympathy with Jefferson and Jackson, both of whom impugned the motives of those who differed from themselves in political opinions. Writing of the period when he himself was in political life, he says: "The press, men of letters, artists, and professional men, of every denomination, and those engaged in subordinate pursuits who live upon luxurious indulgences of the rich, are all brought within the scope of this influence" (p. 225),—the "money power," meaning the Whigs. This latter epithet, used by the Democratic speakers and writers of that day, had the effect of prejudicing one portion of the community against another. And again: "It is perhaps in this way only, that we can account for the remarkable disparity in number between the newspapers and other periodicals advocating Democratic principles, and those which support the 'money power' and its adherents [Whigs] a disparity the extent of which will strike any one who visits a common reading-room, in which, amid the well-furnished shelves and full files of the publications of the latter class [Whig papers], it is rare that we find many of the former [Democratic], often not more than a single newspaper, sometimes not one. Yet those papers which we do not find there, represent the political principles of a large majority of the people" (p. 225). Again : " Although Hamilton's policy was successful with many, it failed signally [in elections] with the most numerous and consequently the most powerful class of our citizens, those engaged in agriculture." Further on : " Farmers and planters are the mainstay of the Democratic party," (p. 227). These leaders always refer to the *number of the votes*, and not to the *intelligence of the voters*. Van Buren ought to be good authority on the subject. Was he aware of the stigma he thus placed upon the intelligence of the members of his own political party, by representing that portion of the people presumed to be intelligent and of refined tastes, as not in sympathy with it, but in intimate relations with the Whigs, whom he for his own reasons, characterized as " rich and luxurious "? The solution of this problem was not found, as Mr. Van Buren insinuates, in the influence of the "money power," as he characterized the intelligent and well-to-do classes, but in the fact that the great majority of the *reading and thinking* portion of the people were not in sympathy with the party to which he refers.

Van Buren speaks approvingly of the planters and farmers of his day, as being the adherents of the

Democratic organization, and in respect to its
opponents, he does not hesitate to impugn their
principles and motives by declaring that they " were
constructed principally of a network of special interests " (p. 226). But the planters and farmers had no
foreign competition, and they needed no measure
as a tariff to equalize the cost of production between
them and foreign owners and cultivators of the soil.
The Northern farmer of that time had no foreign
outlet or market for the produce of his fields, while
the planter had for his cotton. In the England of
that day, the land under cultivation was sufficient,
or nearly so, to produce food for its own people,
but the population has since increased, while the area
cultivated has remained about the same ; hence the
necessity now to supplement their own production
of food by importations from abroad. On the contrary, the American manufacturers had to contend,
not only with the low wages paid workmen in Europe,
but with the acquired skill of ages, in that day even
much greater in proportion than now. Hamilton's
famous report on manufactures in Washington's
administration was the only public document up to
that time that unfolded principles which, if applied,
could remedy these defects. Yet Van Buren laments,
in referring to this report, that " the political seed
sown by Alexander Hamilton has never been
eradicated—it seems not susceptible of eradication "
(p. 227). Of course not ; and why ? Because time has
shown that the wisdom and principles embodied in
that report have had the sanction to this day of

the great majority of the reading and thinking
portion of the American people.

Finally, as to party management, Van Buren says:
"A political party [Whig] founded on such principles
and looking to such sources for its support does not
often stand in need of caucuses and conventions to
preserve harmony in its ranks." (p 226). Certainly
not ; for the members of such political organization
think and act for themselves. The animus of what Mr
Van Buren says in respect to the managing of
political parties, is clearly derogatory to those who
were sufficiently intelligent to comprehend the relations that one portion of the nation has to those
of another, and dared act accordingly; but its practical bearing is the reverse.

For thirty-six years it had been conceded as a
matter of courtesy to the Vice-President, as the presiding officer of the Senate, to appoint the committees and their respective chairmen. During the
administration of John Quincy Adams, John C. Calhoun being Vice-President, a necessary change
(1826) was introduced. Though in quite a minority, Calhoun appointed Democrats on the more important committees in such manner as to give them
the control of each one. Former Vice-Presidents
had made these appointments *impartially*. This
uncalled-for action of Calhoun became the occasion
of the Senate adopting the rule which still obtains
in that body, *to elect its own committees by ballot,
and also designate the chairman of each*. (*Johnston's
American Politics*, p. 96.)

XII.

POLITICAL PATRONAGE.

The " Demand for Spoils."—It is fitting to trace more fully how the custom was introduced into the politics of the country, the principle of which is tersely expressed by the aphorism, "to the victors belong the spoils."

The four presidents immediately preceding Jackson,—Jefferson, Madison, Monroe and John Quincy Adams—were educated and refined gentlemen, and judicious in the exercise of the duties of their office in respect to the appointments of subordinates; in consequence they held the radical Democracy in check. But now the latter were to have their own president—" one of the people," as they put it. In the presidential election of 1824, Jackson had more electoral votes than any one of the other candidates—his vote being 99, Adams's 84, Crawford's 41, and Clay's 37. Although this was a minority of the whole, the Democracy, whom Jackson represented, demanded that the House of Representatives should waive its independent position and choose him president, simply because he had a plurality though not a majority of the electoral votes, as required by the Constitution.

The Kremer Letter.—A few days before the House was to act on the subject, there appeared in a county newspaper of Pennsylvania a letter over the name of a certain "half-educated" member of Congress, named Kremer, from a rural district in that State. This letter stated in substance that Henry Clay, whose name would not come before the House, because only the three candidates having the highest number of electoral votes could do so— had made a bargain with Mr. Adams to the effect that he (Clay) would throw his influence in favor of the former, in consideration of which, Clay was to have the highest position in the Cabinet—that of Secretary of State. This story was known to be absolutely false, and the members of the House, ignoring it, promptly chose Mr. Adams. The letter was not written by its reputed author, but by a more practised hand, as its internal evidence and proof afterward adduced made manifest; but when an investigation was attempted Kremer kept out of the way, and could not be produced before the committee. Nevertheless, certain newspapers continued to repeat the slander during the four years preceding the next presidential election; meanwhile always characterizing its spurious author as " Honest Kremer." This incident is mentioned only because of the influence it had upon the rank and file of the Democracy and its peculiar resemblance to the coincidence of the forged " Morey letter," published in the interest of the same Democratic party on the eve of Garfield's election to the presidency in 1880 —fifty-six years later.

Election by the House.--The House chose

John Quincy Adams because of his superior qualifications as a statesman, and in this view Jackson is
said to have at first acquiesced, admitting that he,
himself, in that respect, had but little experience.
But to be easily influenced by flattery was, unfortunately, one of the traits of Andrew Jackson, and
in addition he was like Jefferson in imputing sinister
motives to those who differed from him in opinion ;
he seemed unable to recognize good qualities in his
political opponents, and to his dying day he firmly
believed the absurd story about the "Bargain."
Says Prof. Sumner, p. (221), "Jackson was a rude
soldier, unlettered, intractable, arbitrary, with a
violent temper and a most despotic will." Morse in
his *Life of Jefferson*, p. 148, says, "In a blind way,
because he was intellectually immeasurably below
Jefferson, but with the same instincts, Andrew Jackson afterward repeated the triumphs of the former
by aid of the same classes of the community."
Which classes Prof. Von Holst characterized as
the "Radical Democracy."

Jackson a Candidate.—Immediately after the
inauguration of Adams, Jackson was taken up, especially by the leaders of the latter, as their candidate
for 1828 ; meanwhile, as a preliminary process, he
was beset by a host of politicians who knew his sus-
ceptibility to flattery, and they so lauded his qualifications to be President of the United States, that he
himself got the impression, in the course of these
intervening years, that he was the most competent
man in the nation, and the only one who could save

the Republic! He seemed also to be irritated;
since he had been made believe that, somehow, he
was defrauded of what was due his merit, in his not
having been chosen by the House instead of Mr.
Adams. As Prof. Von Holst puts the case (II. p.
50).—" A narrow-minded man with absolute faith
in himself." "His election was the triumph of the
radical over the moderate Democracy." And now,
" professional politicians and the crowd" took possession of the White House.

Jackson's Theories Changed.—It may be worth
the labor to trace the influences that produced a
change in the political theories of Andrew Jackson.
This result was the outgrowth of the systematized
efforts of "professional politicians." When James
Monroe was about to assume the office of president,
Jackson urged him "to exterminate that monster—
party spirit," saying that the "chief magistrate of a
great and powerful nation should never indulge in
party feelings." Said he,—" Consult no party in your
choice of your ministry or cabinet," (*Von Holst*, II.
p. 13). Jackson afterward changed his mind on
this phase of appointments to office—not consciously,
it would seem, of his own motion, but from outside
pressure, which influenced him by appealing to his
self-complacency. The leaders of the time were
adroit; they did not dare assail him in a direct
manner, but by availing themselves of this weak
point in his character, they induced him to do what
they wished, and then congratulated him for his
patriotism in saving the country, thus strengthening

his theory that he alone knew what to do in the premises.

"**The Spoils.**"—The evil of patronage being used for political or partisan purposes had been increasing in some of the States, but as yet the demoralizing influence had not reached the administration of the National government. Notably had this custom prevailed in New York; that State was the paradise of politicians. During many years a "Nominating Council" named the candidates, and the rank and file of the Democracy never failed to vote as thus directed. This "Council" was known in political annals as the "Albany Regency," and its presiding genius was Martin Van Buren, who managed the whole organization with marvelous skill. This peculiar method was practised in that State for about twenty years. (Article "*Martin Van Buren*" in *Appleton's Encyclopedia* and Townsend's *Hist. of Politics in New York State.*) Seeing that Jackson was the coming man, and having an inkling of his character, Van Buren began to oppose the administration of John Quincy Adams, and finally carried New York State over to the support of the former, though in the previous presidential election, more than two-thirds of the electoral votes of the State had been given to Adams. From that time forward Van Buren stood in the relation to Jackson of a protégé.

Now, for the first time, appears the "professional politician" at Washington; national politics became somewhat a game, and the principles and a management similar to that which had been successful in the Empire State, were to be applied to the administration of national affairs. In that State originated the custom of appointments to office being made for partisan reasons alone; in which custom the interests of the State were held subordinate to those of the individual who received the office, not because of his fitness to fulfil its duties, but as a reward for services rendered. William L. Marcy, when United States Senator from New York, in commending the politicians of his own party in that State, said,—" They boldly preach what they practise. When they are contending for victory, they avow their intention of enjoying the fruits of it. If they are defeated they expect to retire from office. They see nothing wrong in the rule, that to the victors belong the spoils of the enemy " (*Von Holst*, II. p. 26).

Jackson's New Policy.—Andrew Jackson's intended policy was foreshadowed in the newspapers of his party; a leading one announced,—" We take it for granted that he [Jackson] will reward his friends and punish his enemies; " that is, those who differed from him in political opinion. John Quincy Adams sturdily refused, though urged in justice to himself, and his success as president, to remove numbers of United States officials, who, in an offensive and officious manner, were in the habit of opposing the policy of his administration, because he consistently adhered to his belief in the principle of free political discussion as the birthright of every citizen, whether office-holder or not ; and in four years he removed only *two persons* from office. Mark the contrast! The majority of the United States Senate belonged to the opposition about to come into power, and when toward the close of his administration, President Adams sent in a number of nominations of gentlemen to fill offices that had become vacant by death or resignation, the Senate postponed the consideration of these nominations to a day beyond the 4th of March 1829—on which day Jackson was expected to be inaugurated as president.

The latter came prepared for the emergency, having his list made out of those he intended to remove, and also of those he purposed to put in their places. With him came, likewise, " his friends " in hundreds, who openly demanded that he should "deprive political opponents of their offices and distribute them to political friends." The hitherto unquestioned right of the people to have the affairs of the Nation administered wisely and economically, was made subordinate to this new system of supplying partisans with places. Under the specious name of " rotation in office," lay the assumption that the offices of the government were the property of these partisans, *and to be used by them in turn*—thus there grew up a new order of things. In consequence the most sordid and selfish passions exhibited themselves in distorting and misrepresenting the motives and conduct of those whose places were wanted, and could be obtained by slander.

Intense Patriotism.—Jackson, the victim of systematic flattery, imagined something must be wrong in any statesman who differed from him in political opinion. From this mere supposition, it was easy for one of his peculiarly arbitrary nature to pass over, perhaps unconsciously, to the feeling of hostility toward such statesmen. This manifested itself in acts on his part that sometimes savored of vindictiveness; and, yet *in his way*, he was intensely patriotic, and verily thought he was doing the country service. Under the circumstances, perhaps, he has been censured too much for his adoption of the New York system, as introduced indirectly by Van Buren, who was his Secretary of State and most *confidential suggester.*

As has been noticed, to his inauguration came hundreds of his friends, who were made believe they had saved the country by electing him president, and they were clamoring for their reward, as the aiders and abettors of his election; says Von Holst : "Their most forcible arguments being the erection of 'hickory poles,' and 'hurrahs for Jackson'" (Vol. II., p. 10). His inaugural stated that the "task of reform" was imposed upon the Executive, and he commenced a general and indiscriminate removal from office of those who differed from him in political opinion—*all for the good of the country.*

Removals and Appointments.—The presidents, hitherto, had made appointments to office, because of the competency and integrity of the appointee, and not for partisan purposes. The same principle prevailed in respect to removals, none being made except for cause, and designed to protect or aid the interests of the whole nation. For illustration, Washington removed nine persons from office, John Adams, 10; Jefferson, 39; Madison, 5; Monroe, 9; and John Quincy Adams, 2; in all 74—*this was during forty years.* But Jackson, the representative of radical opinions, and under their pressure, unceremoniously removed, and put his own partisans in their places, 230 officials of higher rank, and 760 postmasters and subordinate officers—*in all* 990. Numbers of these had held office under Madison and Monroe, and were continued under John Quincy Adams because of their competency. Here was the introduction of the most corrupting element in the politics of the Nation. For twelve successive years the rule in the National government, in this respect, was strict and unrelenting; and then for about two years (1841-1843) under Tyler, there was a little relaxation; then, after another four years under Polk, came Taylor and Fillmore, represented by a medley of removals and appointments; then came back the old Jacksonian custom in all its vigor, for eight years, under Pierce and Buchanan, terminating March 4th, 1861, when the circumstances had become radically changed, and many of the incumbents were so disloyal, that it was absolutely essential for the safety of the Union that their places should be filled by loyal men, without much reference to their theoretical political opinions.

Disregard of Constituted Law.—Jackson came to the presidential chair as the idol of the radical wing of the Democracy—one of themselves—and his overbearing character, tyrannical manners, and disregard of constituted law, became *virtues* in the eyes of his ardent followers. From this time forward the influence of statesmen of a high order began to be made subordinate to the crowd of "professional politicians," by being outvoted on the floor of Congress by the adherents and tools of the "professionals." The arbitrary sway of this "idol of the Democracy" was almost unendurable, yet he was sustained and lauded by those who were continually prating about liberty and all that. Said Justice Story—a Democrat: "I confess that I feel humiliated at the truth, which cannot be disguised, that though we live under the form of a republic, we are, in fact, under the rule of a single man." (*Life of Story*, II., p. 15.)

"The Supreme Court had not failed to pursue the organic development of the Constitution, and it had on every occasion in which it was put to the test, proved the bulwark of constitutional liberty, by the steadiness and solidity of judgment with which it had established the interpretation of the Constitution." "No man can be named to whom the nation is more indebted for solid and far-reaching services than to John Marshall" (Sumner's *Life of Jackson*, p. 361). "The master-mind of Chief Justice Marshall laid the foundation of a school of Constitutional interpretation which is now completely in the ascendant." (Edward Stanwood, *Atlantic Monthly*, May, 1884, p. 701.)

At the commencement of his presidency, Jackson proclaimed that he himself would act in accordance with the Constitution, as *he understood it*. This is the first enunciation of that theory in our history. Jackson continued to disregard the interpretation given of that instrument by the Supreme Court, if it did not agree with his own notions. He even went so far, in one of his veto messages, to announce, that "each public officer who takes an oath to support the Constitution, swears that he will support it as he understands it, and not as it is understood by others" (*Von Holst*, II., p. 49). This theory opened a wide field for disregarding constituted law. The influence extended, and we even find Democratic officials sometimes applying the same principles of action and interpretation to the laws and constitutions of the States, that Jackson applied to those of the United States.

Jackson Managed. — Senator Poindexter, of Mississippi, tells how Van Buren managed Jackson. Should he have a scheme in which he wished to interest the General, he would give him a hint of it. The latter would say, "Eh!" Van Buren would adroitly change the subject, but erelong allude to it again. The General, now, would ask, " How's that?" Van Buren would evade the answer ; but he had set the General thinking, who himself would soon after broach the subject; then Van Buren would exclaim, "What a grand, a glorious idea! No man in the land would have thought of it but *yourself.*"

XIII.

UNITED STATES BANKING.

Uniform Currency.—The necessity for some medium by which exchange could be facilitated became apparent toward the close of the Revolutionary struggle, and the Bank of North America was established in 1781 for a period of ten years, at the recommendation of Robert Morris, the celebrated financier of that period. (*American People*, p. 544.) This institution was of immense advantage to the cause of Independence in its closing struggles. Then again at the commencement of Washington's administration, when the United States government was inaugurated, Congress took a comprehensive view of the situation, and on the recommendation of Alexander Hamilton, Secretary of the Treasury, chartered a National bank (1792), for twenty years, with the privilege of having branches in any of the States. This bank was of very great advantage in promoting exchanges in commerce and thus encouraging the industries of the people. When this charter had expired and the affairs of the bank wound up toward the close of the war of 1812, another United States bank was chartered (1816) for twenty years, which charter expired in 1836. This bank commenced operations in Philadelphia, March 4, 1817, and in connection with its

branches—numbering twenty-five—in other States,
afforded the people a uniform currency redeemable
at all times in gold and silver. (*American People*,
p. 686.) These banks, the latter especially, fulfilled
their parts well and were of immense value to the
commerce and the industries of the people in affording facilities in moneyed transactions throughout
the Union.

The U. S. Bank Opposed.—The Southern statesmen for the greater part opposed a United States
bank, " because it would faciliate the borrowing of
money by the government," (*Deb. in Congress* I.
p. 287); and Jefferson was even in favor of an
amendment to the Constitution by which "the
United States government would not have the
power to make loans " (*Works*, IV. p. 260).
Still another objection was " that the bank would
be of advantage only to the mercantile interests."
(*Deb. in Congress*, I. p. 272.) Prof. Sumner gives
one of the current objections to the old bank when
he says : " the Democrats opposed it as aristocratic,
federalistic ; a dangerous political engine, because
its stock was partly held by foreign noblemen "
(p. 229), and Jefferson as expressed in his private
correspondence, held similar views. This unreasonable feeling of hostility to anything English, extending from the leaders, pervaded the minds of
the rank and file of the Democracy. They seemed
unable to comprehend that capital, no matter whence
derived, invested for instance in our internal improvements, was aiding the industrial progress of

the country. The writer, when a boy, once heard two staunch Democrats lamenting that English stockholders owned a portion of the Pennsylvania canal, and what was still more alarming, rumor said, they would soon own the whole. These two worthy men feared that in case of war the English could *use their own canal* in moving their troops and artillery. But was this fear any more absurd than the objections just noted?

In 1815, and for many years afterward, Boston was the money center of the Union. The New Englanders had been industrious in manufacturing, but especially in sea-faring in its various forms, and had managed their financial matters on common-sense principles, and thus were able to continue specie payments. Sometimes they took the notes of banks outside, but at their depreciated rates or intrinsic value, and sometimes, when they were worthless, not at all, and instead demanded coin, hence the accumulation of silver in their vaults, and when it was in excess they exported it. For this legitimate business they were denounced by those parties who through their own mismanagement had brought on the financial distress that existed outside New England.

Jackson Vetoes its Renewed Charter.—A new order of financiering came into power with Andrew Jackson at its head, the latter announcing a most determined opposition to the United States Bank, even before it applied for a renewal of its charter, which expired in 1836. Congress passed a bill renewing its charter, which the President vetoed. Jackson was not reckoned, even by his admirers, to be learned in constitutional law ; yet he had the audacity to declare he did not deem it constitutional for Congress to charter a United States or National bank. There had been three such charters already given, as we have seen—two since the inauguration of the National Government. Their charters were held to be constitutional by an express decision of the Supreme Court—the legitimate authority ; in addition the same was approved by Madison and the most learned jurists of the Nation. Yet Jackson, in his self-complacent ignorance of the fundamental law of the land, placed himself in opposition to these judicial decisions and vetoed the bill to renew the charter of the bank. Jackson "set up his own arbitrary will against the judgment of two congresses, two presidents of great authority, the Supreme Court of the United States, and the general acquiescence of the Nation on a question of constitutional construction." (*Judge Curtiss' Life of James Buchanan*, I. p. 414.)

Chaos.—The Bank had been of immense advantage to the whole country in facilitating mercantile exchanges. Had it not been for certain pet notions of leading Democratic statesmen, a Bank might have been chartered, which in its legitimate functions could have been a "financial agent" for the whole land ; and thus saved annually millions on millions in exchange or discounts to the people in their trade with each other in the different States and sections.

But after a charter was denied the Bank giving it a national character, there sprang into existence an unusual number of banks, under the authority of the several States, and in addition great numbers of *private* ones, that were virtually irresponsible. For the most part the charters given by the States were loosely drawn, and thus afforded facilities for defrauding that innocent victim—the public. Says Prof. Sumner,—" Ninety-nine in one hundred of these banks (outside New England) were pure swindles. They had no capital; by issuing notes they borrowed instead of lending, and they paid no interest," (p. 230). In a thousand ways they were vicious, and lost their credit; the result was a continuous and enormous expense in the way of discounts or exchange, when merchants did business at a distance or out of their own States. This immense tax fell upon the people, who were the consumers, as it enhanced the price of almost every article. The necessity to pay these discounts brought into existence hordes of brokers, who entered upon the business of conducting these exchanges, and their commissions were just so much loss to the people at large, while they themselves were non-producers, but acquiring fortunes in consequence of the financial disorders thus introduced in the commercial world. These banks, for the greater part, were continually going into liquidation and defrauding their customers, while their places were supplied by others which usually went through a similar process.

Who were to Blame.—Why may not these Democratic statesmen be justly held responsible for these immense losses to the people, from 1836 to 1863? Had it not been for their peculiar notions on the subject of the finances, they could have devised a national banking institution, which might have been so guarded in its provisions as to prevent fraud, and have been of almost incalculable advantage to the business interests of the whole land. A bill designed to accomplish this end was introduced and supported by the Whigs; it passed Congress to be vetoed by John Tyler who played into the hands of the opposition leaders. Thus time passed on, and for a quarter of a century the people were enormously taxed in the form of discounts, which enhanced the price of every article supplied from a distance. The theory of not having a financial agent for the benefit of the people of the whole Union, was only another form of the influence of the dogma of State Rights or Sovereignty. A national banking system would have had the effect of binding the people of the different sections more intimately in their business relations, and the moneyed interest of the Nation, thus united, would have been a great impediment in the way of those who, for years, were laying plans to break up the Union. These gentlemen chuckled over every alienation of feeling that grew up between the Free and the Slave-Labor States, whether it was in business, in governmental policy or in church relations.

It may be said any political organization is liable

to make mistakes; that is true, but no party or organization has a right to introduce measures of such doubtful utility, no matter how sincere they may be in their motives. The leading minds among the Whigs—Clay, Webster, Seward and others—and commercial men, bankers, merchants, etc—members of both political parties—in every section of the country, almost invariably pointed out the bad results of such injudicious legislation—but without avail. The prophecies of these statesmen and experienced financiers were fulfilled almost literally. In the days of Andrew Jackson and Thomas H. Benton, the Democratic party prided itself on being in favor of hard money to such an extent that they did not wish the Treasury to transfer funds by check—but it must be done literally by gold and silver. "As there was then "—since the destruction of the United States Bank—"no efficient means by which the Government could transfer funds as they were wanted, from place to place by any paper representative of equal credit throughout the Union, specie had to be moved to and fro in masses and under guard." (*Curtiss' Life of James Buchanan*, p. 410.) The legislatures that were under the same influence forbade the banks having charters from their respective States issuing bills in amount less than five dollars. The design was to compel the people to use silver in mercantile transactions—but the latter refused to subject themselves to the inconvenience, and instead used the notes of smaller denominations, though they were issued by banks in neighboring States, and were often at a discount.

The False Electioneering Cry.—It is proper to notice that the cry of Reform by Democratic leaders, so effective in overthrowing the administration of John Quincy Adams, was based on charges, known to be absolutely false, but they were implicitly believed to be true by the unenlightened, who voted as their leaders dictated. It would not be complimentary to the intelligence of the prime movers of this crusade, to say they believed these charges, while the manner in which they persisted in proclaiming them, and thus gained their end, damages the moral character of their political honesty. This same administration, since the motive for slandering it has disappeared, has been referred to by speakers and writers, perhaps oftener than any other, as a model of economy in expenditure and the general progress of the country. It was a period of four years of unparalleled prosperity when compared with previous administrations; while greatly diminishing the national debt, it left five million dollars as a surplus in the treasury; the same financial influence passed over into the succeeding administration of Jackson, and finally led to the paying off of the entire debt. The people had been gradually advancing in wealth and in the blessings of peace; every branch of industry was prosperous,—agriculture, manufactures and commerce,—while the Nation, thus rapidly gaining in strength at home, was also securing more and

more the respect of the governments of the civilized
world; yet, in the face of this extraordinary prosperity the unenlightened Democracy—the leaders
never—were induced to believe the country was
going to ruin, and Jackson was carried by their
votes into the Presidential chair. It is a remarkable coincidence that in much the same manner,
John Adams had been displaced by Thomas Jefferson.

Reproof of Van Buren.—It is astonishing how
far party spirit will often censure that which appears just and proper in the eyes of posterity. Mr.
Van Buren, when President Jackson's Secretary of
State (1829), had instructed John McLean—afterward one of the justices of the United States Court
—as Minister to England " to reopen negotiations on
the subject of the West India trade," and in so
doing had reflected on the previous administration
(that of John Quincy Adams), saying that the party
in power " would not support the pretensions of its
predecessor." This undignified and unworthy
exhibition of partisanship was not overlooked by
those who had regard to the dignity and self-respect of the Nation as superior to any political organization. Accordingly, when afterward (1831)
Jackson nominated Van Buren as Minister to England, the Senate refused to confirm the nomination,
though he had already set out on the mission. This
they did on the ground of the objectionable instructions to which allusion has been made. The rejection was designed as a " rebuke upon the first,"

and we may say only, "instance in which an American Minister, had been sent abroad as the representative of his *party*, and not as the representative of his *country*." Strange to say the whole Democracy were incensed beyond measure at this dignified and self-respecting action of the Senate in resenting the slight thus thrown upon the Nation itself by a Secretary of State. The cry of persecution was raised. All other considerations were overlooked amid the furor thus excited, and Van Buren henceforth became more than ever the protégé of Jackson, while this reproof had much to do with his nomination and election to the Presidency.

XIV.

IMPORTS AND CURRENCY.

Northern and Southern Tariff Views.—While energy, intelligence and perseverance in the North were carrying forward manufacturing industries with unprecedented vigor, a universal depression brooded over similar industries in the South (1818-1833). In the former the whole people, in various forms, were industrious, while in the latter, with few exceptions, only the slaves worked. In the one section the planters went on from year to year raising only cotton or tobacco, never fertilizing the soil but exhausting it so much that in a short time it became barren and unfruitful; in the other the farmers cultivated all the crops suitable to the soil and climate, fertilizing their fields and making them from year to year more and more productive. In the one section labor was despised—in the other respected. In those days, and after the attempt at Nullification, it was customary for the ordinary slave-owners of a neighborhood to meet once or twice a week, usually Wednesdays and Saturdays, at some central point, a village or Court House, and discuss politics, while the more prominent were frequently engaged in the non-productive enterprise of meeting in yearly conventions and discussing why it was, as Senator McDuffie complained on the floor of the Senate, that in the Southern States were seen "deserted villages, houses falling to ruin, and impoverished lands thrown out of cultivation." This result these political economists attributed to the influence of the existing tariff! It did not occur to them that had they been as industrious and provident as the people of the Free-Labor States, their success would have been equally great, and that in addition they had a decided advantage in a climate and a soil that gave them the monopoly of the world in the production of cotton.

The people of the North—on the whole industrious and economical—paid as they went, while those of the South contracted the improvident habit of being behind hand, at least a full year, and often more; in consequence buying their supplies at exorbitant prices, and on this debt thus enhanced paying usually a heavy interest. This system of conducting mercantile transactions was ruinous in the extreme. But the owners of slaves, assuming that the tariff was in some way the cause of their ill success, and not recognizing the true reason—idleness and want of foresight—determined to break up the industries of the country by lowering the tariff under which they had been so successfully carried on. The remedy they proposed was virtually free trade.

The planters could purchase their main supplies in the Free-Labor States, but an antagonism toward the North had come into existence within a few years, that preferred free trade or nearly so, in order that they might obtain certain manufactured articles

from England—the principal market for their raw
cotton, rather than from the factories of their own
country. They manifested but little sympathy for
National success, as such; even if for obvious
causes, they themselves failed, there was no reason
or justice, why an unrelenting war should be waged
upon the industries of the Free-Labor States, and
the wages of those who worked in factories reduced
to a level with those paid in Europe. The slave-
owners assumed that they would be safe in either
case, as they produced raw cotton which Europe
must buy. This was the animus of the movement,
which, after a few years, led to an attempt at nullification by South Carolina. That State was only
more bold than Virginia and Georgia, as the latter
two professed to be equally opposed to a tariff that
encouraged mechanical industries, except " incident-
ally," as they termed it.

Nullification. — Compromise Tariff. — T h e n
came the decisive contest in respect to nullification,
or the determination of South Carolina not to
permit the United States authorities to collect within
her ports the duties levied on merchandise brought
from abroad. (*American People*, pp. 718–720, and
721–724.) President Jackson, in the crisis, showed
his manly strength in sustaining the Federal dignity;
but Congress backed down in passing the Compromise Act, introduced by Henry Clay as *a peace
measure*. (*American People*, p. 725.) By this Act
the Tariff was to be gradually lowered, to what was
termed a " horizontal tariff " of 20 per cent.—every

article coming in under that rate of duty. The theory was that the tariff thus modified would afford sufficient revenue to defray the expenses of the government and, also, give incidental protection to industry. By this compromise bill annual reductions were to be made of 1-10th per cent. on the value of duties above 20 per cent. for *eight successive years*—terminating Sept. 1842—so that the reduction of all duties was to be brought by that time to a uniform rate of 20 per cent.—except on about 100 articles which were to come in free. When this rate arrived at the "horizontal" 20 per cent. it became our first example of a "tariff for revenue only." In accordance with this duty of 20cts on every 100 or one dollar, it would result from the average wages paid at this time (1883) in Europe, that in producing an article costing one dollar in wages—the other expenses being equal—the English manufacturer would have over the American the advantage of 30cts; the French and German, 47; the Italian, 55. That is, the American manufacturer paid 100cts in wages where the English pays 50; the French, 33; the Germans, 33; and the Italian 25.

Almost immediately on the passage of this bill, those engaged in manufacturing, as a matter of prudence, commenced to curtail their operations (1833), and in consequence, the wages paid workmen began also to decline. Ere long it became known that in making many articles, the American manufacturers could not compete with those of Europe, where the operatives received so much lower wages. Meanwhile the rate of the tariff continued to diminish on all merchandise, and American production of articles competing directly with those made in Europe ceased almost entirely. The whole Nation virtually stood idle; bought in Europe, and went in debt for the class of goods it used to make for itself. Though the tariff was lower than ever before, the revenue was much greater, owing to the vast amount of foreign merchandise that was imported. The National debt was paid off in 1835, and within two years there was a surplus of about $40,000,000 in the treasury. This apparent success was at the expense of the ruin of the industrial interests of the country—the raising of cotton being the only exception. The government was rich, and the people bankrupt. In November, 1836, the people elected, as Jackson's successor, Martin Van Buren, the Democratic candidate.

The Crash and the Uprising.—Congress, at a loss what to do with the surplus revenue on hand, finally decided to distribute $37,468,819 of it among the States in four quarterly installments, and in proportion to their respective population or representation in the Lower House in Congress. Three of these installments were paid. Meanwhile the world was invited to applaud the statesmanship which had brought about this marvel of the Nation's progress. Soon after the first installment was handed over, various speculations sprang into existence; one form of which was State Banking Institutions, besides multitudes of banks owned by pri-

vate individuals, and under such regulations as to
be virtually irresponsible. (See previous chapter.)
Bank notes now flooded the land, together with
"shinplasters"—thus named in contempt—issued
by individuals in denominations as low as ten cents.
Speculation raged; the compromise tariff stimulated
immense importation; manufactures drooped. We
need not go farther into detail. In due time the
bubble burst (1837), and never before in our history
had there been so terrible a financial crash throughout the length and breadth of the land. Industry
was prostrate; laboring men and mechanics were
thrown out of employment; bankruptcies were almost universal. Within two years there were more
than sixty defaulters to the National government:
Swartwout, the Collector of the Port of New York,
leading that band of worthies with a defalcation of
$1,500,000. This latter phase was the outgrowth
of the Jacksonian policy of appointing men to office
not because of their integrity and competency, but
on purely partisan grounds, and also the result of
the measures of the nullifiers of South Carolina.

The excitement was intense throughout the
Union; the people traced these disasters to the
mistakes and the injudicious interference of the
National government with the finances, and in consequence, the breaking up of the industries of the
land. The Democrats nominated Martin Van
Buren for a second term, but at the presidential
election (1840), the people chose Gen. William H.
Harrison, his Whig opponent, almost by acclamation.

Great numbers of the thoughtful and intelligent Democrats voted with the Whigs; while, strange to say, the Irishmen, whom we have seen thrown out of employment, still clung to the party which had cajoled them with promising words, while ruining their interests as laboring men. The new president died within a month after he assumed office; then began a series of tamperings on the part of certain leaders with John Tyler, the acting President. But into this political flirtation we do not intend to enter. We have noted in this chapter the mischief wrought by Democratic and pro-slavery statesmen, when they broke down the protection of the tariff and tampered with the currency—stopping home industry and begetting speculation.

XV.

FINANCIAL REVIEW.

National Banking.—Until 1836 the surplus revenue of the government had been deposited in the United States Bank, which had always returned such funds to the government, as its charter expired at that time, and President Jackson refused to sign the bill for its renewal and the bank had to close up its business. After that the governmental deposits were made in certain favored State banks, at the time called in derision " Pets." The public money thus appeared in circulation in the form of notes or bills, issued by banks scattered over the country, to redeem which bills these banks had very little coin of their own; yet, notwithstanding this lack of basis, the notes themselves were received by the United States Treasury in payment of duties, as well as of sales of the public lands. The " Pets " soon began to utilize the money thus placed in their keeping for their own benefit, by loaning it to speculators; this they did most recklessly on the supposition that the money would not be needed by the government for a long time, since the amount of the importations and consequent revenue continued to be enormous. In consequence of these loans, speculation became even more rampant, especially in the purchase of the public lands; but a change began when, near the close of his second term, President Jackson issued the famous Specie Circular. This Circular demanded that the lands sold should be paid for in gold or silver, and that brought the speculators to a standstill; they could buy no more land nor pay for what they had bought, because the notes which they held they were unable to convert into coin, as the banks had very little or none in their vaults. Meanwhile the importations began to fall off—as the people were out of employment and could not purchase—and of course, also, the revenue. In consequence, the government was soon in want of money to defray its current expenses, and that within a year after it had announced a surplus of about $40,000,000. It called in vain for the return of the deposits, for the "Pets" being unable to return them, failed and became bankrupt, and their credit, always more or less spurious, now vanished entirely.

The Sub-Treasury.— This failure of the banks to pay back their deposits led to the adoption of the Independent Treasury. There was no alternative; by substituting that mode of keeping the public money, the interest that might accrue from it would be lost, but then it would be safely kept. The Democrats passed the law; and afterward the Whigs repealed it, as they believed that the public money under suitable regulations could be safely kept on deposit in banks, and at the same time pay interest; but the former had had such terrible ex-

perience on account of defaulters, that when they
again came into power, they re-enacted the law,
and it still remains unrepealed, because the country
seeing its advantages continues the system. It is
a singular fact, that this is the other measure (see
p. 36), which, originating with Democratic statesmen, introduced and passed by them, has become
the permanent policy of the country. The physi-
cian deserves more credit for preventing disease,
than in curing it ; thus we have seen that the management of the national finances induced a state of
things by which the deposits in irresponsible banks
were lost ; and the remedy for the future was the Independent Treasury. "Ever since emptying its
plethoric purse into the greedy State Treasuries,
the government had not received enough to pay its
annual expenses. Every year it sank a little deeper
into the mire of debt." Thus "in a time of pro-
found peace, the government could not pay its expenses year after year save by borrowing." This
continued until the era of Southern Secession, and
in July 1860, the public debt was $87,700,000, at
the end of a period of many years of peace. "Such
was the miserable ending of the chapter on finances,
while they were managed by the South, under the
quasi administration of James Buchanan." (*Bolles's
Hist. Finances U. S.*), pp. 576, 605.

American Credit.—The credit of the government had been brought so low under Jackson and
Van Buren's combined rule, that one of their Secretaries of the Treasury said in his report : "While

European nations, with not a tithe of our resources
and burdened with debts, could borrow money at
three per cent., the agent of the United States government could not obtain a loan in the same money-
market, when capital was seeking investment at *two
and three per cent.*," and he was compelled to return
home " without receiving a single offer for any portion of a loan to our government at *six per cent.*"
Such was the condition to which the monetary affairs of the country were brought by this peculiar
financiering. "The Tariff of '42 was expected to yield
a larger revenue to the government; but for two years
after its introduction importations were light ; but toward the close of Tyler's administration" [Whig except in relation to the U. S. Bank] "the country had
recovered from its depression, profits were greater,
importations had increased" [they paid higher
duties], "and the revenues were augmented sufficiently to pay the current expenditures, and leave a
surplus," (*Bolles*, pp. 586, 589). Robert J. Walker,
(1845), "proposed to swell the national income still
more by revising the tariff (1842) in such way as to obtain the largest revenue possible from importations."
[This resulted in the tariff of 1846]. Here no respect was paid to the interests of the people as individuals, either as those who worked for wages, or
those who employed them, but only the most money
for the government. Thus, "by lowering the rates
and sinking the receipts below the expenditures,
and doing nothing to extricate the government
from that situation for three years, its credit was

seriously shaken. For such financial mismanagement no possible excuse could be made." (*Bolles*, p. 602.)

The Various Makeshifts.—It may be said, that it is not fair to charge the Democratic failures of those years in managing financial affairs, upon the Democratic party of the present time. But there always seems to have been brooding over that political organization a lack of practical wisdom in conducting financial affairs. Can any of their early blunders compare with their recent resistance to the resumption of specie payments in 1879? First they opposed the bill authorizing the Secretary of the Treasury to resume; then for four years, they persistently did their utmost to prevent resumption; and in the House when they obtained the majority, they actually repealed the bill, but the Republicans having the control in the Senate, threw it out, and resumption took place two months before the Democrats obtained a majority in the latter house. The commercial and industrial world owes no thanks to them for that measure so beneficial in its effects, but to their opponents, who carried it through in spite of their opposition. Again in the same category are their coquetting within the last few years with the Greenback movement, perhaps the most wild and visionary financial scheme ever presented to the American people, and dallying of their leaders with the free traders in their platforms, when perhaps a majority of their party are opposed to the principle of out and out free trade.

XVI.

CAUCUS RULE.

The two Parties.—The Whigs came into power in 1841, for the first time for thirty-six years, not including John Quincy Adams's administration, the Democrats had had control. Up to the second year of Washington's administration there was virtually one party only—that of the whole people. The struggles of the Revolution had united them closely, and the differences of opinion on the acceptance of the United States Constitution seemed to have left but little impression, as all had practically acquiesced in the result after the adoption was completed.

The contrast between these two political organizations—Whigs and Democrats—was in two respects: one in their management and the other in the elements composing them. The one—the Democratic—grew up as we have seen (p. 11); first in opposition to the policy of Washington's administration in regard to Neutrality—that party, under the same name has remained to this day; the other, the Federalist, succeeded by the Whig, and that, as we shall see, by the Republican in 1856 (p. 180), the latter drawing large numbers from the Democratic. The internal management of the great organizations has been quite dissimilar. From the first the lead-

ers held the *one* in hand by means of caucuses and
conventions; the *other* was never thus held, but
only as they, individually, agreed with their party in
political principles. The former had a much larger
number, who were not famed for general intelligence, and who, looking up to their leaders, implicitly followed them; the latter had more who
thought for themselves, and could not be held in
leading strings.

That prince of party strategists—Martin Van
Buren—in his history of " Political Parties " in the
United States, throws light on the subject when he
says, " for more than half a century, with the exception of a single instance, the Democratic party,
whenever it has been *wise enough* to employ the
caucus or convention system, has been successful "
(p. 5). This means that the leaders of that party
dictated and their followers implicitly obeyed. He
then remarks that the " sagacious leaders of the
Federal party, as well under that name as under
others [Whig] by which it has at different times
been known, have always been desirous to bring
every usage or plan designed to secure party unity
into disrespect with the people, and in proportion
to their success in that, has been their success in
elections " (p. 5). This is said *ironically* and savors
of a sneer at the success of the Whigs, because their
leaders failed to hold the members of their party in
hand to do their bidding. Again, in speaking of
the period from 1840 to 1860: " The wonder has
always been that a party, which had at its com-

mand so large a portion of the appliances generally most effective in partisan warfare, should meet with such infrequent success in elections" (p. 226). Did it not occur to Mr. Van Buren that the cases were not parallel? It would have been futile for the Whig leaders, even if they desired, to attempt dictation with their intelligent followers, as the latter did their own thinking, and never obeyed manifestoes of caucuses, unless they were in the main in accordance with their own individual views. On the other hand, a successful management of a political organization by the caucuses of its leaders is necessary where a large number, perhaps a majority, are of those who do not read carefully or think deeply for themselves, on current political questions.

The leaders of the Democratic party were "sagacious," and ever have been, in the use of caucuses or conventions to promote the success of their plans. This system was well adapted, and, indeed, the only one that could hold in hand certain elements of the organization, and make them effective in elections, as in doing so it was essential to use strong restraints as well as strong incentives.

The Material of Parties.—Mr. Van Buren also inquires why the system of caucuses or conventions of leaders "was in fact so much less necessary to one party [Whig] than to the other" [Democratic] (p. 6). The answer is found in the greater intelligence of the rank and file of the former.

Parties—How Managed.—A political organiza-

tion so constituted as to be susceptible of manipu-
lation by caucuses of its leaders, would likely be
made up of three classes: the first, the leaders who
devise the plan of action; the second, the fairly
intelligent, but who, absorbed in their personal
affairs, pay little attention to political questions,
unless in some important crisis; the third, the
illiterate and unintelligent. The first and third
classes scarcely ever change their political relations;
the one because of personal interest, for being in
the habit of influencing their fellows they are loth
to lay aside the power; the other, from distrust of
their own knowledge, obey the dictation of their
leaders: while the second in great crises, when
their attention has been drawn to questions of
National importance, such as the finances or industrial interests, frequently vote independently,
as it is termed, as upon them, the influence of mere
party relations is not strong. A political organization composed of those who read and think for
themselves, cannot be manipulated by caucuses of
self-constituted leaders; for illustration, the Old
Federalist or Whig never could be thus managed,
and the Republicans of these later days in the three
States where it specially prevailed, have recently
repudiated what is vulgarly called "Bossism."

Planters and Farmers.—The classes in the
Democracy of Jefferson's time, and onward for
more than a third of a century, that obeyed the
leaders implicitly, were the planters and farmers.
Jefferson, perhaps unconsciously, attributed much

merit to these, because they manifested faith in his wisdom, and they justified that opinion by following him with untiring zeal in all his theories, whether they understood them or not. In accordance with his conceptions concerning the " goodness of human nature," he seemed to imagine that the simple-minded farmer or planter, being " nearer to nature," had a sort of *political inspiration*, which he characterized as the instinct of humanity. The farmer or planter class of that day was far inferior in general intelligence to that engaged at the same time in commerce and other mercantile pursuits, the mechanical industries, manufacturers or bankers. Yet if compared in the same respect with the farmer of the last thirty-five or forty years the former will be found to be much inferior, because the newspapers of that day, circulating among the country people, were very limited both in number and quality, compared with what they are among the farmers of to-day. In addition the ordinary newspaper of the present time is aided immensely in instructing the people by other appliances of literature and science in the form of periodicals of various kinds.

This change began with the discussions from 1826–1832, and onward, on the subject of slavery, that roused throughout the land an interest in political affairs, which led to more diffusion of knowledge among the people living in the rural districts ; although the absence of common schools in the Slave-Labor States had rendered the country white

population there sadly deficient in the elements of
an education. But the rural class of the earlier day,
followed unflinchingly the political leaders, who
enlightened them by means of stump speeches. On
the contrary the Northern farmers of to-day are
among our well-informed citizens on current political questions, because of their greater facilities in
acquiring knowledge. The class among them that
once unhesitatingly followed old time leaders, have
passed away or changed their views ; their places as
docile voters have been taken by another class, not
preëminently intelligent, but who are of foreign extraction, and who are equally true in their party
allegiance—chiefly found in the large cities and
towns, and along the railways of the country.
From two to three-fifths of the steady voting
strength of the Democracy to-day in the old Free-
Labor States is found in this class of the population.

Sons and Fathers.— Mr. Van Buren, when
speaking of the continuance of party preferences on
political questions handed down from one generation to another, says: " Sons have generally followed in the footsteps of their fathers, and families
originally differing in political principles, have in
regular succession maintained and transmitted this
opposition," (p. 7). Facts seem to be wanting to
establish this theory very perfectly ; it may have
been more correct in the earlier days, when political information was not as widely diffused as since
by means of numerous newspapers, in which national questions are ably and fully discussed, and the

readers have more opportunity to read and reflect
on the opposing arguments.   In later times, it was
strikingly true that many *thinking* sons of Democratic fathers took steps in accordance with the advance of the times, and left the paternal fold.   The
first break was in 1840, when the Whigs came into
control of the government by the aid of advanced
Democrats, but the great and permanent break was
made, when " the young Democracy " refused to follow their fathers any farther in their subserviency to
the slave-power.   Van Buren himself, even, head-
ing the revolt as the presidential candidate of the
Free-Soil party in 1848, in its endeavor to prevent
the extension of the system of human bondage into
free territory.   The majority of these never returned to the political dogmas of their fathers, but
repudiated them by voting for John C. Frémont in
1856, and four years afterward for Abraham Lincoln
When the firing on Fort Sumter took place, there
occurred a still greater desertion of the sons from
the old faith of the fathers, and these *young native*
Democrats either entered the ranks of the Union
army or aided the cause by other means.   They,
also, never returned; afterward they learned some
lessons in political economy, and did not sympathize
with destroying the finances of the country, nor refuse to aid its industries, while they thought it
just and proper to give the freedman a chance to help
himself in his new relation as a citizen of the republic
in good and regular standing.

    The Foreigners.—If the party of to-day con-

sisted only of those lineally descended from the old
line Democracy, there would be few to do it reverence. Take away the foreign element and how
many would be left? Before the Rebellion the Hi-
bernians in the Free-Labor States, especially in the
cities and large towns and along the railroads, were
almost supreme in the Democratic party, but these
Irishmen acted nobly in the Union cause; those
who went into the armies fought valiantly for the
preservation of the Nation's life. But when the war
was over the impulsive fighting Irishmen nearly all
went back to their first love—Democracy. It is
amazing they did not see that the very leaders,
whose principles they had fought against for four
years, were the same who now told them that the
Republicans were their enemies in disguise, and
freed the slaves only to bring them North, by hundreds of thousands to take the places of Irishmen in
their fields of labor. This absurd fabrication had
perhaps as much effect as any other in seducing the
Irishman back to his old allegiance, and to-day the
main strength of the Democracy lies in the foreign
adherents, who obey the mandates of their leaders,
apparently without thinking for themselves at all.
They wish well for the country and for themselves,
but for lack of knowledge they are unable fully to
comprehend all the bearings of the questions of
finance, and the aids that industry needs in our
comparatively new country, and for that reason
they persistently vote against their own interests
as mechanics and laborers. Should a war occur.

these very men would show their love for their
adopted country by volunteering in multitudes.
Now, however, as in the earlier years, a large number of the Democratic party is made up of those
who do not think, but who blindly follow their
leaders under the party whip of caucus-rule.

Servility to "Bosses."—In our political annals
there is no unwritten law so arbitrary and tyrannical
as that of the caucus-rule of to-day in vogue among
the leaders of the Democracy. Van Buren intimates
that the system was peculiarly effective in controlling
unintelligent voters. In order to deter a member
of the party from changing his political relations,
there is held over him the threat of his *losing caste*
among his fellows; this form of punishment has
great influence upon the rank and file of the party
in the cities as well as in the rural districts. The
servility of ignorant voters toward their political
"Bosses" is not less degrading than the subserviency of intelligent and reputable citizens, who obey
the mandates of the same dictators when the latter put in nomination candidates for office that are
unworthy of support in any form whatever. Yet
strange to say, these worthy citizens, perhaps unconsciously trammelled by their associations, often
vote for such nominees for the sake of sustaining
the prestige of the party.

XVII.

WHIG REFORMS.

The Whig Party.—The first business that occupied the attention of the Whig Congress on its assembling in 1841, was to remedy the evils brought upon the country by the legislation of the previous ten years. The members of the Whig party were the earnest advocates of some system by which to develop the industries as well as the resources of the whole country. Though fewer in numbers than their political opponents, they had been, and were in those days, and ever after under another name have been, the party of progress; they were composed of the men who would think and act for themselves, and for that reason would not be trammeled by mere leaders as such; they had too much self-respect to obey implicitly conventions unless the latter's enunciated principles coincided with their own. Hence, only after gross mismanagement of the Nation's affairs by the opposite party, could they come into the control of the government, and only then, by the aid of Democratic voters who were also dissatisfied with the policy of their own party.

Industrial Advancement.—Under the influence of the tariff enacted in 1842, the industries of the

country, so prostrate after a depression of eight or
ten years, as if under some magical influence, sprang
into activity. This progress continued for only
four years. Meanwhile the policy of the Democratic
organization came more than ever under the control of the slave-holding leaders in those States that
raised cotton, and, also, in those that supplied the
latter with fresh slaves. Then by degrees the portion of the party in the Free-Labor States, coming
still more under the same influence, fell into line of
not promoting the manufacturing industries of their
own States, by aiding to pass the tariff of 1846.
This indirect method of retarding the progress of
these industries was to be carried on under the
disguise of a " tariff for revenue and incidental protection." The Nullifiers, as we have seen, took the
ground that protected industry was unconstitutional,
hence as a tariff, however low, must to that extent
be a protection to the American manufacturer of
the same kind of article, it would follow that Free
Trade, alone, was constitutional. Had the question
on which the two parties entered upon the Presidential contest in 1844 been on sustaining the
policy which promoted the industries of the whole
land, the Whigs would no doubt have elected their
candidate, as the manufacturing interests had progressed in two years at such a rate as to attract
attention; the people of the Free-Labor States
were rapidly acquiring skill, and placing their industries on a firm basis, which, had it not been interfered with, would have become permanent. The

evidence of this industrial progress was seen everywhere, while the laboring man found employment
at fair wages with the prospect of its indefinite
continuance; indeed the people began to look forward to a success in the prosperity of the Nation
never before realized. These sanguine hopes were
doomed to disappointment, as we shall see later on.

Cheap Postage.—The good influence of this
Whig Congress was not limited alone to reviving the
industries of the Union in 1842; in it after much
opposition was introduced a measure vastly beneficial to the people and to the Nation at large—
Cheap Postage. There is no item individually
small, so great a boon as this to the " poor man ; "
and indeed all classes in the community, are thus
benefited in their social relations, as well as in the
entire business transactions within the Nation.
The cultivation of the affections of friends and of
families is of great advantage, even when they are
far separated ; this can be done only by means of
letters interchanged, and it is now accomplished
without largely taxing the parties corresponding,
as in the days of dear postage. Says an English
writer speaking of the introduction of their system
of cheap letter carrying : " Our post-office system
is our greatest measure for *fifty* years ; not only
political but educational, for the English mind and
affections."

Cheap postage in the latter respect is much more
beneficial to the American people than to the
English, as the former are scattered over so much

more territory, and from the fact that the members of American families are so liable to be far separated, when settled in life. They often migrate from one portion of the country to another; the farmers' sons and others from the east to the plains of the far west or the mines of the Rocky Mountains. To these persons and their friends at home cheap postage and rapid mail facilities are blessings that cannot be estimated at a mere money value. Cherishing the affections of those friends and relatives separated from each other far over the land, is an advantage of great value to the unity of the Nation at large.

The Opponents.—In the days of dear postage the cost of sending letters was a great tax upon the people, yet the leaders of the Democracy resisted cheap postage for years, opposing it as long as the bill was before Congress, and not until 1863 when that party had but a small minority in the House or Senate, did the people get almost the present rates. The South took the lead in opposing cheap postage; the States of that section, with one exception, *never* paid their own postage. The exception was Louisiana, and it gave a small surplus, while the surplus of Massachusetts was about the same as the deficiency of Virginia. The truth is, in proportion to the number of the inhabitants of the Southern States, a very limited number patronized the post-office, and this portion had but little respect for the wants of others who worked for their living, whether Southern "white trash" or

Northern "mudsills." They argued that cheap postage would deprive *them* of the greater portion of their mail, as the government could not afford the expense, while the advocates of the measure contended that the greater intelligence of the people of the Free-Labor States would supply the deficiency in the increase of the number of letters and papers sent through the mails, in consequence of the reduction of the rate of postage. This result has been attained in the increase of revenue from the post-office, now nearly self-supporting. The efforts in Congress to obtain cheap postage were commenced in 1836 by Edward Everett representing a Whig constituency of Massachusetts, but practically put under way in 1842 by George Ashmun of Massachusetts in the Congress chosen two years before, when Gen. Harrison was elected president. In 1845 the first reduction was made; but it took *twenty-one years* (to 1863) by successive steps to reduce the rate of postage to what it was 1st September, 1883; the Democratic members for the most part opposing the reduction more or less whenever the matter was brought before Congress, though a few individuals—more progressive than their fellows—voted for this boon to the people, while the political organization *as such* was opposed to it.

High Rates.—At the time the agitation on the subject began, the letter which now costs a *two cent stamp*, cost from *three* to *ten* times as much, and even more. The letter was reckoned partly by the distance it was to travel and partly by sheets, not

by weight as under the present system; hence dou
ble letters—no matter how thin or light—were
charged double postage; triple sheets, triple, and
so on in the same proportion. The postage on
newspapers did not differ much from that of the
present time; the great burden was on the letters,
they being so much more important to the mass of
the people. As soon as weight was adopted as the
basis of charge, another improvement came in, that
of envelopes, which, in addition to their convenience,
have been a protection against the necessary annoy-
ance of postmasters prying into letters to ascertain
the number of sheets of which they were composed.

This free intercourse by means of letters and
newspapers is an advantage of almost infinite value
to a nation composed as ours; its people homo-
geneous, and every community having representatives from other communities far distant, but
often united by ties of relationship, as we find in
the wide separation of families. The advantages
accruing from cheap postage to the business relations between the different portions of the Union,
are as obviously beneficial as they are great. It is
due to truth and justice as well as to history, that
the American people should recognize to whose
foresight and statesmanship they are indebted for
this boon, and what influence has consistently opposed it from the earliest to the latest times.

XVIII.

DEMOCRATS AGAIN IN POWER.

The Turn of the Wheel.—Into the presidential canvass of 1844 the South came with the demand that Texas should be annexed to the Union; thus the question of slavery was introduced; by this means James K. Polk of Tennessee, was elected. The annexation of Texas was designed to extend the area of slavery; on that question the Slave-Labor States were virtually "solid," and holding the balance of power between the two political parties, the Democrats succeeded in this national election; as the Northern wing of the party succumbed as usual to the dictation of the Southern, the Whigs of those States were not so much opposed to the acquisition of Texas, but they were unwilling to have it at the expense and moral wrong of a war with Mexico, when it was evident that the same end could be attained in a few years by peaceful measures. (*American People*, pp. 742–749.) Then, for the next fifteen years, slavery held sway in the National government, and the progress and the industry of the country was held subordinate to it.

The Trick.—It had been foreshadowed that the South was hostile to the tariff of 1842; but it was necessary for the Democracy, in order to succeed in the election of 1844, to secure one of the influential Free-Labor States, whose interests were thus involved; Pennsylvania was chosen as the battle ground. That State had always, strange as it may seem, voted against its own interests, but since her industrial progress had been so great, especially in developing her immense resources in iron and coal, under the tariff of '42, it was feared that without strenuous exertions, she would now support the Whig ticket. Her farmers must be induced to vote as they always had done. Therefore on the banners used in that State during the canvass, the Democratic leaders had inscribed the legend,—"*Polk and Dallas and the Tariff of '42.*" Dallas was a Pennsylvanian and the candidate for vice-president. He was a protectionist, and as such was recognized throughout the State; for this reason large numbers having faith in him on that special question, voted the ticket. We shall see how these innocents were deceived,—the State went for the party by a small majority.

Tariff of 1846.—It was soon seen what the revived industries of the country had to expect from the return of that party to the control of the national government. The "tariff of '42," was modified and almost neutralized by the one—"*for revenue only*"—enacted in 1846. The latter was passed under the dictation of the slave-owners; the changes being made in accordance with the recommendations embodied in the report of Robert J.

Walker, of Mississippi, Secretary of the Treasury under President Polk. This report, the London *Times* characterized as the only "properly free-trade report ever made by an American Minister of Finance." This bill was passed by the aid of North-ern Democratic votes; a tie occurring in the Senate, Vice-President Dallas gave the *casting-vote*, by which it became a law. (*Appleton's Enc., first edition. Article, George M. Dallas.*) This was a most wanton and uncalled for interference with the industrial interests of the country, which were rapidly becoming more and more prosperous. All were taken by surprise; not a petition for a change had been presented by the people to Congress; on the contrary all the Free-Labor States were in favor of letting well alone—but slavery commanded and the Northern Democracy obeyed.

Double Invoices.—A principle that wrought immense harm was introduced into this new tariff, as it changed the mode of levying duties in nearly all cases, from a *specific basis* to that of *ad valorem*. The former system prevented, to a great extent, cheating the government, as the article imported had a definite value given it, on which the duty was levied. The latter, as the name implies, was a duty levied according to the *value* assigned the article in the invoices, thus opening a wide field for defraud-ing the government. This was accomplished by the importer using *double invoices;* one on which to pass the goods through the Custom House, the other to pay and sell by. The first was sent with

the merchandise, the second afterward, giving time,
generally, for the goods to be assessed for the
duties before its arrival. The result was, that those
importers who paid their duties on honest invoices
were undersold in the market by their rivals, who,
in this manner, defrauded the government of its
just revenue. Many American firms, importing
merchandise, were driven out of the trade, and
much of this business passed into the hands of
foreigners. The alternative was, for the American
firms either to withdraw from the business, or enter, also, upon the same scheme of cheating their
own government. The *ad valorem* system affords
special facilities to the foreign importer who may
wish to defraud, because, having branch houses in
our seaports, they can easily use *double invoices*,
and with less liability to detection than they could
as correspondents of independent American firms.
In connection with the *ad valorem* mode of levying
duties, great facilities are, likewise, afforded for defrauding the government by *under valuations* of the
merchandise on which duty is to be levied. This is
possible by means of collusion between the Custom
House officer and the importer. (*Daniel Webster's
Speech on the Tariff in the Senate, June* 25, 1846.)

Says Sir Francis Hincks: "Frauds are invariably
perpetrated when there are very high *ad valorem*
rates as duty." (*N. A. Review*, April, 1880, p. 348.)

Government deemed an Enemy.—It ought to
be borne in mind, that, especially on the Continent
of Europe, the people are accustomed to look upon

their government more as an enemy than as a friend; from this sentiment it is easy for many to pass to the belief that to defraud it is neither a crime nor even dishonorable. The English merchant has a much greater respect for his government than his fellows on the Continent have for theirs, and it is exceptional for him to enter into schemes to defraud it of the imposed duties. The same spirit, it is hoped, will yet prevail to an increased extent in Republican France. But what can we say of the American merchant, if there is one, who can be seduced into cheating his own government, which is known to him only by its blessings? This measure of almost universal *ad valorem* duties, with its demoralizing influences, remained in force about fifteen years to 1861, but now, as far as it is possible under the circumstances, the regulation requires specific duties. There are, it is said, some kinds of merchandise imported, upon which *ad valorem* duties can be levied to advantage; these make a small exception.

Ignoring Facts. — Democratic leaders, when praising the "for revenue only" tariff of 1846, uniformly ignore causes that greatly promoted the business of the country in spite of the counter-influence of that tariff itself. *First*, the Mexican War (1846–48); *Second*, the finding of gold in California (1848); and, *Third*, the failure of crops abroad (1847–49), and the Crimean War (1854–55). This tariff finally brought about the crash of 1857.

XIX.

THE MEXICAN WAR.

Neighborliness.—As a nation we have been peculiarly kind in our intercourse with the people living on the eastern coast of Asia—the Chinese, the Japanese, and the Coreans. The same, however, cannot be said of our treatment of our southern neighbors. For the slave-owners and the Northern leaders of the Democracy, when, having control of the national government, and opportunity served, have treated the latter more or less unjustly. Witness the spirit of the Ostend Manifesto, and the several raids of filibusters (p. 138). But these outrages are insignificant when compared with the treatment Mexico received at the hands of the same political leaders—South and North.

If one wishes to investigate the intrigues and bad faith of certain politicians of that day in order to bring about the annexation of Texas, in spite of the reasonable protests of the Mexican government, then at war with that State, and also of multitudes of the best men of our Nation in both political parties, let him read chapter cxxxv. of that sturdy old Democrat Benton's great work, "Thirty Years' View," where the subject is fully and graphically discussed.

Injustice of the War.—The war was forced upon Mexico by the influence of the slave-power which was sustained for the most part by the northern Democratic leaders, while the Whig organization, as such, was opposed to the war, in the first place because they deemed it both unnecessary and unjust, when there was evidence that the same ends could be attained in a short time by negotiation. In this union of sentiment were also numbers of Democrats, who were opposed to a war upon our neighbor, so inferior in strength and still more feeble in the general intelligence of its people. Yet the insatiate spirit of slavery would brook no opposition in the party organization to these high-handed measures of the leaders, who had control of both Houses of Congress and the President. The enlightened conscience of the Free-Labor States rebelled at this injustice toward a weak neighbor, and though the war occasioned the gain of a vast domain, yet the conscience of the thoughtful was ill at ease.

Says Senator Benton, "Texas and Mexico were at war; to annex the former was to adopt the war; while annexation was desirable in itself, when it could be honestly done." Such, also, were the well known opinions of other American statesmen; Mr. Van Buren was in favor of the same, " when it could be done peaceably and honestly." Henry Clay and the Whigs of the South held similar views, as well as many of the same party in the North. But for reasons which Benton explains, the plan of these

leaders was to have "immediate annexation" in
spite of the repeated protests of the Mexican government, which deprecated war, and also "notified
the United States Government three separate times
'that she should consider the annexation of Texas a
just cause of war." But the champions for annexation confidently proclaimed that Mexico merely
blustered and would not fight. "In no period of
our history was the ascendancy of the Slave-Power
more complete; nowhere along its gloomy pathway
did the Nation afford sadder examples of abject
subserviency to its behests." (*Henry Wilson's
Hist. of the Slave-Power*, II. p. 7 and I. p. 587.)
The venerable Albert Gallatin, who during his
political life of more than forty years had been
identified with the Democratic party, characterized
the manner in which Texas was annexed as "contrary to good faith and the law of nations;" of the
war with Mexico he was accustomed to say that,—
"it was the only blot upon the escutcheon of the
United States." (*Stevens' Life of Gallatin*, p. 364.)

The Assumed Boundary.—The joint resolutions
passed by a Congress under the control of the slave
owners and their special allies, *assumed* that the
Rio Grande instead of the Nueces was the boundary
between Texas and Mexico—the area thus unceremoniously seized on paper was about 2,000 square
miles. To this territory Texas had no right; even
if she did, by resolutions of her Congress, Dec. 19,
1836, declare the Rio Grande to be her boundary,
for she had neither ever occupied any portion of it,

nor exercised over it any control whatever. Said
Judge Ellis, president of the convention which
framed the Constitution of Texas, the latter *assumed*
to extend her boundaries to the Rio Grande "solely
and professedly with a view of having a large margin
in her negotiations with Mexico, and not with the
expectation of retaining them as they now exist on
the statute-book." (*Wilson*, II. p. 9.) Strange as
it may seem, President Polk, "disregarding the
rights of Mexico and the amenities of good neighborhood," sent Gen. Zachary Taylor into this very
district, first to Corpus Christi, on the south bank
of the Nueces to take possession, and four months
afterward to build on the north bank of the Rio
Grande a fort, whose guns commanded the public
square of the Mexican town of Matamoras on the
opposite side. Gen. Ampudia, who was in command of the Mexican forces, courteously requested
Gen. Taylor when the latter entered the district, to
retire beyond the Nueces, and not to provoke hos-
tilities. Gen. Taylor declined to comply with the
request, meanwhile referring the Mexican commander to the Government at Washington, under
whose orders he acted. The war was soon after commenced by Mexican troops attacking an American
party of dragoons, who were reconnoitering within
the district. (*American People*, pp. 753, 756, 757.)
Many prominent Democratic statesmen claimed that
Texas had no rights in the territory between the
Nueces and the Rio Grande. Among these were
Silas Wright of New York, Thomas H. Benton of

Missouri, Levi Woodbury of New Hampshire, and others, while it was the universal opinion among the Whigs. But the sentiments of all these were overridden by the advocates of slavery extension, who controlled both the Southern and the Northern Democracy—the latter with but few exceptions. The spirit which animated this war may be inferred from the answer made by Mr. N. P. Trist, who negotiated the treaty of Guadalupe Hidalgo and who had his instructions from Washington, to the Mexican Commissioners when they requested to have incorporated in the treaty a guarantee that the territory which they were about to cede should be preserved in a state of freedom. The reply was the exaggerated statement that if it were "increased tenfold in value, and in addition to that, covered a foot thick with pure gold, on the single condition that slavery should be forever excluded," he would not "entertain the offer for a moment, nor even think of sending it to his government. No American President would dare submit such a treaty to the Senate." (*James G. Blaine's "Twenty Years of Congress,"* I., p. 74).

The Cost of Texas.—Let us look at this operation. The Mexican war, from the battle of Palo Alto to the treaty of peace at Guadalupe Hidalgo (February 2, 1848), lasted about seventeen months, but, in addition, the time occupied in the preparations before and in the disbandment of the soldiers afterward covered altogether at least two years, if not more. The vast naval armament to invade Mexico on the east, and also another sent round

Cape Horn to make an attack on her western borders, cost an immense sum; then the volunteers —50,000 in number at once accepted—one-half to be mustered into the service, and the other held as a reserve. Within a few weeks, 200,000 men had volunteered. The expenses of this war are not at all covered by the nominal sums expended by the government, such as pay to the soldiers and expense of their equipments, etc., but, to be strictly accurate, there must be included the loss of time by the volunteers, in their being thus withdrawn from the active duties of life for nearly two years; and, also, the large sums privately contributed by individuals to their friends who volunteered; and, in addition, we have been paying pensions to the soldiers of this war down to this hour. But considerations of wounds, and sufferings, and deaths, are not deemed worthy of estimate by those who recognize only the value of the money expended, while the varied demoralizations incident to war, and losses of friends and relations, came home to the people at large, and were viewed by them from a different standpoint than that of the heartless one of money alone. " In the Mexican war, 120 officers and 1,400 men fell in battle or died of wounds in the United States army, while 100 officers and 10,800 men died of diseases contracted in the war." (Gen. Egbert L. Viele). After what had been paid out in current expenses during the war itself, there remained a debt in round numbers of $130,000,000, but, when we take into consideration all the expenditure that fell upon the people them-

selves, with this immense sum and the interest
upon it, the entire cost of the Mexican war to the
people of the United States must have been
$250,000,000, if not more. However, we will put it
at $200,000,000, which is certainly below the actual
amount.

The area of Texas is 274,356 square miles—thus
being about 70,000 square miles larger than that of
France. Seven years after annexation (1852) its
number of inhabitants was only *one to three square
miles*, as based upon the number of their votes cast
in the Presidential election of that year. Not an
acre of this immense domain was asked by the
United States government as a part remuneration
for the expenses incurred in this war, which was
undertaken at the call of Texas for protection;
neither did the State thus defended offer an acre!
Slavery demanded the whole, though with comparatively little expense to itself, and Northern Democratic leaders sustained the demand. As a matter
of justice to the whole people of the Union, some
such arrangements for remuneration ought to have
been made, since, perhaps, four-fifths of the expenses of that war were borne by the people of the
Free-Labor States.

The number of square miles in Texas is 274,356,
but by deducting the water surface along the coast,
—three miles out—and that within the State, which
may be estimated together at 2,500 square miles, there
would be left of land, available for use, 271,856 square
miles. The cost of the Mexican war, at its lowest

estimate, being $200,000,000, it would follow that the people of the United States paid for Texas at the rate of $736 per square mile, or $1.15 per acre —this price per acre being only *ten cents* less than that asked by the government for its own unoccupied lands outside railroad grants.

Cost of California, Louisiana, and Alaska.— Compare this $1.15 per acre with the prices paid for other territory, in some respects more valuable. The amount paid for California, including the Mesilla Valley, was $25,000,000; to this is to be added the $3,500,000 due from Mexico to American citizens, which was assumed by the United States, making in all $28,500,000; this was at the rate of $46.65 per square mile, or *seven cents an acre.* The purchase of Louisiana was at the rate of $14.20 a square mile, or *two cents an acre.* The cost of Alaska, purchased in 1867, was $7,200,000, or at the rate of $12.47 per square mile, or not quite *two cents an acre.* The Alaska Fur Company pays annually about $300,000 to the United States government for the privilege of capturing fur-bearing seals on the Prybiloff Islands, belonging to Alaska in Behring's Sea. This is $12,000 more than the interest on the purchase money at 4 per cent.

The people of each political party willingly acquiesced in the purchase of California, as thus, in connection with the Territories of Oregon and Washington, already in our possession, our domain would extend across the Continent from ocean to ocean. This mode of obtaining territory was legitimate, though it did grow out of the contingency of the Mexican war, and was in accordance with a sense of justice. The providential discovery of gold in California afterward enhanced the value of the purchase immensely. The price per acre was three times as much as that paid for Louisiana, by far the most valuable purchase ever made by the United States (*American People*, p. 558—Map). The latter's rich soil, genial climate and rainfalls, combine to produce abundant crops of cereals and afford pasturage for domestic animals, and in addition it includes our gold fields north of the parallel of 42 degrees and those of Colorado south of that line. But when the mines of precious metals in both regions shall have been exhausted, this immense territory of arable and grazing land will be still increasing in value, as its soil, growing more and more fertile, under proper cultivation, will continue to bless the Nation by its abundant crops—and thus go on forever.

XX.

KANSAS.

Increased Greed.—Thus in 1848, was Texas annexed and the war with Mexico brought to a successful issue ;—yet, here was the beginning of the end of slavery! On account of this success the arrogance and the demands of the exultant slave-owners became still more exacting, while their Democratic allies in the North remained true in their allegiance. Instead of being content with the acquisition of Texas, with its area larger than that of Kentucky, Tennessee, Georgia, Alabama, Mississippi and Louisiana combined, and also in a latitude and climate in which, if anywhere, slavery could flourish, the advocates of its extension demanded still more territory. It would have taken more than half a century for that wasteful system to exhaust the virgin-soil of Texas, as it had already reduced to sterility that of the old Slave-Labor States on the Atlantic slope. Notwithstanding, they cast longing eyes upon a territory of fresh and fertile soil, lying directly north of Texas, and west of the State of Missouri. It was about 550 miles distant from the center of Texas to that of the territory, and in a climate that was not deemed well adapted to slavery; yet they determined to have it. Within a few years they set in train a series of

plottings, which resulted in events that roused the
indignation of the people of the Free-Labor States,
including great numbers of Democrats, whose self-
respect was touched, when they saw how they had
been used as tools in the Texas affair and in the
Mexican war. We give the account here, to preserve the connection.

Fugitive Slave Law.—These indications called
into existence a determination in the minds of
many influential men in the Free-Labor States to resist, in a legal way, the further aggressions of the
slave-power. One of the outgrowths of that power
was the famed Fugitive Slave bill of 1850 ; the most
cruel enactment found among the statutes of the
Nation. Its harshness excited in the North a still
stronger feeling of hostility against a system whose
influence could produce such a law. The humanity
of the people led in some of the Free-Labor States to
the passage of laws known as Personal Liberty bills.
These were designed to protect free colored men
from being seized as though they were fugitives and
carried into slavery, as well as to afford arrested
negroes themselves a fair trial, to establish whether
they were fugitive slaves or not. There is not an
instance on record, in which it was ascertained that
the person thus arrested was a fugitive, but that the
individual was given up by a decree of the court
or commissioner ; yet perhaps there was no other instance during this period, in which certain leaders
in the North played into the hands of the slave-
holders as much as they did by their *misrepresenta-*

tions of the intent of these Personal Liberty bills, which were simply protective of the plainest individual rights.

Squatter Sovereignty.—As a measure preliminary to the seizure of Kansas, the Missouri Compromise was repealed in 1854. This measure, passed in 1820, after long and exciting debates, had admitted Missouri as a Slave State on the condition that the territory west of it should be forever free : a compact as solemn and binding as any covenant ever was. And in 1854 it was deliberately violated by the Democratic party, at the demand of their Southern allies ; who, with their accustomed tact, used as their agent a celebrated Democratic Senator from the North, whom they allured to introduce the bill into the Senate. The history of this breach of faith on the part of the slave-power with the people of the Free-Labor States, ought to be better known, but we cannot in this connection go into detail. Let it be sufficient to say, that with this repeal was also connected another enactment, organizing the two territories Kansas and Nebraska; the design being to obtain possession of the former in the interest of slavery, although it was included in the land set apart and agreed upon in the Missouri Compromise as to be free. In the enactment just mentioned was incorporated a principle, afterward known as " Squatter or Popular Sovereignty," which was intended, so its authors said, to enable " the people of the territories to be free in their political action, and when they came to frame their State

Constitutions and ask admission into the Union, they could *exercise* this right, *and adopt or reject slavery.*" At first, the Southern prime movers of this scheme apparently took but little interest in the matter, and left its management to their Northern allies; the former even intimating that it was a Northern rather than a Southern movement; but they were too sagacious not to be on the alert.

"Bleeding Kansas."—The bill having become law, and Kansas thrown open for settlement, emigrants began to pour in from the Free-Labor States in order to found permanent communities and homes for themselves and their families. The time had now come for the advocates of slavery-extension to act, and they also sent men into the territory, not with their families and to found permanent settlements, but *men armed*, with the intention to control the elections and make the future State slaveholding. These men—characterized at the time as " Border Ruffians "—crossed over the line from Missouri; drove off the legal voters, took possession of the ballot-boxes, and in the first territorial election (Nov. 1854) chose a delegate to Congress, and four months afterward by similar means chose a Legislature—all in the interest of slavery. Afterward these worthies were joined by great numbers of the worst class of roughs from some of the Southern cities. The Free-State men were taken by surprise at this outrage, but they soon rallied and began to arm themselves in order to maintain their rights. They were reinforced by still greater numbers of

emigrants from the Free-Labor States who remained
as citizens, while those who came in the interest of
the slaveholders did not, as they came only to control elections. "Outrages of almost every kind
were committed, robberies, murders, illegal arrests
and property destroyed, most of which belonged to
the Free-State men." These disorders lasted about
three years.

The Political Result.—The delegate to Congress, chosen in the manner mentioned above, presented himself (Dec. 1855) to be admitted. The
House refused his request, but appointed a committee to investigate the charges of fraud in the elections in the territory. The committee after full
investigation reported that the charges of fraud
were fully sustained. The House of Representatives
passed a bill declaring the acts of the "Territorial
Legislature" that had been thus fraudulently elected
to be null and void, both on the ground that its enactments "were cruel and oppressive," and that "the
said Legislature was not elected by the legal voters
of Kansas, but was forced upon them by non-residents
in violation of the organic act of the territory."

Now what was the attitude of the leaders of the
Democracy in the Free-Labor States on these doings?
They gave the perpetrators of these political crimes
moral encouragement. Their newspapers apologized
for these outrages; when they could not deny the
facts, they belittled the crimes, as exaggerated, and
raised the cry of horror because the Free-State men,
who went there with their families as *bona fide* set-

tlers, dared defend themselves with arms against the maranders from across the Missouri line.

The pro-slavery aggressions, lasting from the inception of the Mexican War and the annexation of Texas, and continuing on into this struggle for freedom in Kansas, were the occasion of an indignant uprising in the Free-Labor States, that in the end led to the extinction of their primary cause— slavery. The opposition to the extension of the system into the territories became embodied in the formation of the Republican party in 1856. Its primary object was to prevent such extension, but not to interfere with the system in the States where it existed. This organization was composed of Whigs and self-respecting Democrats, who refused to submit any longer to the dictation of the Democratic organization under the orders of the Southern slave-owners. To this new organization was also attracted the great majority of the thinking young men of the Free-Labor States.

XXI.

FILIBUSTERING.

Cuba.—After the Mexican War, about the time that Gen. Zachary Taylor became President (1849), —the Candidate of the Whig party,—a scheme, having its origin in the Slave-holding States, was set on foot to secure the annexation of Cuba to the United States. The motive for this movement is not difficult to divine. The honest President issued a proclamation, cautioning the people against violating the laws by engaging in such enterprises. Yet, in less than a year after its issue (1850), six hundred men—nearly all Americans—under Gen. Lopez, a Spaniard, eluding the subordinate United States officers, got to sea, and landed at Cardinas in the island of Cuba. Finding the people hostile instead of friendly,however, they thought it prudent to reëmbark at once, and make their way to the nearest United States port, Key West, Florida. They did so, but were closely pursued by a Spanish war steamer. The following year Lopez found means, it was said, again to elude the United States officers at New Orleans, and to sail from that port to Cuba with four hundred and eighty men. But this expedition was still more unsuccessful than the former, for it was attacked and totally defeated,

Lopez himself being taken prisoner and speedily executed. It was evident that Cuba could not be " annexed " by means of filibustering expeditions; some other plan must be adopted.

The Ostend Manifesto.—Three years afterward by direction of the Democratic President Franklin Pierce, three American foreign ministers, James Buchanan, John Y. Mason and Pierre Soulé, accredited severally to Great Britain, to France, and to Spain, met Oct. 9, 1854, in consultation at Ostend in Belgium, and thence issued a sort of proclamation, known as the " Ostend Manifesto " from the place of its issuance. This " manifesto," in relation to our government seizing Cuba if Spain would not sell it to us, is of the same objectionable character, though not precisely in form, as the expeditions just mentioned, the difference being in the dignity of those proposing in this manner to obtain the coveted island. The purchase, or the seizure as the case might be, was designed for the special benefit of the slave-owners, who had obtained Texas for themselves alone some dozen years before. The threat thus unblushingly made of appropriating a neighbor's property in this peculiar style, astonished the world, as well as the best men of our own land who deemed the Nation dishonored by the proceeding. The plea given was, that if Cuba was likely to become similar to San Domingo—that is, its slaves become free—it would be for the interest of the United States to take possession of the island in self-protection, lest the slaves in the Southern States might thus be induced to rise in rebellion. Every intelligent person knew that the latter would never hear of Cuba becoming like San Domingo, or anything else, but their masters would learn if such were the fact, and act accordingly, with the aid of the National government then under their influence. Of course those in the United States, who would decide on the condition of Cuba, were the slave-owners themselves and those in sympathy with them, their Northern allies. We can easily imagine, if there had been opportunity, in what manner that decision would have been made. It is a singular fact that the United States Government never disavowed this Democratic " manifesto " nor explained it to the world.

Other Raids.—Soon after the issue of this manifesto and evidently encouraged by it, another phase of this disregard of the rights of our neighbors was exhibited in the many raids made into Central America and Cuba, which were either permitted or connived at, if not by the authorities at Washington, by their subordinates. These raiders under the pretense of being *philanthropists* proclaimed their wish to aid the poor down-trodden people to obtain their liberty. Yet the latter, unfortunately, did not realize their sad condition, but were the first to oppose the invaders, who professed to have come with such benevolent intentions.

Responsibility of Democracy.—These outrages, by which the Nation was disgraced in the eyes of Christendom, were the outgrowth of the plottings of the slave-owners, with the connivance of their Northern allies, to extend the area of slavery, and for that purpose to seize the rich island of Cuba, to which they could send their surplus slaves from the border States, as well as from the cotton fields, with the expectation that their labor would thus be much more profitable in raising sugar and tobacco. The same holds true of Central America, where Walker and his maranders attempted to overturn the existing government. These crimes were encouraged by the Democratic leaders, but repudiated by the better portion of the party itself and also by the Whigs. These leaders in their national convention of 1856, called to nominate a candidate for the Presidency—James Buchanan—adopted a resolution commending in plain terms the raid then in progress in Central America by Walker and his fellow-filibusters, saying: "The people of the United States cannot but sympathize with efforts which are made by the people of Central America to regenerate that portion of the Continent." We need no further evidence of the utter disregard of the rights of our neighbors in these proceedings, nor of the animus that inspired them.

XXII.

FOREIGN RELATIONS.

Protection of Adopted Citizens.—There are also two instances in which our dealings with other foreign governments may be noticed; one in respect to the protection of our foreign born-citizens, the other for political effect. The Democratic party has deserved well of the nation in its prompt protection of American citizens in foreign lands; no difference is made between the native-born and the adopted. Such was the case of Martin Koszta, a Hungarian (1853), who had been engaged in a political revolution in 1848 in Austria, and had fled to this country, and in legal form had declared his intention of becoming an American citizen. Having occasion to visit Smyrna, on the coast of the Mediterranean, he there placed himself under the protection of the United States' consul, but, notwithstanding, he was seized by an unauthorized band of men and carried on board an Austrian ship as a criminal. He appealed for aid to the consul, but the commander of the Austrian vessel refused to set his prisoner at liberty. Captain Ingraham, of the sloop of war St. Louis, happened just then to come into port, and after investigation he found that Koszta was entitled to the protection of the

United States, thereupon he demanded his release. The Austrian naval officer hesitated to comply, but on being warned that he would be fired upon, he released the prisoner. Captain Ingraham was sustained by his own government in the position he had taken. From that day to this, the precedent has been established, that our adopted citizens under all circumstances will be protected in foreign lands in their rights as such by the government of the United States.

Political Brag.—Sometimes, however, the Democratic party leaders have make mistakes that savored of bluster, as in the presidential canvass in 1844, when the object evidently was to make sure of the support of certain classes of our foreign population, whose prejudices against England were usually of a most pronounced character. The occasion was in respect to the boundary line between Oregon and the British possessions in the Northwest. The question had been an open one for a number of years, and had hitherto been treated by both parties in their discussions of the subject in a courteous and amicable manner. But now the Democratic leaders introduced into their platform the assumption that the United States had a "clear and indisputable" title to the territory up to 54 degrees 40 minutes north, which statement was rounded into the electioneering phrase : "fifty-four, forty; or fight." This show of belligerency secured the votes of large numbers of those who were willing to twit England, and might have passed as a stratagem to captivate Hibernian votes, but when President Polk embodied the same sentiment in his first annual message to Congress, the relations were changed from a mere newspaper or electioneering statement, to what now became little short of an insult to a neighboring nation. England made no demonstration, but preserved a dignified silence. At length the President and his advisers stepped down from the position thus uncourteously assumed in the canvass and in the message, and proposed to have the line run from a point on a tributary of Lake Superior on the parallel of 49 to the Pacific—that is *five degrees and forty minutes*, or about *four hundred miles south* of what was originally assumed to be the correct boundary. The whole proceeding was undignified in the eyes of other nations, and came near involving the country in war. (*Benton's Thirty Years' View*, II, chaps. 156–159; *American People*, pp. 755–756.

It is the opinion of many that this "electioneering slogan" was the occasion of the Americans losing the territory of the present British Columbia. The Northwest Company was quite indifferent to the influx of settlers, as in that region there were very few fur-bearing animals. The joint occupation would have probably continued as it had done for years; meanwhile American settlers in large numbers would have found homes therein, and a mutual arrangement between the governments might have amicably settled the difficulty.

XXIII.

TARIFF RECORDS.

1846 and 1857.—William H. Seward, Senator from the State of New York, said on the floor of the Senate when the Democratic tariff of 1846 was enacted, that within ten years its effect would be seen in the prostration of the industries of the country. He judged from what had, hitherto, been the effect upon these industries when they were made to succumb to the low wages paid operatives abroad. He knew we could not compete with Europe without a tariff that would equalize these rates of wages, or, that not doing so, we must put the wages of our workingmen and women down to the mere pittance paid by the foreign manufacturers. To avoid the latter evil, as well as to develop the resources of the country, the Whigs, with far-seeing policy—for it was successful—had, in 1842, imposed a tariff intended to raise the needed revenue, and also making it sufficiently high to enable the manufacturers to pay their workmen liberal wages. The capitalist cannot afford to invest his money where it will not pay a fair percentage, nor should he be expected to put his capital where it would be lost, any more than it should be expected of the laboring

man or skilled mechanic to work for half-price, or
for nothing.

The lowered Democratic tariff of 1846 did not
immediately have its full effect in causing the industries of the country to languish, as, in spite of
that influence, they were at first kept up by the necessities induced by the Mexican war, and the acquisition of California—the latter leading to the finding
of gold in 1848. The excitement in consequence of
this discovery, and the immense immigration thither
from the old States, carried forward the industries
of the country, especially those pertaining to transportation and furnishing supplies. Tens of thousands
of laboring men went to California, and when there,
had to obtain their supplies from the older States,
while their places thus vacated in the eastern fields
of labor were filled by others, and at advanced
wages. " Every means of conveyance was called
into requisition, from the emigrant's pack-horse and
wagon, to the sailing-vessel and steamship. Some
went in caravans over the plains and the Rocky
Mountains ; some crossed the Isthmus of Panama,
and made their way up the Pacific coast ; others
took ship and passed round Cape Horn. The fer-
ment extended throughout the civilized world.
Multitudes of gold-seekers were soon on their way
from the different countries of Europe and South
America, and even distant China sent her thousands." This discovery "touched the nerves of
industry throughout the world," infused new life
into commerce, and awakened a spirit of adventure

and individual exertion never before known. (*American People*, p. 825). The energy which developed the requisite industries to supply these demands was preëminently great; while so many laborers and mechanics went to the land of gold, that those who remained in the old States received higher wages in consequence.

When treating of the industries of this period, certain writers ignore both the influence of the high Whig tariff of 1842, the Mexican war, and the revival of business in consequence of the discovery of gold, but attribute the industrial development to the revenue tariff of 1846, and to that alone. This has been strenuously argued within a few months. The plan of that tariff, as stated by one of its friends, was "to charge a lesser duty on partly manufactured goods in their various stages, and a higher rate of duty as they ascended to a state of perfection." (John S. Morse before the tariff commission, October 3, 1882, N. Y. Tribune.) The low rate thus imposed, when we had *not acquired skill*, would have the tendency of crushing out our feeble beginnings; when, if the higher duty had been laid on the *imperfect* article, we could have advanced toward "perfection," at which stage we would be better able by means of acquired skill and machinery, to withstand the effect of a lower rate of duty.

The Democratic advocates for revenue-only admit "the superiority of our labor-saving machinery," but claim that it "neutralizes the great bugbear of pauper labor." The purport of this assertion is, that the American manufacturer must sacrifice the advantage which he has gained by his inventions and use of labor-saving machinery, transfer that advantage to the foreign manufacturer, and take away the higher wages paid his employees, or in other words, give a premium on ignorance and low wages. The period immediately succeeding the tariff of 1846 was one of intense activity and commercial success so long as the needs of war and the California excitement continued. But the low customs finally had their natural effect; the country was flooded with cheaper-made foreign goods, our manufacturers, stimulated by the excitement of the times, produced more than they could sell under that competition, and within ten years the inevitable financial crash did come in 1857. Such has been invariably the result, when we have attempted to compete with the low wages paid those who work in factories in Europe. This crash led to the amending of the tariff from time to time, and the industries began again to revive, as an outlet for their products still continued in supplying the miners in California and the adjacent regions. Then came the war of the rebellion, and this led to the adoption of the tariff of 1861.

When we put a tariff so low as not to cover the difference between the amount of wages paid workmen in this country and that paid in Europe, our industries invariably decline, and our working people are thrown out of employment. How do we otherwise account for their unprecedented success since 1861 ?

The financial revulsion in 1873 was an exception; as it " was a necessary consequence of the speculation and over-production incited by the inflated currency of the ten previous years." (*Wayland and Chapin's Political Economy*, p. 158.) Since January 1st, 1879, business has been conducted on a basis of specie payments, and the inflation of the currency in the nature of the case cannot occur. The tariff should be so adjusted as to pay revenue, and encourage manufacturing, and thus give employment to our own working people at living wages, while, at the same time, developing the material resources of the land. But our free-trade friends would levy no duties on foreign made articles, and thus throw out of employment our own workpeople, who may be engaged in manufacturing the same class of goods, as it would be impossible for our capitalists or manufacturers to contend against the low wages paid in Europe; while almost to the same extent, the advocates for-revenue-only would deprive them of employment, flood the country with foreign merchandise, fill the public treasury, and bankrupt the people themselves.

The Tariff Commission.—The Democratic leaders, after a lapse of fourteen years (from 1861), obtained control of the House of Representatives in 1875; but, the Senate being Republican, it was useless for them to attempt lowering the rates of the tariff established in 1861, under which the industries of the country had prospered marvelously. Notwithstanding this result, they had inveighed for

the last ten years against this tariff, but preferred
to postpone action on it till after the presidential
election in 1876. In 1878 it was evident that on
the fourth of the following March they would also
control the Senate by a majority of nine, but two
months before that time, resumption of specie payments would take place, and this might possibly interfere with the expediency of changing the rates
on imports. They, however, resolved to make the
attempt to introduce a tariff "for revenue only."
The chairman of the Committee of Ways and
Means prepared a bill making reductions in order
to reach that standard, and likewise imposed duties
on many articles of raw material used in American
manufacturing, which had, hitherto, come in free of
duty. The chairman in presenting the bill to the
House prefaced it by saying : "If I had the power
to commence *de novo*, I should reduce the duties
fifty per cent., instead of less than fifteen per cent.
upon an average, as now proposed." This was at a
time when the wages paid by our manufacturers
were, on an average, about sixty per cent. higher
than those paid in Europe. This bill did not pass
the House, a sufficient number voting against it of
those who are nominally Democrats, but on the
tariff and the banking question, in their political
opinions sympathize with the Republicans.

Meanwhile the tariff question continued to be
discussed in the newspapers and in the canvass for
members of the XLVIIth Congress (1881–1883).
The Republican majority of that Congress at its

first session, authorized the President to appoint a "Tariff Commission," consisting of nine members. It was their duty "to take into consideration and to thoroughly investigate all the various questions relating to the agricultural, commercial, mercantile, manufacturing, mining and industrial interests of the United States, so far as the same may be necessary to the establishment of a judicious tariff, or a revision of the existing tariff, upon a scale of justice to all interests." The members of this Commission were recognized as men of great intelligence on these special subjects. In their investigations they spent several months in receiving testimony and opinions. They also visited throughout the country, the different centers of mercantile, manufacturing and mining industries, and invited intelligent gentlemen, who were engaged in these various avocations to appear before them and give their views; they also solicited information from writers and experts or those who took special interest in studying the subjects under investigation.

The "Commission" made their report to Congress at the commencement of its second session, and after due consideration the latter adopted the "Report" with but few changes, and enacted the tariff as thus revised, which revision was based on the general principle that it produced more revenue than we needed. In addition at the same session Congress endeavored to take off about $70,000,000 of import and revenue taxes—leaving, with little alteration, the tax on whiskey and tobacco, they being deemed luxuries of doubtful utility. It may be noticed that the Democratic leaders in this Congress persistently opposed this revised tariff, but made efforts to have the tax on whiskey and tobacco removed or reduced.

Present Party Attitudes.—No thoroughly organized party in the country can be said at this writing to be in favor of absolute "free-trade" as a practical working basis; but the Democratic leaders have for years worked in this direction rather than toward the protection of American industries, and during the presidential campaigns of 1876 and 1880, in the former announcing themselves in favor of a tariff "only for revenue," and in the latter, "for revenue only." This simply means that duties should be imposed so as to produce revenue for the National government expenses, without regard to the needs of American mechanical industries. It is perhaps not correct to say that the Democratic party leaders as such favor a strictly revenue tariff, for having an inkling of the unpopularity of that line of legislation, they hesitate to avow anything definite on the subject; but on the one hand they wish to cultivate the "Solid South," which for the most part believes in free-trade, and on the other to give the working man the impression that they are his special friends. Thus lacking the courage of their convictions, are they not likely to fail in securing the confidence of either the pure free-trader or the strict protectionist?

XXIV.

"THE POOR MAN'S PARTY."

THE Free-Traders of the XLVIIIth Congress, (1884), made a desperate effort to embody the general feeling of the Democratic party in a bill reducing the Tariff. This was under the leadership of Mr. Morrison, Chairman of the Ways and Means Committee. But it is the year of the Presidential election; it was widely believed that the "For-Revenue-Only" cry lost the Democrats the election in 1880; and the party, as such, was divided in feeling, in policy, and in action. About one-fifth of the Democratic Congressmen joined with the Republicans, and the bill was lost. There can be no doubt about the free trade tendencies of most of the Democratic leaders; but while there is a question of their being entrusted or not entrusted with power in a near election, there will always be doubt about their *action*. And this uncertainty is for business men and interests about as bad as a certainty of the worst.

Some Notorious Facts.—The Democratic leaders have nearly always induced the organization as such, to vote against measures designed and adapted to be specially beneficial to the "poor man,"

while at the same time proclaiming themselves his
only true friends. This ardent zeal in his behalf
and great love for his interests, have been proclaimed
especially every four years in their National conventions when a presidential candidate was about to
be nominated, and the "poor man" must be conciliated; the echoes of the same sentiment are heard
throughout the land in the State conventions of the
party during the intervening years.

It may be asked, if these leaders wished to hold
in hand on election days the man who worked for
wages, why did they not aid him by promoting the
mechanical industries of the country and thus give
him employment? Reasonable answers may be
given to this question: one is that the party was
under the control of the slave-holders up to 1861,
who were more or less opposed to the manufacturing
interests in the Free-Labor States. The Whig party
of that period was in favor of developing the resources of the land, and in this policy the present
Republican party is its legitimate successor; the
design is, to protect our National industries, and in
so doing keep up the wages of the laboring man;
affording him aid indirectly, and at the same time
fostering his self-respect, by giving him employment,
and an opportunity to support himself and family.
A second answer is: as this ground of thus aiding
the workpeople was already occupied, the leaders
of the Democracy seem to act as if they hoped to
secure certain results by prejudicing the unenlightened portion of the laboring classes against their

employers, and thus induce them to vote in opposition to whatever the latter may favor. *This fact is more or less notorious.*

An Instance in Point.—The famous tariff of '42 revived the industries of the country in a remarkable manner, and brought into existence many new manufactures and works. In Pennsylvania an iron furnace, which had been long in existence, was owned and operated by a gentleman proverbial for his kindness toward those whom he employed. This furnace under the influence of the tariff just mentioned was much enlarged, and it was threatened that if the Democratic organization succeeded in electing its candidate for the Presidency and a majority of the members of Congress in 1844, this tariff would be repealed, and one enacted instead more in accordance with the notions of the slave-owners. Under these circumstances the proprietor thought proper to call together the men in his employ, and explain to them the effect this proposed tariff would have upon his special manufacture, and upon the men themselves in respect to their pay, as he would either have to curtail his operations or reduce their wages. He expressed the wish that they would consider the matter, and vote in such manner as to aid themselves as well as himself; showing them that in the coming issue their interests and his own were mutual. Time passed on; the leaders of the Democracy sent their orators to harangue the workmen on the great privilege of voting as freemen, and all that. They especially exhorted

them not to be influenced by their employer, who
belonged to the "silk stocking gentry," that being
the epithet then used to prejudice the "poor man"
against those who gave him employment. The
election came off; of the workmen, the sons of the
Emerald Isle almost to a man voted the Democratic
ticket. In due time the tariff of 1846 was enacted,
and it inflicted a severe blow upon the general industries of the country, but especially on the interests involved in the iron manufacture. Nearly one-
half the furnaces in Pennsylvania in the course of a
year or two had to curtail their operations or close
their fires entirely.

The furnace just mentioned was compelled after
a while to reduce the amount of its operations, and
a portion of the men were of necessity dismissed.
The owner dispensed with the services of those
who had voted both to injure his interests and their
own. Throughout that whole region this benevolent iron-master was unmercifully abused, not because he had dismissed those workmen who did
all they could to injure him in his business, but as
the partisan newspapers put it, because he had
done it for *opinion's sake*—that jewel of inestim-
able price, so dear to these leaders.

This instance is not unlike many others that
could be named, when workmen have ignorantly
voted against their own interests, while being the
dupes of cunning demagogues. How is this evil
to be removed? Only by education; but the application of that remedy seems almost hopeless, so

long as ignorance and mere partisanship have so much sway.

The Working Man's Capital.—If the laboring man or mechanic or whoever works for wages, would avail himself of proper information, he would labor to promote the general industry, and uniform development of the resources of the country. Prosperous industry in its varied forms is a god-send to the man who works for his living, because he can then obtain employment. *The brain, the hand and the mechanical skill* of the working man, are his *capital*, as much as the *money* invested in the factory or iron foundry and their equipments of machinery, are the *capital* of the proprietor. The owner of these factories derives his income or dividends from the *application* of his capital in the business of manufacturing; just in the same respect the *capital* of the mechanic is brought into practical development when he is employed, and his dividend or income is his wages. The former would have no income if he did not invest his capital, nor would the latter have wages paid him unless he invested his capital, or in other words, *worked.* But the former, having his capital in available funds, can live upon it; the latter, on the other hand, cannot live on his capital—his brains, muscle and skill—he must labor, or invest them; the one party can put his money in a bank or business and derive interest from it, the other cannot deposit his muscle and skill at all. If labor should cease there could be no income from the money, any more than from idle

physical strength and skill. That legislation therefore, is humane, which in its influence aids the capital of both parties to be employed, and thus produce dividends.

The Working Man's Income.—The workman
or laborer obtains employment only when the capitalist invests his money in agriculture or in some
kind of manufacturing, in which persons are needed
to work in order to make the investment pay : the
result is a mutual benefit to both the employer and
those employed, and a dependence of the one upon
the other. In truth, the greater advantage accrues to
the working man, as he receives absolutely more in
proportion—it is estimated by practical men to be
from 80 to 90 per cent—to the amount of his capital than the employer, though they may labor
equally. The latter may deny himself luxuries
when he does not actively employ his money, but
with the mechanic it is a far more serious matter,
for when financial troubles come and manufacturing
industries languish or cease, the misfortune falls
peculiarly hard upon the working people. The
owner of factories can fall back upon his capital for
individual wants, when he cannot derive an income
from it, but the " poor man " has no such resource,
he must live upon his *income, i.e. his wages,* and if
he has no employment he must suffer. For this
reason that large class whose only capital is their
brains, skill and muscle, suffer the most whenever
commercial troubles sweep over the land.

Mutual Interests.—The investment of money

in a manner to give occupation to the "capital" of the working people, is one of the greatest boons conferred upon that class,—about three-fourths of the adult population,—as they otherwise could not support their families. The perfect industrial development of the resources of the United States, depends upon the harmony and good will existing between these two kinds of capital—the one in the form of *money*, and the other in the form of *physical strength and skill ;* the harmonious blending of these two classes of investments in energetic employment, secures the success of the people, and their happiness, and thereby indirectly promotes the interests of the whole Nation.

There should be the greatest harmony and kindness of feeling existing between those employing and those employed. The interests of both parties are involved in such enterprises, and both ought to be governed by the principles of the golden rule. If such were the case many difficulties would vanish. The fault of disagreement is not always on one side alone. It is hard upon the workmen to find the corporation, or individual proprietor, who employs them, refusing what the former deem sufficient wages ; they then have a right to ask more, and the request should be heard respectfully, and granted, if consistent with the best interests of both parties. On the other hand, it is no more pleasant for those who employ workmen to find them manifesting no special interest in their employers' business, but oftentimes indifferent to it, even sometimes looking upon their employer as inimical to them rather than friendly. Were it not, however, for outside influences, arbitrary rules of busybodies, the troubles that sometimes occur between those who pay wages and those who receive them, would be easily adjusted.

The Working Man's Choice.—It cannot be too deeply impressed upon those who are employed in factories, in which the articles produced are in direct competition with those of foreign make, that it is for their interest that such industries should be sustained, that they themselves may be employed. They should resist, in self-defense, the policy of any political party that would, by its measures, have a tendency to lower their wages, as those employed have an unquestionable right to demand a fair remuneration for their labor. To secure this, the workingmen, for their own protection, are in duty bound to study this question, and labor to attain that end; yet how often they unwittingly vote against their own interests! The Democratic party has, from its birth to the present day, striven to prejudice the workman against his employer, and also—chiefly at the demand of the South—to discriminate *against* American industries; thus doubly crippling the poor man's only source of success and improvement. Yet, there is no denying that the great majority of our unskilled laborers, and even numbers of skilled workingmen, under the leaders of the Democracy, almost invariably vote that ticket;

we see this to-day, especially in our Northern cities and along our railways. It is astonishing how these working men have been seduced into voting against their own interests; this was the case in years gone by in the times of the old Whig party, that strong advocate for developing the natural resources of the country, and of affording employment to the working people. A similar spirit prevails when they oppose the Republican organization, an advocate to-day of the same policy of improving the industrial interests of the whole land, and of aiding the laboring classes in the only way consistent with the latter's self-respect. Yet the majority of the workingmen, especially the unskilled, and we must say the unintelligent, always vote against that political party whose measures of statesmanship have given them employment; while they have invariably supported its rival, to whose lack of practical wisdom in managing the finances in their varied forms, history attributes, with only one exception, that of 1873—the commercial failures of the nation.

A Word of Warning.—This is not the place for extended argument for or against the general principle of a Protective Tariff, or one that equalizes the cost of production, but it may be admissible to urge working men—whether they labor with hand or brain—to study this question carefully; to note the condition of laborers in Europe, for instance, Great Britain, their low wages, their squalid homes, their social degradation, the increase of pauperism among them, and then decide whether Americans are prepared to pave the way for a similar downward course for their workingmen.

The animus of the South toward the commercial industries of the North may be inferred from the following :   Through the influence of Senator Robert Toombs, of Georgia, aided by certain Democratic members from the North, " Congress passed an act (June 14, 1858) limiting and forbidding the Postmaster-General to make a contract for carrying the ocean mails to run for more than two years." This law was designed to break up the " Collins Line " of ocean steamers, which then received a moderate sum from the National government for carrying the mails to and from Europe. Within two years this noble American line of ocean steamers disappeared. At the above date the Cunard Line was running under an *eleven years' contract*, calling for an annual subsidy of $957,000.   Mr. Cunard testified before a committee of Parliament: " If I had got the contract three months sooner, there would have been no American line." The committee asked :   " You are aware that the line (Collins) ceased because the American Government withdrew the subsidy ? " (*Denslow's Economic Philosophy*, p. 657.)

XXV.

FREE AND SLAVE LABOR.

Sectionalism.—It is well for those interested in questions of labor to trace further the influence of the Slave-Labor States and their right hand, the Democratic party, on the industries of the whole Nation, during the period 1832–1861. From the time of Nullification onward the South, instead of laboring harmoniously to develop the resources of the whole country, acted for their own section alone, and in this they had the sympathy of the greater portion of the Democracy of the Free-Labor States. This was the struggle between the North and the South; the one to develop the country in its industries, and the other by the extension of slavery to increase the political power of their own section; the one by the increase of industrial facilities to benefit all, especially the "poor men" or laborers, the other by strengthening the bonds of slavery to gain for the slave-holding class power and influence. The latter literally held all the political offices within their own States, and an undue proportion in the services of the national government; with them the "poor men" were simply

" white-trash," whose only use was to vote for the candidates whom the slave-owners chose to nominate.

As the slaves failed their masters in not being intelligent enough to work in factories, the latter determined to go into Free Trade or nearly so, and raise only the raw material—tobacco and cotton— which Europe must buy, and pay for in manufactured goods, though in this case the National government would receive but a small revenue, and on some merchandise none at all. This was to be the policy without reference to the industrial interests in which so much capital had been invested in the Free-Labor States, and in which great advancement had been made and much skill acquired. The friends of these industries argued that the Slave-Labor States themselves had unrivaled facilities for manufacturing in their immense and available water-power and mineral resources, and that operatives could be obtained from the non-slaveholding whites. But the owners of slaves had a special contempt for that class of their fellow-citizens, and were unwilling to promote their advancement in respect to education or acquiring mechanical skill in manufacturing.

From the year 1803 when Louisiana was acquired, and after the Missouri Compromise (1821) was passed, but more especially after the attempt at Nullification (1832) the Southern statesmen acted preëminently for their own interests with little regard to those of the other portion of the Union. The student of our history can see that after the time mentioned, their congressmen and senators bent their energies to secure the supremacy of their own section. The dream of Calhoun was under all circumstances to have the Senate equally divided in its members between slave-holding and free States. The admission to the Union of territories if they were free, no matter how populous, was opposed, unless offset by slave-owning ones. This result they could not obtain without assistance from the Free-Labor States, which had the majority in the Lower House because of their greater population, though the South had from ten to twenty members in consequence of the representation of two-thirds of the slave population. They were aided in carrying out this policy by the Democracy, North, the members of which for the most part played into the hands of the slave-holders from one presidential election to another, and meanwhile by their votes in Congress.

The slave-owners, as was natural, had a secret contempt for those Northern men who proclaimed themselves believers in the righteousness of the system. They were willing to use them in order to carry out their plans, but they did not implicitly trust them. Thus, when they fired on Fort Sumter, their indignation was of the sublime order, at finding that numbers of the Northern Democratic leaders did not sanction that proceeding. They then charged, but unjustly, the whole party North of treachery, as having led them on by expressions of sympathy, and deserting them when the hour of trial came. This was true in respect to some of the mere political leaders, but not of the non-political

Democrats—the latter were not in the secrets of the would-be disunionists. The rebels sneered scornfully at this newly developed love and reverence for the "Stars and Stripes." Since the rebellion the ex-Confederates and their sons in trampling upon the rights of defenceless freedmen and ex-Union men, have had the sympathy and connivance of the Northern Democratic leaders as fully as the old slave-holders had it in the palmiest days of the system.

The True Progress.—The true and general progress of the country always has been in the Free-Labor States, especially from 1842 onward. The intelligence, the industry and economy of the people of that section, in spite of hindrances in the form of unfriendly legislation, urged them forward in national prosperity, at an unprecedented rate. The people were so much engaged in the avocations of life, that they neglected too much the interest they should have taken in National affairs. With them the office of being a Congressman was not deemed of so much importance as it was in the Slave-Labor States; but if they had valued it more, they might by their intelligence and votes have diminished the number of Northern Democratic Congressmen who followed the lead of slave-owning members, and saved their own industries from many reverses.

The South as a section advanced very little in manufacturing pursuits, and even in cultivating the soil little improvement was made; in truth, under the wasteful system of slavery the cultivated lands grew poorer and poorer. The poor whites or "trash" as they were contemptuously called, were too ignorant to make much progress in those occupations that required mechanical skill, while the slave-owners and their sons thought it beneath their dignity to engage in industrial pursuits. The ruinous system of slave-labor meanwhile was impoverishing the whole region; like some malign power it moved steadily forward, soon exhausting the virgin soil and never making it more and more fertile. For example in Virginia, which had the possibilities of being the Garden State on the Atlantic slope, could be seen the ruins of the fine mansions of other days, in the midst of farms once flourishing, but now exhausted and overgrown with rubbish. Instead of going industriously to work and availing themselves of their magnificent climate and fertile soil, as a general rule, the Southern gentlemen or slave-owners mostly spent their time in complaining that the merchants and manufacturers of the Free-Labor States, were growing rich out of the percentages on their cotton and tobacco! The latter by their industry and economy obtained the means to purchase and pay for these products at their market value, and either manufactured them or sold them in Europe. What would be our estimate of the wisdom of Western farmers, that, to-day, should upbraid the produce merchants, who give them the market price for their wheat and then send it to supply the wants of the Eastern States or of Europe, even if at the the same time they made a fair profit? The burdens of these complaints were often sent abroad from Southern conventions, and manifested themselves from time to time on the floor of Congress. The main remedy proposed for these evils was to extend slavery to new and fertile soils.

Did not this influence extend still further, and even blunt the political acumen of certain American statesmen? History shows that for the last half century the statesmen whose writings live, and whose memory is linked with the promotion of the now recognized best interests of the nation, were not in sympathy with the Democratic party. The political theories which the latter advocated could not, from their nature, promote policies, humane in character and calculated to benefit the whole people of the Union. Instead, these statesmen drifted into a negative position—one of apologizing for wrongs, such as the continuance and extension of slavery, and indirectly, as a collateral of the same wrong, encouraging filibustering raids against our Southern neighbors; while in another direction, under the plea of opposing fancied "sumptuary laws," they catered to the liquor interest. In contrast is the manly vigor with which statesmen not thus trammeled opposed these wrongs. This influence entered into the higher and more intellectual walks of life. The reader may ask himself, with what political organizations have sympathized the great majority of the brightest names in our literature?

XXVI.

DEMOCRATIC ORACLES.

Jefferson and Jackson.—It is said the savage who comes in contact with the civilized man copies the latter's vices rather than his virtues. The Democracy claim two men—Thomas Jefferson and Andrew Jackson—whose names they use somewhat after the manner the ancient conjurers used great names when they performed their enchantments. Jefferson they never imitated in his generous sympathies for humanity, and his repugnance to the system of slavery, so contrary to his better nature ; but his views on State Rights they adopted, and quoted him as an authority and an infallible oracle on the subject. But Jefferson—radical as he was—never held the *extreme views* of State Rights or Sovereignty attributed to him by certain leaders who ruled the Democratic party, neither would he have thrown the Nation into the convulsions of a most cruel and uncalled for war, to continue, much less extend, slavery. These leaders endeavored to carry out the State Rights theories of John C. Calhoun, rather than those of Jefferson, but they unjustly attributed them to the latter, in order to secure greater influence by the authority of his name, as the great majority of the party North, even

if they so desired, had not the intelligence to detect
the subterfuge, nor, afterward to unveil the de-
ception. This had been the policy of these leaders
for a third of a century, but more systematized in
the latter portion of the time. Calhoun's influence
had waned very much, except in his own State,
South Carolina; his connection with Nullification
excited a feeling of distrust in the other States—
hence the necessity of giving a certain tinge to the
views of Jefferson.

As to Jackson, the Southern wing of the Democracy, and quite a portion of the Northern, rejected
his dogma as expressed by himself: "The Union
must and shall be preserved," and also his views as
to the development of the industries of the country;
but adopted his theory that subordinate officers of
the government ought to be removed, if their political views were not in accordance with those of the
executive, and, also, of not enforcing a law which
he deemed unconstitutional. Jackson was consistent, as he removed from office during the period
he was President, 990 persons, and appointed in
their places decided political friends of his own.
During the previous forty-four years of the government's existence, the Presidents had found it
necessary to remove only 74 persons from office,
and that for definite reasons. From this innovation
of Jackson was derived nine-tenths of the partisanship and unseemly struggle for office that thenceforth prevailed in the Nation's politics. The influence in the mean time being most demoralizing

and corrupting, the leaders having adopted the comprehensive aphorism of Wm. L. Marcy: "To the victors belong the spoils." The evil extended; and we find the Whigs to some extent, but partly in retaliation, carrying out the same system of change, though only in respect to important and influential offices. Strictly speaking, the latter had really control of the national government only four or five years out of the twenty-four from Jackson's time to the commencement of the Rebellion. Nor should be overlooked the injurious influence of Jackson's violating the laws because he himself deemed them unconstitutional, in opposition to the decisions of the legal expounder of that instrument —the Supreme Court of the United States. This baleful influence has permeated the minds of the leaders of that party, and we have seen them, even in municipal affairs, endeavoring to resist the enforcement of State laws, in accordance with Jackson's theory of personal interpretation of any constitution—National or State.

Disloyal Incumbents Removed.—When the Republicans came into power (1861) the circumstances were peculiar; great numbers of the subordinate officers and employees of the government were found to sympathize with the Secessionists, soon to be in open rebellion. In view of the condition of the Union struggling for life, it was expected, and the case demanded, that among its officers there should be no half way loyalty to the preservation of the Nation's integrity.

Since the Union has triumphed, the reform of the Civil Service has been steadily advancing, and the indications are that the affairs of the government will be conducted hereafter on the principle of employing only competent and honest men, and removing only for malfeasance in office. True patriotism deprecates blind partisanship, and appointments to office on that principle only. If a mercantile firm or a manufacturing company were to conduct its business as the United States did when "to-the-victors-belong-the-spoils" theory was the rule, it would lose its credit and become bankrupt.

XXVII.

CONSTITUTIONAL INTERPRETATION.

The Real Interpreter.—The legal interpreter of the Constitution of the United States is their Supreme Court. But Andrew Jackson, when President, announced that he would enforce the laws as *he understood* them, without reference to the decisions of that court. The influence of this political vice, or revolutionary spirit, has had a baleful effect from that day to this, as seen whenever his admirers wished to prevent the enforcement of a law, which in their wisdom they deemed unconstitutional, or of which they wished to get rid.

The Nation's gratitude is due to the Supreme Court of the United States, whose influence up to the death of Chief Justice Marshall did much in moulding our institutions by its decisions; thus standing as a bulwark against which dashed the machinations of theorists and partisans, demagogues and factions. Its efforts in behalf of constitutional liberty, and in training the better class of citizens to true ideas of order, were beyond calculation in their benign influence upon the stability of the Nation. One advantage was, that the judges of that comparatively early day were familiar with the understanding which the framers of the Constitution themselves had of its meaning. The court's decisions were pure and legitimate.

Jackson appointed more judges than any one of his predecessors in office, and apparently more because they coincided with him in his peculiar notions and prejudices, than for other considerations. The decisions of this court have been sometimes tinged, unconsciously no doubt, with certain theories, rather than pure deductions from the Constitution and its principles. The last of this class—the famous " Dred Scott decision "—was in its character more political than legal. It is said that chivalry went out amid the laughter of Europe, when Don Quixote was published; thus, amid the disgust of the unprejudiced thinking minds of the Nation, vanished the influence of such decisions as the " Dred Scott." Nevertheless, in the vast majority of cases, the Supreme Court has commanded the confidence and the approval of the entire Nation.

Unauthorized Interpretation.—The great riot to resist the draft in the city of New York (July, 1863), was encouraged by the assumption that the law under which it was ordered was *unconstitutional.* This opinion was proclaimed in the Democratic newspapers for weeks before the draft was to take place, and it was also announced that the Democratic Governor of the State coincided with that view of the law, and this statement was not contradicted by himself nor even by his friends. According to the favorite Jacksonian mode of dealing with obnoxious laws, this assumption was sufficient

reason for the mob to resist the draft. I say
"Jacksonian mode," for although he grandly crushed
the would-be Nullifiers of South Carolina, it was
chiefly because he did not agree with their opinion of
the unconstitutionality of the law they resisted; he
himself was a remorseless Nullifier whenever he did
not like the law. It was evidently known to a
number of these political leaders that some form of
violence was about to be used in preventing the
enforcement of the draft law, yet the Governor did
nothing, did not even issue a proclamation warning
persons against committing such acts of violence.
At this very time Lee with a rebel army was in
Pennsylvania, in the vicinity of Gettysburg, and
the National Guard was absent from the city in
order to aid in repelling the invasion.

On the third day of the riot the Governor met
great numbers of the rioters face to face in the City
Hall Park and said: "Let me assure you that I am
your friend; you have been my friends," and ended
by promising "to see to their rights." Instead of
denouncing them as violators of law and liable to
punishment—for he well knew that murders had
been already committed by the rioters then in his
presence—he took the ground that he would endeavor to have the draft "suspended and stopped,"
and for this purpose he had sent his Adjutant General to Washington to confer with the President.
He then asked the mob to desist till he could hear
from Washington. This implied that the rioters
were justifiable in their resistance to a law, which

they were told by their leaders and newspapers was *unconstitutional.*

At this time multitudes of innocent and helpless persons had been wantonly murdered, and whole blocks of buildings burned to the ground, while an asylum for colored children—an institution managed by benevolent ladies—was pillaged and burned and its little inmates driven into the street. It was a hideous crime in those who, knowing better, urged on the ignorant and vicious by false representations to commit these terrible outrages.

Congressional Nullification.—In the extra session of Congress in 1879, the Democratic majority attempted to nullify a law by refusing to make an appropriation to pay the salaries of the United States marshals, because they and their deputies, by laws passed by a former Congress, had included in their duties that of keeping the peace at the polls, when Congressmen and Presidential Electors were to be chosen. This refusal was under the plea that the law by which this duty was enjoined upon the marshals was *unconstitutional;* in the same category they placed the law of Congress authorizing the judges of the United States Circuit Courts to appoint supervisors at the same elections. The Supreme Court has since decided that both of these laws are in accordance with the Federal Constitution, which says (article 1, section 4) in respect to regulations of elections for representatives in the Lower House: "Congress may at any time by law make or alter such regulations." In this instance

the majority in Congress attempted the Jacksonian method of nullifying a law, which they
opposed but could not repeal. This virtual annul-
ment of these election laws was attached to the
requisite appropriations, and passed Congress; but
the bill was vetoed by President Grant. The plan,
as announced, was to stop the wheels of government
by not voting the necessary supplies of money
to defray its expenses, and thus compel the president to sanction the repeal of laws which the
majority in Congress, on their own authority,
assumed to be unconstitutional. The effect would
have been to remove almost every guard against
fraudulent voting, when Congressmen and Presidential Electors were to be chosen. (*American People*,
p. 1083, and Ch. XLI *of this monograph*.) Immediately after the decision on this law was made by the
Supreme Court, a representative on the floor of the
House (March 10, 1880) and a leading member of
the majority (which at that time happened to be
Democratic), is reported to have proclaimed his
defiance of the authority of the Court and of its
decision on these laws—the sentiment, it seems, was
applauded vociferously by the members of the
majority present.

Summary of Faults.—It would seem as if the
political faults of Jefferson and Jackson had been
embodied in certain prominent characteristics of
the Democratic organization, namely : States Rights
or Sovereignty leading to secession; extreme partisanship in removals from office and in appoint-

ments to the same; attempts to nullify laws which
they dislike, on the plea of their being unconstitutional : while on the other hand stand out the
rejection of Jefferson's humane sentiments in relation to slavery; and the repudiation of the doctrine
of Jackson in respect to the promotion of the
industries of the nation and the development of its
natural resources, and the preservation of the Union.

XXVIII.

OPPONENTS OF THE DEMOCRATS.

The Federalists.—To more fully understand one political organization it is sometimes essential to study the character of its opponents. The Democratic party has had during its existence three prominent contemporary and antagonistic ones—the Federalist, the Whig, and the Republican. The first, the honored organization under Washington, John Adams, Alexander Hamilton, James Madison, and that galaxy of eminent men, practically laid the foundation of the government. They and their compeers framed the Constitution—and on the principles embodied in it, based a government which has stood the test from that time to the present. The policy of Washington's administration, especially in three respects, has been acted upon by the national government ever since; First, in relation to neutrality or the non-interference in the quarrels of foreign nations. This policy appears so rational to-day, that it seems surprising it ever could have met with opposition (see p. 9); Second, the protection to American industry, as set forth in the preamble to the first tariff passed by Congress and signed by Washington; and third, notwithstanding the opposition continued for many years, the financial measures inaugurated by the first Secretary of the Treasury—Alexander Hamilton—

which in principle virtually remain in force to-
day, in the financial policy of the Nation.

The Whigs.—When the Federal party, to which
the American people owe so much, passed out of
power (1801), its spirit still lingered in the minds
of multitudes of the intelligent and thoughtful of
the land. The War of 1812, which had united the
people as patriots and obliterated much of the partisan feeling that ever existed, was followed by what
was termed the "era of good feeling." In time
the progress of the country demanded new measures
to meet its wants. The most prominent was that
of easy communication from one portion of the
country to another for the purpose of commercial
intercourse and travel. The spirit of the old progressive Federalists gradually revived, but under another name, for a time that of National Republican,
then that of Whig—borrowed from the days of the
Revolution. This party grappled with the question
of internal improvements, and contended that the
national government ought to aid in the cause;
while the Democratic statesmen of the time were
in the main in opposition to that policy, they being
worried by abstract theories on the question whether
Congress had the constitutional power to aid such
improvements. In that day there was comparatively
little surplus capital in the hands of individuals to
invest in internal improvements such as canals, and
in turnpikes or macadamized roads; at that time
the only effective—but, owing to the manner of their
construction, expensive—means of transportation.

But inter-communication, the Whig party contended, was one of the most effective measures to
develop the resources of the entire country.

The Whigs were, also, preëminently the promoters of all measures having an elevating influence
upon the mass of the people; they were, especially,
the advocates of schools of learning, and of all forms
of industry. These statesmen saw that in a young
nation like ours, where the laborers or those who
exchange their services for hire were few in comparison with the whole population, wages must
be comparatively high. The situation was very
different from that of the Old World, and they
thought it useless to attempt any industry in competition with Europe, if great numbers must be
employed, unless some means were devised to
counterbalance the low wages paid workmen there.
This was the principal point of contrast between
the political parties. The Whigs proposed to
remedy the evil by a legal measure *to equalize* this
difference in amount of wages, and thus put the
American workman in manufacturing industries on
a level with the foreigners by means of a tariff—
called "protective" for want of a better designation.

The Republicans.—Numbers of the purest and
ablest statesmen of the Slave-Labor States were
Whigs, and were also slave-owners. In process of
time political questions arose which involved the
system of slavery; this led to the alienation of the
Southern wing of the Whig party, because on that

subject the portion North for the most part did not sympathize with the policy of extending the system to the territories. Thus deserted, the party as such became powerless. This accession of Whig strength thus derived made the Democratic slave-owners still more exacting in their demands in behalf of human bondage, while as a natural result, a stronger opposition arose in the Free-Labor States. The Whigs of the latter chafed under these demands, and a new organization arose from the wreck of that party, for the present Republican party sprang spontaneously out of the political chaos ; drawing to itself the advanced men of the Whigs, and many of the Independent Democrats who *would think for themselves,* and refused to be dragooned into voting at the dictation of the Southern wing. These gentlemen from the first took ground against the extension of slavery into the territories, and were known as the " Free Soil" party. They finally affiliated with the Republicans, and with them remained identified in its struggles against the Southern wing, which endeavored to found a confederacy whose "chief corner-stone" was to be slavery. They aided in putting down the Rebellion; in preserving the Union; in blotting out slavery; and in placing the Nation in a position in Christendom for which its people need never blush.

Let us consider some of the measures of public benefit introduced and fostered by these opponents of Democracy, while obstructed by the "friends of the poor man."

XXIX.

LAND LAWS.

The Year 1863.—No measure in respect to the public lands ever passed Congress that has been so fraught with blessings to the "poor man," or settler with limited means, as the *Homestead Law*. This law went into effect on January 1, 1863—that year so remarkable in our annals—on the same day slavery was abolished. During that year a Republican Congress cheapened postage still further, to what it was as late as 1883, or nearly so, and inaugurated the National Banking system; this year was also noted for the Union victory at Gettysburg and the Union capture of Vicksburg and of Port Hudson—so that within ten days (July 1-9) the Confederacy lost between seventy and eighty thousand men, and war material in proportion,

How to Get a Home.—Under the Homestead Law a settler can enter 160 acres upon any unoccupied lands of the United States, by paying ten dollars to cover incidental expenses; but the settler must live upon the land thus entered and cultivate it for *five years*, at the end of which time he receives a *title in fie* for the land thus occupied. The government has also given grants of alternate

sections of land to aid the construction of railways
through the territories, and in some of the new
States where there may be public lands. In the
territories the grant extends *twenty* miles on each
side of the road, and *ten* miles in the States. Within these grants the Homestead given is only 80
acres, because the land in the vicinity of railways is
rated at *twice the value of that outside the grant.*
The result is the Government *loses nothing* by its
grants to railroads, as the lands within them are
held at twice the price of those outside. Did the
statesmen or newspapers who opposed this beneficent measure ever publish this fact ?

These Homesteads can be obtained by the head of
a family, male or female, by complying with the
above conditions. The same regulations, also, apply
to foreigners who are already citizens, or have
declared their intention to become such.

The Timber Culture Act.—A later enactment
likewise enables persons as heads of families to
secure homesteads. If they "plant, protect, and
keep in a healthy growing condition for *eight years,
ten* acres of timber, on any section of any of the
public lands of the United States, they shall be entitled to the whole of such quarter section," or 160
acres. If the settler plants trees on *five acres*, on
the same condition, he receives a patent for 80
acres, and so on in proportion. Residence on these
claims is not required by the Timber Act. This act
is limited in its operation much more than the
Homestead, as it applies only to the portions of the

public lands where there may be a scarcity of
timber.

It shows the intention of the statesmen who
enacted these laws to encourage the settler and industrious man, that they made the homesteads
obtained under both of them *exempt from seizure*
on account of debt or debts contracted previous to
the date of the entry, and also exempted them from
taxation until after a *title in fee* had been given the
settler.

Blessings Conferred by the Homestead Law.
—Since the Homestead Law went into effect, as
shown by the successive reports of the Secretaries
of the Interior for twenty-eight years, to July,
1891, there have been taken up in homesteads by
settlers under this law, 141,606,400 acres, or
221,260 square miles.   This equals in area the
five New England States, the Middle States, and
the State of Virginia combined.   The ordinary
enumeration of the areas of these States includes
the surface of their lakes and rivers, and also their
shore line extending three miles out, altogether
estimated at 7,000 square miles.   Deduct this
latter area, which is not included in Homestead
surveys, and we have the amount of land occupied
by *free farms.*

As has been said, the Homesteads outside the
railway grants contain each 160 acres, while within
the grants it is only 80.   The government averages
the amount of land under these two arrangements,
belonging to Homesteads, at 120 acres each.   At

this rate the number of homesteads would amount
to 1,180,053, while at the average rate of five persons
to each, the population thus supplied with home
comforts amounts to 5,900,265, lacking not quite
one hundred thousand of being equal the population of the State of New York in 1890. Already
there are numerous and flourishing villages located
on lands originally taken up in Homestead grants.
The denser population in these villages makes the
average number for each Homestead in the whole
area occupied, perhaps, more than *five* persons.
The happiness of families growing up as citizens
successful in life, and the moulding influence they
exert on the Nation's future, are not to be reckoned
in dollars and cents, but in the wealth and growth
of great communities of moral, industrious and self-
respecting people. These results are well worthy
the attention of the political economist, and of the
patriotic statesman.

Homesteads are located all over the new States
and territories; and whole settlements have grown
up and become prosperous, and no doubt will thus
continue, for it is a fact well known, that the great
majority of those who settle on these Homesteads
are young married people. They are also energetic
and industrious, and determined to make an independent living, and set before their families an
example that will tell on their future happiness and
success. None but the energetic go so far from
their native homes in order to obtain a competency,
and their habits of diligence and economy will cor-

tinue to influence for good future generations by means of their children, thus properly trained. The same may be said of the many thousands who have settled alongside the occupants of the Homesteads on lands purchased from the railway corporations or the government.

School Funds.—The government has also provided the funds for the support of schools in all future time, if they are properly husbanded. This fund is furnished by giving the *first and the thirty-sixth* sections of each township of *thirty-six* square miles, to be reserved and sold when the territory becomes a State, and the proceeds invested for the benefit of schools. This regulation was in existence before the passage of the Homestead Law.

How Lands Are Given to Railways.—A portion of the unoccupied public lands, of course, lie along the three routes of railways across the continent The National government, especially since the Homestead Bill was passed, has granted lands to railways, in order to aid in their construction through the public domain, with the twofold object of making these lands accessible, and of extending three belts of settlements along these roads across the continent. These grants of land are given to the roads on this condition. The school lands are *first* reserved; then of the remainder the *odd* numbered sections are given to the railway, and the *even* numbered the government retains, either to sell or to give to the settler in Homesteads, each of *eighty acres*. The land within these railroad grants, when sold costs $2.50 an acre—double the price demanded outside the grant. In theory as well as practice the national government loses nothing by these grants to the railways, as it sells the lands retained for as much as the whole would have sold for at one-half the price.

Under the present system these lands virtually build the roads, as the funds to be derived from their future sale form a basis of value, which become a guarantee for the remuneration of the stock and bondholders, who have furnished the capital for building them. The benefits are immense which these roads across the continent have already conferred, and will confer, upon the whole country; they are peculiar in their character, inasmuch as they make cheap homes accessible to multitudes of families, and at the same time extend three belts of settlements toward the Pacific.

Speculators.—Before the Homestead Law was passed, speculators were accustomed to buy up whole counties and districts of the best public lands. This was the case, especially, in the States of Iowa, Wisconsin and Minnesota, where the settlers in purchasing farms were forced to pay enormous profits to the speculators. This extortion retarded the settlement of these States; though thus hindered at first, their progress was the marvel of the time; what would that progress and settlement have been if the people had been protected by a Homestead Law?

The difficulty in Congress was that the slave-owners, constituting the landed aristocracy of the South, were opposed to the Bill, because it opened the way for small farms. As slavery could not exist except on large estates, they were "solid" against any measure that would distribute the public lands in limited quantities to those who would cultivate them by means of their own labor. Even if the lands lay in a latitude or a climate where slavery could not exist, these gentlemen disliked the *precedent*, and seemed unwilling to aid any measure, whose influence would promote the interests of the " poor man," " white trash," or " mudsill," no matter in what section he lived. We infer this from their votes in Congress ; witness their opposition to cheap postage, to this Homestead Bill, and to the fostering of the industries of the entire Union. The Democratic members in Congress from the Free-Labor States almost universally voted with them in respect to these beneficent measures.

Opposition to the Homestead Law.—This instance is so striking that it deserves further notice. There had been measures adopted by Congress from time to time in respect to the public lands—but this is not the place to go into detail. It may be said, however, that the principle of *free homes or lands* had been before Congress for some years, but the Democrats—South and North—always voted it down. Meanwhile, the matter was more or less discussed, especially in the Free-Labor States. At length an amendment was offered to a bill (in 1859), which embodied the principle of *free homesteads.*

This amendment was adopted in the House by a vote of 98; every Republican and 13 Democrats voting in favor of it—the negative being all Democrats. But when the Bill with this amendment came up for its final passage, the vote stood 91 in favor of free homes, *all* Republicans; 95 against the principle, *all* Democrats. The latter, who changed their votes on the amendment, were from the South (*Congressional Globe*, p. 492, *et seq.* for 1859).

In the session of 1860–61, the Bill was brought up again, and after much discussion, finally, by a small majority, passed both Houses of Congress; nearly all the Democrats voting against it, especially those from the South, while upon some of the party from the Free-Labor States, public opinion among their constituents was so strong, that they did not follow their leaders, but voted for the bill, knowing, perhaps, that it would be vetoed. The Republicans to a man voted for the beneficent measure. This Homestead Bill failed to become a law, for, sure enough, James Buchanan, the Democratic President, on the last day of his presidential term (March 3, 1861) vetoed it. This was the end, after a struggle for years—killed by the special "friends of the poor man."

Lands for Colleges.—Another beneficial measure which, after much labor and debate, passed Congress, had been already vetoed (Oct. 24, 1861)—the bill granting waste lands in aid of Agricultural Colleges. Since that time Congress has passed the

Bill, and the advantages to the colleges, and indirectly to the country, have been large.

Finally, under the incoming administration of Abraham Lincoln, this *same Homestead Bill* was passed in 1862, and went into effect Jan. 1, 1863. We have seen that the good effects of this law are almost innumerable, in the founding of Christianized communities having the advantages of schools and churches. From these elements spring industry and economy, and moral influences that multiply themselves through all coming time. These settlements confer great benefits upon the older States; the former cultivate the soil and aid by their products in furnishing food and raw material to those portions of the country, where, in proportion to the number of the inhabitants, there is less land under cultivation. The latter are more generally engaged in manufacturing interests, because of the greater amount of population who can be thus employed. The benefits are reciprocal; the agricultural sections of the Valley of the Mississippi have become, and will continue to be, the future storehouses of food for the older portions of the country. These mutual advantages should hold us together as a Nation.

The Advantages of the Measure.—The advantages to the people themselves of having these settlements, on this vast amount of once waste territory, are far beyond the value arising from the sale of such lands paid into the treasury in money at the rate of $1.25 an acre. In the first place, the sales

would have been very limited in comparison with
the amount of territory brought under cultivation
by means of the Homestead Bill. But these are
trivial considerations when compared with the blessings conferred upon the tens of thousands that have
thus been enabled to start in life and to be the
ancestors of future millions of industrious citizens.
These lands were once so inaccessible, that there
was no special inducement to found homes upon
them. But the government's policy of aiding to
build railways through the public lands since 1863,
has made these vast territories available for the
people's use, who have founded on them large communities, prosperous and happy. If the Democratic
leaders had had their way, neither these settlements
to any extent, nor the railways extending across the
country toward the Pacific, would have been in
existence. But since the Homestead Law has, for
the last thirty years, proved and been recognized
as a great blessing to the "poor man," they proclaim that all grants of public lands in aid of building railways must cease; and instead these lands
must be given to the "poor man." Every intelligent American that has kept up with the times,
only half-way, knows that railways thus built through
the public domain far more than pay the market
value of the land granted them, in their being the
occasion and cause of the unprecedented development of communities of successful and industrious
people in regions useless to the Nation, because of
their being inaccessible. How could it be possible

for the productions of these distant settlements to reach the East, were it not for the railroads? As for the lands given the railways, the greater part would not have been sold perhaps for half a century; neither would there have been so vast an immigration from continental Europe of the better class of farmers, scarcely one of whom is unable to read and write—and all seem to be industrious—had it not been for the free gifts of lands under the Homestead Law.

True statesmanship does not limit its view only to a few years or Congresses, but to the future development of the Nation, which is limited only by time. That is the reason why those who advocated and passed the Homestead Law, and aided the building of railways, wished to put in train great communities to develop into a population—moral, educated and industrious. When a people have these characteristics, they, from choice, improve in refinement, and obey the law instituted by a higher authority than Congress—that man must labor for his own support. It may take a score or more of years to so mould youthful communities, in order that the germs of intellectual and moral progress may bloom in future generations.

Mingling of the Settlers.—It ought to be taken into consideration, that along the routes of these railroads the land belonging to the railway companies themselves are sold on very liberal terms to settlers, the payments being so arranged that the purchaser can easily, if prudent and industrious, pay for his farm. This portion of the settlers are as energetic, industrious and moral, as those located on Homestead grants, and are generally better off in respect to wealth. The purchasers of railway lands mingle with those who live on Homesteads obtained from the government, and the two soon become able from the number of the population to sustain schools and churches. These communities will continue to cultivate and improve the soil, and send to the East their products, in the form of food, such as grains, cattle and sheep, also metals, gold and silver, receiving in return what they may need of manufactured articles.

One Dollar and a Quarter Per Acre.—The leaders of the Democracy in Congress, who opposed the Homestead Law, for the most part based their opposition upon the loss of the comparatively trifling amount of money paid into the treasury from the sales of the public lands. They appeared unable to comprehend the immense advantage accruing to the Nation at large, by opening the unoccupied lands of the public domain, to moral and industrious, and happy communities. They ignored the principle that *the people constitute the State.* On the contrary, the advocates of the bill did not refuse to recognize the benefits that might accrue to the National Treasury from the sale of these lands, but contended that from the sales being so limited, these benefits would be very small when compared with the blessings that would be conferred upon hundreds of thousands of young American farmers, who were

unable to buy these lands and also stock their farms,
but might be able to do the latter, and occupy and
cultivate them and found homes for their families.
How infinitely better for these young farmers to
thus settle in new States and Territories, than to
have remained in the old ones, to eke out a dis-
couraged existence! But with this humane feature
of the Homestead Bill—the aiding of poor men by
giving them a chance in the world—these leaders
gave no sympathy, but ridiculed the idea as the off-
spring of a "morbid sentiment."   To them it
would seem the all-important consideration was—
one dollar and twenty-five cents an acre! Imbued
with this dollar and cent theory, they also seemed
unable to take into account the advantages conferred
on our working people by having plenty of employment at fair wages in our factories; the comfort
and happiness of those thus employed was over-
shadowed by the extra dollars and cents they expected the United States Treasury would gain by
putting our mechanical industries in competition
with the low wages paid abroad.

Absence of Humane Sentiments.—It has been
charged that in the platforms issued from the Democratic Conventions—State or National—there is
an absence of humane sentiments, unless it may be,
occasionally, "glittering generalities" in respect to
"poor Ireland;" that previous to 1861 there is
found in these manifestoes no special recognition of
genuine civil liberty, but, on the contrary, much to
encourage the advocates of human bondage.   The

question has also been asked, where in our history
is the instance recorded, in which these leaders
originated measures in Congress humane in their
characteristics, and which were calculated to confer
great and lasting benefits upon the mass of the people, or when did they not oppose such measures
when introduced by others?

[*Since the above charges are so serious, we leave
this blank that we may be able to insert authenticated
examples of their refutation when found.*]

**Benefits Recognized, Transportation of Pro-
ducts**—It is now become evident that railroads
have been essentially necessary in order to develop
the public lands, by inducing farmers to settle upon
them, either on Homesteads or on farms purchased
from the government or from the railway companies.
Our policy as a nation, is not to have vast landed
estates in the hands of a few, as in England, and
as was attempted in the late Slave-holding States,

and, consequently, very large landed estates will never be possible to much extent in regions where the Homestead law originally prevailed. Such with us do not remain unbroken, as a rule, beyond the second or third generation, as we have no laws as in England, by which land is *entailed for the heir.*

After opposing as long as they could the giving of public lands to those who were unable to purchase them, the Democratic leaders now declare most zealously, they are unwilling that an acre of these lands should be diverted from the landless, and given to soulless corporations for building railways. The true plan, as the result proves, has been to blend the two systems in founding settlements upon the public domain by means of the Homestead law, and by grants of land to aid in constructing railroads, in order to render these lands accessible. Had the making of these railways been postponed till the country was occupied by farms purchased from speculators or even from the government itself, and then built by unaided private enterprise, this century would scarcely have seen one of them finished, and to-day we have three extending from the Mississippi to the Pacific, and in addition are seven connecting branch roads. When all along these three routes settlements shall have been founded, perhaps ranging from twenty to forty miles wide, then will private capital still further build cross roads, running north and south, as the case may be, uniting these settled districts.

These roads so speedily built, and these settlements so rapidly founded,—the latter in consequence
of the facilities afforded by the roads—have had
almost from the start, many of the comforts enjoyed
in the States. This progress is one of the marvels of
the age. These farms—originally Homesteads—and
others within the railroad grants, are to-day furnishing much of the grain and other supplies of food to
the Middle and the Eastern States, while the surplus
is carried to the sea-board and shipped to Europe.
Could the Territory of Dakota have astonished the
world by sending annually so many million bushels
of wheat to the Eastern markets within the last
year or two, if the Northern Pacific railway had not
penetrated its borders? Had it not been for that
road, or the prospect of its being built, there would
instead have been scarcely a settlement within her
boundaries.

The grants of land to the railroads across the continent have secured their completion, and thus
paved the way for these belts of settlements along
their lines from the Mississippi to the Pacific. Now
it is thought by the political organization which
originated and carried out this combined system—
of giving Homesteads to settlers and grants of land
to railways—that the cross roads, hereafter, uniting
these three belts, can be built as needed by private
enterprise and without aid from the National
government, and therefore they propose to reserve
its remaining lands for the landless, saying that
"no further grants of the public domain should be

made to any railway or corporation," (*Platform—Republican—etc., adopted at Chicago—June* 4, 1880). This comes with a good grace from the organization that has accomplished so much for the people by giving them homesteads, and making their numerous settlements accessible by railways, built by funds derived from the sale of lands hitherto waste. Yet, after all, what is the objection, if the government continues to *lose nothing* by giving lands under the usual conditions to aid in building railways?

XXX.

NATIONAL BANKS.

Financial Security.—Relief in the management of financial affairs came to the people on Jan. 1, 1863, when the present National Banking system was introduced by the Republican Party, and for thirty years it has truly been what its name implies. By recent enactment of Congress the system is to be continued. In contrast with the former miscellaneous and irresponsible banking—incorporated and private—within the States, the notes of the National Banks are at par all over the Union, and they are so on their own merits; being secured by United States bonds held on deposit at the Treasury at Washington for that purpose, they are worth everywhere in the land their face in gold. The United States Treasury stands guard that these banks shall not over-issue, as such institutions frequently did under the comparatively irresponsible systems of former days, when great numbers of them often failed and defrauded the public.

The law permits only nine-tenths of the capital—all of which must be paid in—to be issued in the form of notes, and to prevent fraud the Treasury Department itself prints and issues these notes in due form, and keeps an account of the same with each bank, and in addition holds in its vaults the bonds representing the entire capital of the bank in order to secure the holders of its notes in case of failure or of winding up. The U. S. Treasury thus stands as a responsible receiver to pay on demand every note issued by any National Bank. The excellence of this system has attracted the attention of financiers abroad. Says the *London Times*—by no means an admirer of our affairs or policy—"The genius of man has never invented a better system of finance than the National banking system of the United States."

No Monopoly—These banks, from the nature of their constitution, cannot become a monopoly, as has been charged by their opponents, because they are organized under a general law, of which any who choose can avail themselves. If *five persons* think proper they can comply with the conditions, and establish a bank. If they find there is not sufficient business in their vicinity to warrant the enterprise, or make their investments pay, they can take the legal measures, and " wind up their bank," lift the notes they have issued, and withdraw their pledged bonds lying in the United States Treasury, and no one can possibly lose a dollar. There can be under this system no more monopoly than there is in farming or sailing on the ocean; it is only requisite to have control of a farm or of a ship.

The great numbers who can avail themselves of the advantages afforded by these banks precludes another feature of a monopoly. Frequently a large share of the stock in these institutions is held in trust by trustees for minors, and charitable institutions. In the main, it is estimated that one-third of their stock is thus held by women and trustees. Not one laboring man or woman or boy or girl, has ever lost a dollar of their earning by taking in payment a note of a National Bank. Banks are mercantile agents for facilitating the exchange of products; an outgrowth of the best industrial and social development, and in consequence the business interests of the community are deeply interested in their existence and management.

In the future when our national debt may be paid, leaving no United States bonds upon which to base the security of the banks, other measures must be devised to keep them National as they are now, as well as to make them equally secure. It will be essential that the notes of these future National Banks should be kept at par throughout the Union and be received, at all times, by each other. The Secretary of the Treasury, as at present, should supervise the issue of their notes in order to prevent fraud; having the different denominations engraved and stamped distinctly, and properly authenticated before being issued. This arrangement, with proper liability of the stockholders and officers, ought to secure the confidence of the public. In lieu of the commercial benefits conferred by these banks upon the people, their stock should be exempt from taxation, since they derive no income from it, except that from the portion issued in notes. The future will take care of itself; but for the benefit of the commercial interests of the whole people, the National characteristics of these future banks should be ever preserved.

Inflation and Contraction.—As to the amount of notes issued, it must be sufficient, and no more, to supply the needs of trade—if more, it becomes inflation, if less, it becomes contraction, both of which are financially injurious. The National banking law makes these extremes self-adjusting. If a bank is needed at a certain center, capitalists are quick to see it, and they will organize one; and if there is too much money afloat in proportion to the business carried on, they will as quickly see that, and act accordingly—either moderate the issue of their notes or discontinue their bank. The people themselves in their representative men, as intelligent farmers, manufacturers, merchants and bankers are the best judges of the wants of the business of the country, in respect to the amount of money necessary to carry it on. Now the amount to be issued is regulated by an unwritten but infallible law, which the wants of the commercial community dictate. This is infinitely more practical, and more in accordance with common sense, than it would be for Congress to determine by law how much money is necessary for that purpose. That power, should it be entrusted to Congress, would be *Centralization* in its worst form—this feature is opposed by the Republican party, and is indirectly encouraged by the Democratic; yet the latter in some resolutions found in their platforms cry out lustily against such power being lodged in the National Government, and in others seem to sympathize with the Greenbackers or Inflationists, who proclaim their intention to destroy the conservative system of National Banks, and instead authorize the *central government* at Washington to issue notes to any extent. In accordance with this theory, Congress could expand or contract the currency to suit the political interests of the party that happened to be in power; thus continually interfering, directly or indirectly, with the legitimate business of the whole Nation. In times past, the "*wild-cat*" schemes of issuing money in the form of notes were highly conservative in comparison with the visionary ones under consideration.

The details of finance we cannot here enter upon, but merely note the National Banking System as one of the public benefits created and fostered by the Republican and vehemently opposed by the Democratic party—which almost succeeded during the late Congress in compassing its end.

XXXI.

EVILS OF PARTISANSHIP.

City and Country Democracy.—There is now quite a difference between the views and characteristics of the country and the city Democracy; yet in the rural districts, numbers are of the party because of their traditions. Their fathers having been Democrats of the old school, while they themselves grew up in the ranks, and when becoming of age voted as their fathers had done, and, asking no questions, continued to jog along, indifferent and almost neutral as to what was going on outside their own immediate neighborhoods. At first the change began when multitudes of rural Democrats *waked up*—from nullification times onward—under the influence of the persistent and spirited discussions on the subject of slavery; for lectures on that theme, and pamphlets and newspapers, invaded the hitherto quiet country neighborhoods, and thousands of these native-born sturdy Democrats threw off their indifference to national questions, and began to realize that the political party to which they had fallen heirs was under the control of the astute leaders of the Southern wing, and that the whole organization was committed to their interests. Having more vividly realized this fact during the discus sions preceding the annexation of Texas, they afterward threw aside the shackles of tradition and became out-and-out opposed to the slave-power.

Again, when to-day the accusation is made that in the cities the leaders of the Democracy are the main supporters of the Liquor Interest, and of the evils which naturally grow out of the traffic, and also that thereby thousands upon thousands of the rank and file of the party are terribly corrupted, the rural Democrat is indignant at the charge. He looks round upon his neighbors of the same political faith, and who are as temperate as himself, and he feels assured these charges must be untrue. He knows, for the most part, absolutely nothing concerning the disorderly elements—principally foreigners and their direct descendants—in the cities and large towns and along the railways, that constitute the main portion of the party's unwavering adherents, and who are completely under the influence of political leaders.

The rural Democrat is often an opponent of intemperance and of the liquor interest ; he himself is temperate and sometimes even a prohibitionist, and he frequently finds his Democratic neighbors holding similar views. Thus, when statements are made that in the cities, perhaps, ninety-nine hundredths of the liquor-dealers, gamblers, and keepers of gambling saloons are invariably supporters of his traditional party, he very naturally discredits the charges. In addition, his trusted county paper assures him these statements are falsehoods, and backs up its argument with editorials and a multitude of garbled extracts.

Issues of Past and Present.—The reason that the organization has survived its great mistake of 1860-1861 is not because its principles have in themselves a vital and intrinsic merit. On the contrary the issues which it has since brought to the front, have been only in direct or indirect opposition to measures proposed by the party in control of the National government; which measures, having been put in force, have been sanctioned by the people because of their influence in promoting the onward progress of the nation. In the previous period, down to March 4, 1861, the spirit that labored for the preservation and extension of slavery, was the great stimulator of the party's measures and gave it life; though John C. Calhoun irreverently said it was held together by the "cohesive power of public plunder." Be that as it may, it is evident that the main element that supported the organization before the rebellion was the slave-holding interest, with which the Northern wing sympathized, and as the slave interest was a unit on that question when it was at issue, the party was sure to win in elections. On the score of apology, it is said that these measures and mistakes are of the past, and that they should not be charged upon the Democracy of to-day; but they belong to the *history* of the party, and as such should be noticed. The next question is: What are the issues—what is the stimulus of the Democratic Party to-day? Is it anything else than party opposition to the Republicans for the mere sake of opposition?

The Tweed Ring.—It is one of the strange problems of politics, so called, that we sometimes find even intelligent men voting against their own interests as citizens, especially of municipalities. This frequently occurs from an indefinable sentiment of partisanship; a desire that the party—right or wrong—with which they have hitherto acted should be successful. This is an unwise and wrong principle that may not be limited to one political organization alone. As a striking instance of this sort of partisanship may be cited the famous "Tweed Ring" of New York City. The persons composing this "Ring"—a set of low fellows—swindled the citizens of the city for about three years. The members appropriated absolutely to their own use, it is carefully estimated, not less than $13,000,000, very little of which the city ever recovered by legal process; meanwhile these worthies for the most part fled the country. In addition, in consequence of the "Ring's" extravagant schemes, under the guise of improving the city, they left its taxpayers to meet an extra debt of nearly $100,000,000. Yet after these enormous swindles were so thoroughly unmasked by the *New York Times* as to convince every intelligent voter of the truth of the exposure, Tweed himself was elected to the State Senate by ten thousand majority of Democratic votes. This famous "Ring," whose rascalities have become proverbial the Union over, was elected and kept in office by the votes of respectable Democrats. If that class had joined with other respectable voters, with no reference to National politics, but only to municipal affairs, the Tweed Ring would never have had an existence, much less have stolen more from the city than has been taken fraudulently from the United States Treasury since the days of the numerous defaulters in Van Buren's administration. The city is still reaping the fruits of such fatuity in the debt under which it labors. It is worth noting that the cities throughout the land have suffered very much from this form of partisanship, that is, in putting into office men of doubtful character and dishonest deeds, only because they were partisans. There are large numbers in the cities who live by catering to the vices of men; these and their adherents cling to the political organization that most favors their interests.

How Countenanced.—The members of this " Ring "—except, it is said, one or two—were Democrats, and were countenanced and kept in office by the party's voters; not only by the votes of the lower orders, such as liquor-sellers of every grade, as well as nearly all their patronizers, gamblers and keepers of gambling dens and the haunts of the vicious of both sexes, but also, strange to say, by worthy Democratic citizens. These statements seem severe, but their severity arises from the fact that they are *notoriously true.* These respectable gentlemen did not associate with, nor

invite socially to their homes, the members of this
"Ring," yet for no higher motive than to keep the
party intact, they would vote for them to fill municipal offices. The men thus entrusted with the
management of the city's affairs frequently appointed their friends and retainers to bogus offices ;
the latter drawing money from the treasury under
the pretense of pay. These gentry would dress
themselves as laborers, and step up to the office,
and, under an assumed name, draw pay as if
for work done. At one time, thus elected by
respectable Democratic voters, every prominent
office in the city of New York, except that of
mayor, was held by a son of the Emerald Isle.
This never could have been the case if these "respectables" had, united with others, voted as
citizens of the city and not as members of a political organization.

At this writing, owing to some striking ex-
posures in the *New York Tribune*, there is going
on in the city of New York, a series of investigations in respect to the management of certain
departments of the city's affairs. The results of the
investigation recall to the taxpayer's memory the
bad old days of the Tweed Ring. Will respectable
citizens of both political organizations reflect that
the occasion for such exposure and investigation
was brought about by partisanship in National
politics influencing municipal elections?

There is no reason nor common sense in intro-
ducing purely National questions into municipal

elections; were it not for this, our cities and large towns would be better governed, taxes lowered, less defrauding, less crime and more surety of its punishment. Those who are themselves in favor of good and pure morals could to a great extent neutralize the votes and influence of bad men were it not for the partisanship kept up by designing politicians. This extreme party spirit is injurious in its moral aspect, and every honest and intelligent patriot ought to be superior to it. But as nine-tenths of those who corrupt the morals of the community vote one way, it does seem strange that respectable gentlemen should consent to being placed in a position where they are liable to be pointed out as giving some sort of respectability to these roughs and their associates. But if worthy men indirectly aid these parties by voting for their candidates—asking no questions as to their character —they have their reward in the satisfaction that their party in politics has succeeded, though the officers elected have been the nominees of caucuses, composed of a class of men whom they despise.

Figure Heads.—Why upright citizens, Christian men even, should be so trammeled by party ties, is indeed a marvel, and difficult to explain. How often, especially in cities, tickets are nominated for purely local offices, when it is essential to have honest men, yet the voters apparently are not governed by that consideration, but on the contrary it would seem by that of preserving intact the party prestige. These leaders are wise in their tactics;

they keep *figure heads* of respectability before the public, and compel the good citizens thus placed to do their bidding. Nearly all the unenlightened in the Northern States are within the ranks of the Democracy, and this class clings to the party organization. No amount of reasoning can reach them; their very lack of knowledge precludes their being convinced, as they have not the intelligence that is requisite in order to examine the bearings of the political questions that often arise. The strong fortress of the party is in the votes of the many persons of foreign birth and their direct descendants, who follow implicitly the dictation of their leaders. No matter whom the caucus nominates or what principles it professes to advocate, they never on election day swerve from the ticket. It is the *misfortune* of these men if they know no better; but their *crime* if they are the willing tools of designing demagogues.

Spurious Civil Liberty.—It is a disgrace to any man of our day not to vote somewhat intelligently when he has so many opportunities to inform himself on political questions that may arise, be they local or national. Nearly all—much more than is thought by non-observers—of the disorderly elements of the Nation are found in the ranks of the Democracy. Let the intelligent reader examine the truth of this statement for himself, taking his own neighborhood as the field for his investigation, especially if it is a city or large town, and he will learn that this assertion in the main is correct.

Where belong politically the keepers of drinking
saloons of various grades as well as the great majority of those who patronize them? And where the
men of violence who take the law into their own
hands and to secure their ends engage in riots?—
How many "Molly Maguires" were not of this
party? These facts are *undeniable* as illustrated in
our cities, and no less *notorious* in the country,
though not met with so often. Let a question of
morals come up in a rural district or village, be
it concerning temperance or Sabbath desecration, and
you will find for the most part the Democracy taking sides against that phase of the question. They
do this under the plea of being the advocates of the
greatest liberty of the individual; this means that
the rights of the community must be held subordinate to that theory of the rights of the individual. At
one time, under the plea that the "world was governed too much," "the proposition to introduce police into cities was resented [by the Democracy] as an
assault upon liberty" (Sumner's, *Life of Jackson*, p.
365). The practical working of this fallacious theory
of liberty is, that if any one wishes to make his living
by selling intoxicating drinks, by all means permit
him, it is his *right*; if he spends the Sabbath—the
legal day of rest and quietness—in a boisterous and
rowdy manner, it is only the exercise of this *civil
liberty*. The number of drunkards he makes or the
families he ruins, or the people he disturbs in their
worship, are only of secondary consideration, in
comparison with this interpretation of the citizen's

individual liberty. The leaders proclaim themselves opposed to " Sumptuary laws; " that unusual word has the desired effect in making " the rank and file " opponents to temperance movements or any measures calculated and designed to promote the public good by restraining the vicious.

Responsibility of Voters.—It is time intelligent voters had a more exalted conception of their responsibility; even Christian citizens sometimes exhibit to outsiders a singular and inconsistent feature of our politics. They will sometimes join, we hope thoughtlessly, with the corrupters of society, such as liquor-sellers and gamblers of every class, in their votes on questions of doubtful propriety, only because these are party measures. This is their right, certainly, on questions devoid of moral character; but is there not a higher obligation resting upon these good citizens? It is for them to explain how they can support party managers, who frame measures in order to secure the influence and votes of the undesirable elements of society. As in days past, the South held the balance of power between the two great National parties of Democratic and Whig, so, especially in the Northern States, between the law-abiding and intelligent members of both the main political parties of to-day—Democratic and Republican — the disorderly elements of society hold a similiar balance of power. The Republican has, unquestionably, a better record in respect to its efforts to elevate the people by moral forces; it is more in favor of temperance, and takes in that re-

spect higher moral ground, and demands more order
in the community.   We would not detract one par-
ticle from the meed of praise due the good and generous found in any political organization, and we
would deem the highest compliment paid such, to
consist in the fact that neither the disorderly
classes, nor those who countenance them belong to
it, but hate it with an intensity that enhances the
value of the compliment.

If the law-abiding and upright men of the leading political parties were to join hands on questions
that partake of both a political and a moral character, such as temperance and the sale of intoxicating
drinks, and others of a similar kind, as gambling
establishments, the disorderly classes, and those
who abet them, would get little encouragement;
and soon find themselves in a helpless minority.   It
is notorious as a rule, that notwithstanding the
many good citizens that are in the Democratic
ranks yet as an organization it often legislates to favor
these classes, or negatively aids them by not legis-
lating.   Can there be any mystery why those persons whose business has a corrupting effect upon
the community vote as they do?   Now the question arises how can moral and Christian men, who
really abhor evil, vote for and with an organization
within whose fold such elements find a welcome?
Were it not for this encouragement, these classes
would soon lose their influence even in the party
itself.   But what are we to think of the grade of
patriotism that leads respectable gentlemen to con-

nive at these evils, and quietly avail themselves of
the votes of such persons, merely to keep up the
prestige of the party, or even as candidates some
times act as *figure-heads of respectability?* But
something more is required to secure the votes of
these equivocal classes—they must be "conciliated."
It will not be politic to have a prominent member
of their own class as a candidate, lest the respectables of the party should rebel. The leaders know
how to secure both ends; they often nominate for
the office in municipal affairs a *respectable* gentleman and amiable of temper. This opens the way to
office for the leaders and at the same time gives them
an opportunity to reward their retainers. On questions that are truly National, such as the tariff or
free-trade, foreign policy or the management of the
finances, as the case may be, voters have different
views, and in that case their sense of duty leads
them to vote in accordance with their own sentiments and with the organization whose views on
these National questions coincide with their own.
But why should good citizens so vote on questions
of a local nature as merely to secure the supremacy
of a party as such?

Party Material Again.—It is a notorious fact
that at the present time as it was in the earlier days.
(p. 41), the great mass of the Democratic voters
fail in comparison as to their general intelligence
with the similar class in the Republican ranks.
This is not said in derogation of the former, as if
they themselves were entirely responsible for their

misfortune, though there is little excuse for the lack of political knowledge we sometimes see in *young men who are voters.* The management of the former organization is confined to comparatively very few leaders, who hold the conventions, pass resolutions, construct platforms, and wind up by nominating the candidates, and demanding that the rank and file should vote as thus directed; and the latter very seldom fail their leaders. This is undeniably true; for that reason at first Van Buren and more recently other political strategists have acted on the principle that the mass of the voters, asking no questions for the sake of information, should take for granted that the dictum of the leaders must be obeyed, and that they vote the ticket. Though demanding this obedience to their behest, the managers hitherto have not usually enunciated clearly and explicitly in their platforms the varying political theories held by the different sections of the party. Was this because an inconsistency so striking would lead the intelligent nominal Democrats to hesitate in implicitly obeying? However that may be, the leaders have carried out the most perfect despotism known to our political annals.

It is equally notorious that the leaders of the present Republican organization could not if they desired lead the great mass of their members, because the latter are readers, and think for themselves, and in consequence can never be led as an unthinking crowd. Hence the latter party strives to be consistent with itself; knowing it must clearly and distinctly lay down the principles which it advocates, whatever their bearings. Neither does its intelligent following tolerate on the part of the organization, political dickerings with factions of other parties, whose principles are not in accordance, in the main, with those of their own organization. It is essential therefore that the enunciations of the party in its platforms, should be so clear and distinct, as not to admit of double or doubtful meanings; they never did nor do they tolerate repudiation, in any form, of the public debt principal or interest; they are clear in their statements on the tariff, and on the subject of education, while they do not hesitate to express themselves on the importance of restraining intemperance.

Republican Independence.—The most striking instance we have seen of the intelligent members of this organization asserting themselves was when they recently rose and annihilated the power of certain political "Bosses" as they are vulgarly called, who wished to manage it in their own interest. The main portion of the party were moving along in the even tenor of their way, politically speaking, when suddenly they realized that a comparatively small number of members had by various means gradually obtained control of the inner management of the organization. The great mass of the members, indignant that they should be deemed by these gentlemen fit subjects to be thus held in hand, made short work with the "Boss" system and in spite of party discipline the "Independents" rapidly assumed the controlling hand. They determined to retain in their own hands the control of the selection of the members to the State and National Conventions. The "Bosses" had been in the habit of virtually appointing through the county committees, the delegates to the State Convention, and the latter, the delegates to the National Convention. The design was to have the latter obey the instructions of the State Convention, in preference to the will of the people themselves of the districts, which these delegates were chosen and presumed to represent.

The Republican party is by no means perfect; yet one custom it deserves credit for, that is, when abuses have grown up among government officials, or members of Congress belonging to it, the charges are investigated and the delinquents brought to trial; for example, the cases of those who were connected with the "Credit Mobilier" scheme, and the "Star Route" affair; while it is just as stringent in relation to its internal management; witness the short work it made of the "Boss" system. Every political organization is liable to be imposed upon by selfish and dishonest men, who connect themselves with it for the purpose of carrying out corrupt or selfish measures. But we judge of the organization itself by the manner in which it treats such delinquents.

XXXII.

SOUTHERN AND NORTHERN DEMOC-RACY.

Old Lines Redrawn.—The intimate relations ex. isting before the Rebellion between the Democratic leaders in the Free-Labor States and the leaders of its Southern wing are worthy of notice because they *still continue.* During the period just mentioned—from about 1824 onward—were blending two dissimilar elements, whose united influence was thenceforth felt in sustaining each other in political relations. These were the slave-owners and the Irish immigrants in the Free-Labor States; the latter nearly all voted the Democratic ticket with the majority of the former. These two classes of voters had really no bond of sympathy with each other, and therefore the connection was incongruous; the slave-holder looked with the greatest contempt upon the poor laboring Irishmen, while the latter in his never failing vote, often in respect to his own interests most blindly given, was essential to the political success of the leaders, both North and South. These relations still remain, though the circumstances are somewhat changed. In the former case, in the language of the time, the slave

owners "cracked the whip;" in the latter the
Northern leaders, caring less for repairing the waste
places of the South and the development of its
natural resources, than for obtaining the control of
the National Government, go hand in hand with
the present Southern wing—known as the "solid"
South. The leaders in the Rebellion would never
have entered upon that project, had they not had
the connivance of the Northern Democratic politicans; but when the crisis came a large majority
of the *rank and file* of the party declined to follow
these gentlemen any further, but promptly took up
arms and nobly defended the life of the Nation.
Great numbers, also, of the thoughtful, intelligent
and leading men of the party, but not politicians,
who were never taken into the secrets of the con-
spiracy, indignant at the insult offered the Nation
at Sumter, burst the meshes of partisan toils, and
joined those who were determined to defend the
integrity of the Union. The native born of the
latter have rarely returned to the fold of Democracy; they understood why they chose to be loyal
at that time, and why they now preserve their
present political relations. The same may be said
in respect to the native born private soldiers, numbers of whom were originally Democrats, but were
equally indignant at the insult offered the "Stars
and Stripes," and who came to fully understand
the principles involved in the contest. There were,
however, other private soldiers from the same
Democracy—generous and brave Irishmen—great

multitudes of whom, after the close of the war returned to the party and are to-day its staunchest adherents, right or wrong. After the war they were much influenced by their old leaders, who purposely appealed to their ancient prejudices against the colored people. They were made to believe, among other absurdities, that the Freedmen were to be brought North for the express purpose of depriving the Irishmen of their opportunities for work. These inducements and old associations have brought them fully back, and they are now depended upon, as in the olden time, to vote the ticket under all circumstances.

It is but fair to say that even during the Rebellion there were native Northern Democrats who were loyal and yet honestly in the opposition; and since the war, too, many old-time Democrats have returned to that party and from sincere conviction oppose the measures of the Republicans. Nevertheless, the general lines of the statements above stand as correct.

Northern Aid for the South.—Almost as soon as the war closed, there arose a strong sentiment among the humane of the North to aid the mass of the people of the South, who had suffered so much, and who were not thought by these benevolent persons to have brought this ruin upon themselves, but believed to be the victims of the political ambition of certain leaders. In accordance with this feeling, efforts were made among the benevolent of the North to aid the educational institutions

of the States recently in the Rebellion. The largest
donations were made by men who had been loyal
to the Union—witness the money raised to aid the
colleges—Washington and Lee, and William and
Mary in Virginia, Vanderbilt university in Nashville
—the latter a personal gift—and the Slater fund.
This aid has continued to be given ever since to
various institutions of learning; besides, funds have
been given to schools to promote a common English
education. Meanwhile, the Northern Democratic
leaders manifested but little sympathy for the poor
suffering Southern people; for the most part they
stood aloof, making no movement; and seemed
anxious only to secure the assistance of the ex-Confederate *leaders* in order to regain the political
power they had lost in 1860.

Northern Sympathy for the South.—In addition to money given, as we have seen, to colleges,
and to aid the cause of education in the South at
the close of the Rebellion, was a more general uprising in the minds of the loyal and benevolent of
the North to aid their poor brethren, whose homes
had been made desolate. They looked upon the
great mass of the Southern people as having been
the victims of a despotism, inaugurated by the
would-be secessionists, unequalled in its tyranny to
any similar rule in modern Christendom. Their
sympathies went out toward these innocent suffer-
ers, and they were willing to aid in repairing the
material ruins incident to the war by furnishing the
means to repair the railways, and, if need be, estab-

lish manufactories. This was not offered as a mere
gift to the people of the States recently in rebellion,
but in the end to benefit both sections of the land.
The development of the resources of the whole
country was the object to be attained, irrespective
of location, or of the fact that certain leaders had
endeavored to destroy the National Government,
in which unnatural contest the mass of their own
people had been made to suffer the horrors of war
for four years. It was well known that the majority
of the Southern people themselves were opposed to
breaking up the Union, and if the bare question of
union or disunion had been submitted to them in a
fair and free election, they would have voted for
preserving the integrity of the Nation by over-
whelming majorities, except in the State of South
Carolina. On the contrary, by a series of manœu-
vers and misrepresentations of politicians, their
wishes were overruled and they themselves, in great
numbers, driven into the army to fight for what they
did not approve, and even abhorred.

The Rebuff.—After the close of the Rebellion
there were thousands of households in the Northern
States who were ready, under these changed relations, to cast in their lot with the Southern people.
The same households would have been attracted
thither long before the war by the genial climate
and rich soil of that region, but the insuperable
objection in the way was slavery, the evil influence
of which, in respect to material progress, was not
to be compared with its ruinous effects upon fami-

lies in their moral and domestic relations. Intelligent and worthy heads of households knew this, and they were unwilling to subject their families to such prospective evils. The war over, great numbers of energetic and intelligent men of the North transferred their property and families to the Southern States, intending there to make their homes. Capital was, to a certain extent, furnished for repairing railways and building new ones, and to be used in renewing the waste places. These efforts were not appreciated. Could not the ex-Confederate leaders see the advantage of these extended railways, of farms well cultivated, of mines of mineral wealth such as coal and iron, opened and worked and manufactures established, affording in time employment to thousands of persons, male and female? These leaders seemed unable to comprehend the idea, that when a well meaning and industrious man comes into a neighborhood, bringing with him his family, it must be with the hope of bettering his condition, and of finding a permanent home. Instead of truly welcoming these moral and industrious men and their households, who proposed to cast in their lot among them, the ex-Rebels looked on them with suspicious eyes. In consequence a series of petty annoyances were put in train—a kind of social ostracism. Especially was this the case if the new comer exercised the presumed rights of the American citizen, of thinking for himself, and voting in accordance with his convictions, or instructed the colored children in Sabbath or in other schools.

Then followed in many places maurauding expeditions of the Ku Klux, to terrify and commit outrages on the Freedmen, on the natives who had been Union men, and on these new comers. These bands were made up of the younger ex-Rebels and the sons of former slave-holders.

Southern Outrages and Northern Democrats.

—It may be asked what had the Democratic Party North to do with these outrages? The answer is that they encouraged these crimes by conniving at them. Their papers and leaders in the North either apologized for them, or proclaimed that the accounts of assassinations and kindred outrages were greatly exaggerated. The facts in the case are embodied in a report of a committee (*Senator Teller, Chairman*), appointed by the U. S. Senate; this voluminous report contains the sworn testimony of numerous witnesses to these outrages. The pertinent question may be asked, were the Northern Democratic leaders careful to have a fair account of these outrages published in their recognized organs? What would have been the result if these leaders and their organs, certain newspapers, had denounced these outrages, and proclaimed to the ex-Confederates, that while they sympathized with them in their recent contest with the government, the Democracy of the Northern States would not tolerate such crimes nor countenance their authors; can there be a reasonable doubt that these marauding expeditions would soon have ceased? We are able to understand the spirit which animated the leaders of the Northern Democracy, from the fact that when President Johnson vetoed that benevolent measure, the "Freedmen's Bureau Bill," which was designed to aid, also, the *poor whites* of the South in their unparalleled distress, and likewise when he vetoed the "Civil Rights Bill," these leaders and papers applauded the vetoes. The latter being overruled by Congress, both the bills became laws, but that applause gave encouragement to the ex-Rebels, and they proceeded in the attempt to neutralize the effects of the laws, by committing outrages on innocent persons. Is it uncharitable to suppose that the ex-Confederate leaders hoped and expected, through the aid of their native allies, and of the latter's unfailing foreign vote to obtain control of the National Government? It is scarcely worth while, as the fact is so well known, to show how completely the former carried out their part of the programme in securing the control of the ex-slave-holding States. These acts of violence, thus encouraged, unquestionably retarded the material progress of those States more than any other cause for the time being. The late Hon. Reverdy Johnson, a Democrat, and an eminent lawyer of Baltimore, was induced to undertake the defence of some of these marauders at Charleston, S. C., but when he learned the truth as to the atrocities of their crimes, he withdrew in horror from the court and would not plead.

The Presumed Political Reasons.—There is no disguising the fact that the Northern leaders of the Democracy confidently depended for "aid and comfort " upon the great majority of the ex-Confederates, while the latter seem to have been blind to their own interests. This was manifested as soon as they recovered from the dazed condition in which the total and sudden collapse of the Rebellion left them. Had they let bygones be bygones, as the loyal people of the North wished, and fallen in with the progressive portion of the people—the Republicans and loyal Democrats—how different would have been their material progress! Capital would have poured in from the North, as it did for a while, and the waste places would have been made to flourish again ; railways repaired, and new ones built. But no ; the disloyalists in the North, who had favored the Rebellion as much as they dared, did nothing to aid the ex-Confederates materially ; but soon it was found that by some mysterious influence, an understanding was existing between the leaders of the Democracy in the loyal States and the ex-Confederates, especially those who had figured as politicians. The object of that coalition was to secure the control of the National Government. To be sure they called into existence a " Solid South," but in the process of doing so, lost irretrievably a whole decade or more of active industry that might have been full of promise.

XXXIII.

SOUTHERNERS AS STATESMEN.

Sectional Narrowness.—It has been said by their admirers, especially among certain politicians, that the southern leaders were born rulers of men. Yet when they came to rule by the force of education and genuine statesmanship, they signally failed. They managed affairs in Congress previous to 1861, not by the power of a comprehensive policy that carries with it conviction, but by tact; their national statesmanship after the failure of Nullification, was dwarfed for more than a generation by Sectionalism. Since the acquisition of Louisiana, and the raising of cotton became important because profitable, they never introduced into Congress or supported a measure of comprehensive National character that would benefit the entire people; instead, they opposed every effort of the kind. Witness Cheap Postage and the Homestead Law, etc. They were politically selfish; that is, every measure before Congress, was made subordinate to the continuance and extension of their " peculiar institution." The annexation of Texas, was preëminently of this class; the acquisition of California was an afterthought, and the discovery of gold an event which no one contemplated.

Taking Time by the Forelock.—It shows the

astuteness and tact of these self-constituted rulers, that they took time by the forelock, and made the charge of *Sectionalism* against those in the Free-Labor States, who opposed their plans of aggrandizement. This hue and cry was taken up by the Northern Democratic leaders, who by means of their newspapers filled the air with these accusations to such an extent that honest, but timid people began to think, that by opposing the extension of slavery, they had in some mysterious way committed a sort of treason against the Nation. Since the close of the rebellion similar tactics have been brought into requisition in order to divert attention from well known outrages and crimes, even those of murder that have been used to intimidate voters in some of the recent slave states and thus gain political ends. The newspapers which dared censure these crimes and urge Congress to investigate them are charged with: "Waving the Bloody Shirt" a vulgar phrase whose import is well known.

Sectionalism.—The people of the Free-Labor States had no sectional schemes for their own aggrandizements. They wished, it is true, to succeed in their varied industrial and commercial pursuits, and also to promote the education of the children of all classes; the latter ambition—outside the foreign population, was a sort of useful hobby. This is evidenced by the interest universally taken in the subject, and in the vast amounts of money, which during the period from 1833 to 1861, were voted by their State Legislatures to promote education, and likewise

the numerous munificent gifts of individuals to the
same cause. There could be nothing sectional in
this. On the contrary the benevolent and religious
societies located in the Free-Labor States did all they
could to give these advantages to their Southern
brethren, till the spirit of slavery inspired the politicians to interfere with the work (*American People,* p. 861,862). Unfortunately, on the contrary, this
spirit of sectionalism had become so deeply rooted in
the minds of Southern statesmen, that some of them
when afterward ex-Confederates could not realize
that the conditions of affairs were radically changed
after the rebellion was crushed, and they still hoped
to rule by means of their old associates the disloyal
faction in the Northern Democracy. The opinion
prevailed, and was cherished among the people of
the North, that the ex-slaveholders, after their terrible experience, would enter upon a course of industrial life such as had prevailed in the Free-Labor
States. The argument adduced in support of this
theory, was that they had superior advantages in soil
and climate, which, with appropiate labor, would
make that the richest section of the Union in the
steady sale of the products of the soil—such as cotton
and tobacco, while its highlands were unrivaled in
their water power, and its mountains were rich in
minerals. This was before the opening of the great
trade to Europe in grain from the plains of the
Northwest. But these philosophers were doomed
to disappointment, and more became fools than the
one who wrote the "Fool's Errand."

Mismanagement of Private Affairs.—In the olden time before the civil war the leading planters for the most part gave up the management of their plantations to overseers, while they devoted themselves to politics; meeting in conventions and passing resolutions, which often berated the people of the Free-Labor States, as if the latter did wrong in buying the former's cotton at its market value, then paid for it without asking credit, and either manufactured it themselves or sent it to Europe, and made a living profit by the operation. The North never went in debt to the South, while the latter through improvidence was always in debt to the former. This relation of mercantile affairs may have aroused, though unconsciously, a feeling of obligation on the part of a portion of the people of the Slave-Labor States, in respect to Northern business men, that finally degenerated into hostility. Meanwhile, the people of the Free-Labor States continued to progress in their varied industrial interests, and in the rapid increase of their population as revealed from census to census. We have seen since the close of the Rebellion a phase of the same characteristic improvidence on the part of a certain portion of the Southern people; while others, who had not been in politics, nor influenced by its traditions, but had been ruined by the war, went to work in a true nobleness of independence and in a legitimate way, to retrieve what they had lost; the former class, mostly "idle young men of the first families," took different measures. They formed themselves into bands of midnight marauders, as we have seen, and under the name of "Ku Klux," roamed over the country, abusing the freedmen and the native white men who had been loyal to the Union ; thus retarding the material progress of that section so much, that it has not yet fully recovered from that direful influence.

Blunders in Public Affairs.—Of similar character is the famous boast often heard that the material progress of the country during the greater portion of the Nation's life, from Thomas Jefferson to Abraham Lincoln, was owing to the superior management of the national affairs by Democratic statesmen. On the contrary, the history of our industrial progress in every respect during this period, shows that this advancement was due to the *inherent energy of the people themselves*, which compelled success in spite of much crude legislation by the statesmen of those times. The National government was for the greater portion of this period under the control of the slave-power, and to such an extent that all public measures were either stifled or moulded by that influence. They had before them one steady aim, especially from the time of Nullification onward ; that aim was to strengthen the power and influence of slavery, and preserve its integrity, and felt but little interest in the progress of the people at large. This may be accounted for on the principle that the Southern statesmen seemed never to take in the full import of the small amount of wages paid to operatives in Europe, when compared with that paid to similar workpeople in the United States. The only plausible solution of this mistake is, that as they did not pay their slaves wages, they had but little sympathy for those who worked for hire. This defective element entered largely into their states-manship, when they endeavored to introduce Free-Trade or nearly so, by not taking into consideration the effect of the low wages paid in Europe, upon those paid our own workpeople in the Free-Labor States, when employed in manufacturing the same class of goods. The custom of paying no wages at all, as in the case of their slaves, put the slave-owners on an equality with those who paid low wages in Europe. The support of the slaves in place of their being paid, about counterbalanced the low wages paid operatives in Europe, out of which the latter supported themselves. Had the slaves only been able to manufacture or work in mills, the result would have been the utter prostration of the higher wages necessary to secure competent work-people in the factories in the Free-Labor States.

Tact in Management.—It may be asked why the South, with comparatively a smaller number of members, exerted in Congress so much influence down to 1861 ? It was not because of their greater learning in law and political principles, for in that respect, taken as a whole, they were inferior to the Northern members; nor from true statesmanship, for they never were the promoters of comprehen-sive measures beneficial to the people in the various sections of the land, taking in the diversities of

climate in our vast domain. The measures they
specially promoted, directly or indirectly, were
planned and designed to be in the interest of their
own section and of slavery, either in strengthening
it where it existed, or of extending it, so as to make
it National. It was their *tact* in managing men;
often measures were carried through Congress by
means of their superior parliamentary tactics alone.
They acquired this skill, because the politicians of
that section sent to Congress usually the same men,
from session to session, and always, without exception, from the same class—slave-owners—and
thus they acquired by continuous experience, the
power of managing that body, and of moulding a
majority of the members for their own interests—
as in voting they held the balance of power.
Especially was this the case with respect to the
Democratic leaders and members from the Free-
Labor States; the latter having a following at
home that did their bidding, in a class of citizens of
foreign birth, who invariably voted in accordance
with the dictation of these subordinate leaders.
This unenlightened class never changed; they
voted continuously the same ticket, and oftentimes
indirectly for measures which were clearly against
their own interests, as laboring men or mechanics.
This fact was well known to the Southern leaders;
they had only to secure the Northern Democratic
members in Congress, the latter being sure of their
own following at home. During the period (1829-
1861) there was not a comprehensive measure to

benefit the people at large introduced into Congress by a Southern member, except the Homestead Bill by Andrew Johnson—he seems, as a Southern member, to have stood alone or nearly so in that movement. Witness the persistent opposition of the Southern members and of their allies from the Free-Labor States, to the introduction of Cheap Postage and to the Homestead Bill, and every measure designed to encourage the mechanical industries or the commerce of the whole nation.

Lack of Practical Wisdom.—It was little short of madness for the ex-Confederate leaders not to accept the situation in good faith at the close of the Rebellion; meanwhile, going vigorously to work in repairing the waste places of their own land, and cordially welcoming all those who came to live in their States as upright and thrifty citizens. But instead, they stood aloof, as did the Democratic leaders in the Northern States. The latter, as such, seem to have had but little intention of aiding their Southern brethren in recuperating their strength in material progress, and in enabling the mass of the people to recover their desolated lands and rebuild their ruined houses; seemingly, their only object was to secure in their favor the political influence of the former leaders in the Rebellion. The latter, it was said, at the suggestion of these Northern leaders, abstained from voting at some important elections, which pertained to bringing back their States into the Union under what was termed the policy of "Reconstruction" (*American People*, pp. 1,033,

1,044), which was adapted to secure the rights of the Freedmen as citizens, and to afford facilities for education to all classes. The Democratic leaders preferred the "policy" of Andrew Johnson, known as that of "Restoration;" "that was to receive the recently rebellious States back into the Union just as they had been before the war, taking no note of the relation now held to the general government, and to the whole Nation, by those who were once slaves, but now free men and, as such, citizens."

It is a mystery why the ex-Confederates at the close of the war had so little self-respect as to affiliate with the Northern disloyal leaders, who, as the former charged, had encouraged them to make the attempt at seceding from the Union, but when the effort was made, for the most part, unceremoniously deserted them. As honorable men, they must have had much more respect for those who met them face to face on the battle-field, than for these who professed to have their cause at heart, but when the hour of trial came were found wanting. The soldiers, both Union and Confederate, who "tried each other's mettle" in deadly conflict, after the struggle was over, were one and all kindly disposed toward their recent opponents; they were animated by mutual respect. If the majority of the ex-Confederate soldiers alone of the South had had their wish, they no doubt would have welcomed emigrants from the North to settle among them with their families. It was those belligerent gentlemen, "chimney-corner soldiers" or politicians,

who were the unreconciled; but Gens. Robert E.
Lee (*Child's Life of Lee*, p. 331), Longstreet, and
Joseph E. Johnston, and many such honored officers of the Confederate army, were willing in the
spirit of patriotism to let bygones be bygones, and
counseled all to labor in making the whole country
prosperous and happy.

The Infatuation.—The ex-leaders of the Rebellion seemed to be infatuated in listening to injudicious advice, and in ignoring the fact that the much
greater portion of the capital in the Northern States
was under the control of the Republicans—who
were progressive both in theory and practice—and
only with their assistance could the ruins of the
South be repaired; and that this capital properly
invested, and combined with the labor of their own
people, constituted the true basis for a rapid development of the resources of that section. Had they
not listened to selfish advisers, but let politics—in
a bad sense—alone, and voted intelligently, as common-sense citizens availing themselves of the aid
thus offered to promote the material interests of
all classes, the result might have been far different.
As it is, the progress of the entire South has been
retarded many years, because of this insane hostility
to citizens from the Northern States settling among
them and *exercising their rights* as intelligent freemen. The only explanation of this infatuation is
in the fact that, perhaps nine-tenths of the more
active leaders of the Rebellion were *mere politicians*
—not statesmen—and who, after its close, were

actuated by no higher patriotism than the acquisition of political power, to attain which they affiliated with the leaders of the Democracy in the Northern States. This hope had already dawned, for after their terrible losses at Gettysburg, Vicksburg, and Port Hudson in July, 1863, the political leaders in control of the Rebellion still held out because, it would seem, they hoped the Democratic party would elect a president in 1864, whose candidate, it turned out, "was regarded as more favorable to the Southerners" (*Life of Lee*, p. 291). The Southern leaders had scarcely ever actively engaged in the ordinary business of life or in personal labor, and to them it must have been exceedingly irksome as well as difficult to earn their bread by the "sweat of their faces;" they naturally preferred to live by politics, and the emoluments of office, since the unrequited toil of slaves was no longer available.

A Better Way.—On the other hand were thousands and thousands of blameless men and women, reduced by the results of the war from affluence to poverty. Their lands remained, but their slaves that cultivated them were gone, and they themselves were compelled to labor for subsistence. To them the change was equally great, but they displayed under their misfortunes remarkable energy and self-reliance, for which noble traits they have won the regard and sympathy of every true and generous-hearted man and woman in the Northern States. They went to work and did not waste their time looking to a recent disloyal faction in the loyal

States to aid them in regaining political influence.

It is strange the ex-leaders of the Rebellion did not recognize in all its bearings, the fact that the slaves had become free, and they had been given the privilege of suffrage, as a matter of expediency, as well as of necessity, in order that they might protect themselves from unjust laws, the form in which their oppressions would be the more likely to come (*American People*, pp. 1,036, 1,040). The freedmen were in their midst and must remain; they could not be driven away, nor was it desirable; they were absolutely essential, so long as the special agricultural products of the South were to be cultivated. The true and common-sense policy for these ex-leaders was to make the best of the situation; encourage the freedman and his children, as well as the children of the poor whites, to avail themselves of the advantages of education—never enjoyed before—as now provided in the free schools, introduced through the influence of the National government. These people could at once have been put in the way of bettering their condition, and consequently in time have become better educated, and more competent to take their part in industrial pursuits, such as working in mills and factories, as well as engaging more intelligently and more successfully in farming and planting. How much wiser would have been the policy of trying to elevate all classes of the community by the various means of education thus afforded, than that of

placing impediments in the way of the general progress of that section of the country, by not protecting
the freedmen in their effort to improve, and by
discouraging intelligent and industrious immigrants
from the States, where common schools had had
their due influence. It is more than probable from
indications prevalent for some time after the close
of the war, that the ex-Confederate leaders, with
but few exceptions, would have accepted the situation, and have fallen in with the designs of the government to aid the people in every way consistent
with its authority, had they not come under the
malign influence already noticed.

The Present Policy.—We can only conjecture
what "it might have been" if Mr. Lincoln's life
had been spared; what he could have accomplished
by means of his wonderful power of conciliating men
of different, and even hostile views and theories.
He had inspired confidence in his integrity, tact, and
goodness of heart, not only among his immediate
friends, but among his political opponents in the loyal
States, and even of those then in arms against the
government, the more thoughtful had come to appreciate these peculiar traits, and after his death had
recognized under the circumstances, that they had
lost their best friend. He would have drawn around
him the leading men of the South—not the incorrigi-
ble politicans—but such minds as Robert E. Lee, A.
H. Stevens, L. Q. C. Lamar and others of influence in
that class, and no doubt he would soon have had the
sympathy of the intelligent and patriotic among the

non-political portion of the Southern people. The latter had already begun to suspect they had been grossly deceived by their leading politicians who represented the non-political people of the North as being for the most part hostile in feeling toward their southern brethren. It was well known in the North that the great majority of the latter had been opposed to the breaking up of the Union, but after the war commenced human nature asserted itself and they determined to fight, and they did it bravely too. Meanwhile, the extreme doctrines of State Rights were harped upon so much that they finally came to believe that the States in rebellion had a right to secede from the Union in spite of the protest of their sisters. But under what doubtless would have been the conciliating policy of Mr. Lincoln had he lived, the game afterward entered upon by the Democratic leaders of the North with the ex-Confederates of the South, would never have had an existence.

Johnson's Plans.—During the space of about seven months, from Mr. Lincoln's death till the meeting of Congress, certain influences produced results that astonished loyal people, and equally surprised the members of Congress, when on their assembling, President Johnson announced in his message what he had done. In the furtherance of his "policy of Restoration" he had proposed conditions with which, if the recently rebellious States would comply, he virtually took upon himself to restore them to their former relations in the Union. Consistently with this proposition, he had recommended the election of members of Congress in these States, and also of Legislatures, the latter to choose United States Senators, that all might be in readiness to take their places in the Congress about to assemble. For this action the President had no authority, expressed or implied in the Constitution. The Executive branch of the government had usurped the province of the Legislative. We cannot here go into detail in respect to the controversies elicited in dealing with the questions that grew out of the war, such as those pertaining to the protection of the Freedmen and their descendants as well as others equally important. (*American People*, pp. 1035—1044.)

Who were Responsible.—What were the influences to which allusion has been made? It is evident that Andrew Johnson would never have taken the position he did, had he not been tampered with by Democratic leaders, backed by ex-Confederate politicians, and in consequence the famous "Restoration policy" would never have been announced, much less attempted to be put in force, had he not been *Tylerized*. Here is the germ of the irritations which grew up during his administration, and the Republican leaders, in defence of their policy of "Reconstruction," denounced him as the organ and representative of the clearly defined combination of the recent disloyal faction of the Democratic leaders in the North with the ex-Confederates in the South. Had it not been for this combination, so patent to all intelligent readers of the time, the many harsh speeches in Congress in respect to the ex-Confederate leaders and their Northern allies, would never have been made. On the contrary, the danger loomed up, that nearly all that the war had gained for humanity and the prospective advancement of the Nation, was about to be virtually lost under the guise of "Restoration," in accordance with which no guarantee was given that the Freedmen and their descendants would not have been continued in a condition of vassalage little less than that of the olden time—save they could not be bought and sold. In proof of this general statement, may be cited the laws passed by several Southern Legislatures, that were elected in accordance with President Johnson's recommendation, and who expected that his theory of "Restoration" would be fully carried out. (McPherson's Handbook of Politics, pp. 29–44.

This great wrong was, however, prevented by a Republican Congress adopting over President Johnson's vetoes the theory of "Reconstruction," by means of which the Freedmen were made voters in order they might have a voice in making the laws under which they and their children were to live, and this right was guaranteed to them as far as could be done under the circumstances. The Freedman could now enter upon his new relations as a citizen, encouraged by the hope of success if he himself made the proper exertion. How different would be his condition to-day if the leaders of the Democracy had had their way. It is almost universally conceded that, in the main, it is better that these States were brought back on the principle of making the colored people citizens, and then training the latter by education to fill well their part, than to have deprived them of such privilege and launched them forth without an incentive, only to be kept in ignorance and to toil, subjected to the caprice of those who employed them, and to live under laws that they had no hand in making.

The Mistakes.—In the light of political history we can see that many mistakes were made on both sides at the close of the war; the Republicans were not free from error, neither were the Northern Democrats, while the Southern leaders failed in not repudiating the disloyal faction in the North, and instead, falling in with the progressive element among the Northern people, whose heart began at once to manifest sympathy for their Southern brethren, and were willing, and even anxious, to let bygones be really bygones, and to aid in recuperating the wasted material strength of the South.

XXXIV.

CASTE, AS A POLITICAL FORCE.

Class Antagonisms.—Immense injury has often been done to the kindly and sympathetic feeling that ought to and would naturally exist among the American people, by the influence of certain political leaders in arraying one portion of the community against another, especially to incite the uneducated and the class that works for wages, against the educated and those who employ workpeople. To that custom, thus persisted in, may be attributed nearly all the unreasonable and dangerous class antagonism—especially in the cities among the people. This feeling is more than usually injurious to a nation constituted like ours, where popular will governs, as the unthinking are so liable to be led astray by designing men under the guise of patriotism, when they are only partisans. Under a monarchy or kingly rule, where the authority is outside the mass of the people, it would be different, but here, where all are equal as citizens in their rights and privileges, the injury is much greater and more dangerous. The Democratic clubs—in the origin of the party—were very effective in exciting prejudice against the Federalists or supporters of Wash-

ington's administration by stigmatizing them **as**
Aristocrats. Indeed, so much has been made of
what they call in contrast democratic equality, as
to give the impression that there is a merit in being
slovenly dressed and vulgar in habits; this may
explain in some measure, why the rough and rowdy
elements of society, for the most part, gravitate
toward the Democracy—though, whatever the explanation, the fact remains.

This antagonistic feeling between classes in the
community, has been inspired and increased by the
same influence as shown in political speeches and
manifestoes in platforms of their Conventions, both
State and National. The spirit has been the same
at all times, and has been exhibited on all occasions
for a purpose; for instance, directly or indirectly,
representing the well-to-do classes of the community
as hostile to those of limited means—especially if
the former were manufacturers and employed the
latter. To fan into flame what latent hostility there
may be among different classes in American society,
has been the systematized plan of the leaders,
especially when a president is to be elected or Congressmen chosen. This influence is by no means
exerted by all their speakers and writers, yet it is
unquestionably true that a majority of them, whatever the motive may be, do prejudice the unenlightened by such misrepresentations. The National
Congress having the control of the affairs of the
country in its general intercourse with other nations,
and also in respect to tariffs and financial measures,

that affect the interests of all classes; the Presidential canvass calls forth more than usual the energies of parties; and measures of doubtful propriety in both cases are sometimes, sad to say, resorted to.

The term *Aristocrat*, as we have seen, was applied for a purpose to the Federal party, which supported the policy of Washington's administration, but this term of reproach lost its power as time wore along, and the prejudices against the aristocracy of England began to fade away. Meanwhile another generation had come on the stage of action. A political organization had grown up during these years, which, because of the elements that composed it, became the successor of the old Federal party. This organization assumed the name of Whig, and within its fold were found at that day, great numbers of the most progressive and intelligent portion of the Nation. They were the advocates of every improvement that could be introduced to benefit the country in its industries and general development. They were in the main well to do in a worldly way; they thought for themselves, and had no great mass of the unenlightened to follow them and vote for their measures, right or wrong. This very independency of thought caused them to differ frequently among themselves in respect to measures of public policy, yet they would never compromise with cliques nor coquette with them to secure their votes. Under these circumstances, it was only when the glaring mistakes of their opponents, as a party, were obvious to nearly every one, that the Whigs obtained control of the National Government, and when great numbers of the intelligent and independent Democrats voted with them. For instance, the numerous mistakes the latter made in relation to the finances of the country, which led to the great commercial revulsion in 1837, enabled the Whigs to succeed; the latter having persistently opposed these measures and foretold the results which followed.

The True Aristocracy.—The lower grade of political leaders likewise often apply the term *aristocrat* as a nickname to those holding in society a higher social position than themselves. This is designed to excite the prejudice of that class which, perhaps, by no fault of its own, has not yet attained to a similar social position. Instead of stimulating these envious feelings in the latter, would it not be more patriotic to encourage them in laboring by industry and correct moral deportment, to attain for themselves as high a grade of excellence as possible, and by their example and influence, aid their children to reach a plane still higher? Above all price is the aristocracy of that family, in whom are blended the physical and moral characteristics which, in the course of generations, become the outgrowth of an upright ancestry. This is a higher grade of excellence than has ever been possessed or even claimed by the so-called aristocracies of the Old World; because it is based on moral and intellectual worth, and will command the respect of the bad, and attract the love of the good. Its ranks are open to all those worthy of the honor, and the qualifications are, in time, within the reach of all—poor and rich. An aristocracy of that character is worthy of any people, as it is based on the eternal principles of truth and excellence, while against it will be arrayed the prejudices of the vicious alone. Such unreasonable antagonism can be removed but in one way, by improving the moral tone of the morally low classes of the community. How much better it would be if political leaders would make efforts to raise the standard of morals and education among those classes, than cajole them in order to secure their influence at the polls.

Prejudice and Nicknames.—In the presidential canvass of 1844, two definite plans of operation was adopted by the leaders of the Democracy: one to introduce the slavery question, another to secure the vote of an influential Free-Labor State (already noticed, p. 117), the third, from the efforts that were made we are justified in inferring was *to prejudice* the laboring classes against those who employed them. This very injurious phase of electioneering was then carried on to an extent never witnessed before. For illustration, the Irishman leaves his native isle with strong prejudices against the English people and their government, and he finds in this land of his adoption certain political leaders so far professing to sympathize with him in this antagonism, that he is confirmed in his original prejudices, and is led to imagine that those who employ him here are as much his enemies as he deemed his employers were in his native land.

Silk Stocking Gentry.—In the time of Jackson's presidency, while the contest was raging in respect to the United States Bank, the business men, merchants, and bankers—those who had had experience in financial affairs—who were in favor of chartering the bank as a measure of commercial importance to the business of the whole people—were characterized as the "*moneyed power*," with the implication that they were the enemies of the "poor man" who worked for wages. Of course this led the Irishmen to vote the ticket of the party to which his employer was opposed—the latter for the much greater portion being Whigs.

The Democratic leaders put themselves forward in this canvass (1844) as the special friends of the "poor man," for whom their hearts went out in sympathy, while the Whigs, whom they now styled "The Silk Stocking Gentry," they represented as the enemies of the workingman, and charged them with growing rich out of the toil of those whom they employed. These epithets, which took the place of the "aristocrat" of the earlier days, had their effect, and were evidently chosen for the express purpose of prejudicing especially the foreign poor and ignorant against the well-to-do and the intelligent. It was really an insult to the self-respect of those who worked for wages, to attempt to influence them by using such epithets. The result showed they were thus influenced, as, for the most part, they voted for the Democracy, and, as it proved in the end, against their own interests, but in obedience to the behests of their leaders.

Locofoco—Bourbon.—One nickname—" Locofoco"—was current for a number of years, but it had no political significance outside the party, as it was not given by the Whigs but by one faction of the Democracy to another. There existed a difference of opinion on some points in the famous society known as " Tammany." A meeting of the society had been called (October 29, 1835), and the regulars, as they termed themselves, secretly gained admission to the hall by a side door, before the hour appointed for the meeting. The other faction coming at the designated time, found their brethren in possession and a meeting organized. The new comers, being in the majority, made short work with the progress of the session, by outvoting its members. The regulars were forced to retire, meanwhile, before leaving, they shut off the gas, and the others, perhaps anticipating such a result, came provided with candles and " *loco-foco* matches," which enabled them to strike a light and organize their meeting and nominate their candidates. The regulars took their revenge by nicknaming their opponents " Locofocos." The term "Bourbon," as used to-day, also originated within the party itself.

Black Republicans.—The Free-Soil Democrats and liberal Whigs united in a new political organization under the name of Republican (1855). This party wished by legal and just measures to prevent the extension of slavery to the territories, lest it should prove to them in future generations, the

moral and economical curse it had been to the then
slave-holding States. To excite prejudice against
this new party the Democratic leaders at once, and
with one consent, characterized it as *Black Republican.* This opprobrious and suggestive nickname
was purposely chosen, as the object was to secure
influence with those who were unable from their
want of knowledge to fully understand the vast importance of the questions at issue. It shows the
cunning of these leaders, inasmuch as that epithet,
under the circumstances, had an immense influence
upon certain classes of their followers, and induced
thousands to vote their ticket, and meanwhile de-
terred other thousands from voting with their opponents.

Recent Efforts.—In later years we have seen the
same political organization endeavoring to prejudice
the laboring man against those who employ him.
The favorite epithets used being : " Bloated Bondholders," " Coupon-Clippers," " Gold-Bugs," " Blood-
suckers," and other vulgar terms, while those who
work for wages were characterized by one single
term—the " Downtrodden." The former epithets
were applied to all those who by economy and industry have obtained a competency of this world's
goods. Were not these ignominious nicknames
designed and used for the express purpose of arraying one portion of the community against another?
Can there be another explanation? What intelligent reader of the day can fail to divine the motive?
Do these demagogues credit the numerous rich men

thus characterized, with the immense sums they have given and are giving to-day for the purpose of founding or aiding institutions of learning, in which the sons and daughters of those of limited means can receive gratuitously a practical education? This antagonism, thus engendered and promoted, of the less wealthy against the well-to-do-classes, is an ominous sign of future evil ; but there is only one political organization that encourages this, and as such expects to profit by it. The capitalist, instead of being characterized as an enemy, ought to be hailed as a friend of the working man; since he alone furnishes the means and the occasion by which the latter obtains employment and derives dividends from his own capital—his skill and his muscle.

In connection with this may be noted that the great majority of the manufacturers and prominent men of business do not—unless in theory—belong to the Democratic party; this may account for the worldly wisdom of the lower grade of their leaders, who endeavor to create antagonistic feelings between the employers and those employed. To be sure, it does not argue much, for the practical wisdom of the working men that they permit themselves to be thus fooled—that they are thus liable, is their misfortune—but how are we to estimate the position of the respectable portion of a political organization, which connives at taking advantage of this misfortune ; and appealing to the meaner instincts of human nature in order to array one class of the people against another, and thereby gain a partisan triumph?

Every true patriot deprecates the *hostile* feeling of one portion of the community toward another, when, on the contrary, their mutual benefits depend so much upon good will toward each other. What antagonism there may exist has frequently arisen from such misrepresentations as we have noted.

Copperheads.—The loyal men, originally of both parties, must, at least, plead guilty to one charge of calling naughty names. During the Rebellion, large numbers of Northern Democrats were disloyal; that is, were in sympathy more or less with the enemies of the Union. They manifested their zeal in underhand and secret ways; such as exaggerating every reverse of the Union arms and extolling every victory of the so-named Confederates; commending the skill of the latter's commanders, while depreciating that of the Union generals. They labored to destroy the credit of the government, and when it wished to obtain money by issuing bonds, they refused to buy them, and endeavored to discourage others, by proclaiming the bonds would never be paid. If they had property, which the government in its emergency needed, they would take in payment, not its bonds, but gold; with the latter the more astute speculated, and the more ignorant—expecting the Union to go to pieces—kept it on hand till they were forced to admit the Nation was still intact. Some disloyal editors, by means of *personals* in their papers, made the latter mediums of communication between the rebels and their sympathizers in the

loyal States (*Jacob Thompson's Report to Jefferson Davis—dated Dec.* 3, 1864, *at Toronto, Canada.
Thompson was Sec. of the Interior under Buchanan.*) Many of these gentlemen engaged, secretly,
in blockade-running; some went abroad, principally to England, to carry out their schemes of
making money, and of aiding the enemies of their
own country by furnishing them supplies. One of
the most blatant of these patriots was sent by
President Lincoln across the lines, but after a time
he made his way from the Confederacy into Canada,
and while on its soil was nominated by the Democracy of the State of Ohio for the office of governor.
The chief leaders, meanwhile, were proclaiming
themselves innocent of disloyalty, in truth were ill-
treated, were martyrs, and were complaining, about
illegal arrests, when they were all loose. There is
found in some states a serpent in its nature very
poisonous—not like the rattlesnake, giving warning
of its presence, but concealed in the grass awaiting the
opportunity to sting the passer by. Was it strange
that the indignant loyal men of the time characterized these secret but active enemies of the Union as
copperheads.

Platform Statements.—The Democracy habitually word their platforms in such manner as to
give the impression that they are the peculiar
friends of the " poor man." As a case in point
their National Convention of Cincinnati, (June 24,
1880) adopted the following: "The Democratic
party is the friend of labor and of the laboring

man, and pledges itself to protect him alike against
the *cormorants and the commune.*" We presume it
was left to their orators to explain what is meant
by these *two enemies* of the poor man who works
for wages. Then again : "The Democratic party
being the natural friend of the working man, and
having throughout its history stood *between him
and oppression*, renews its expression of sympathy
with labor and its promise of protection to its rights."
[Dem. Con. of Penna., April 29, 1880]. Many
more instances might be cited couched in similar
terms. These statements are in the face of the
facts of the party's history in respect to what this
"natural friend of the workman," has done for the
latter in times past. Similar assertions have been
made, and that systematically, in their speeches,
papers and platforms, from year to year, and unfortunately, too often, the unenlightened working
man believes them, perhaps because they are so
often brought to his notice. While the close reader
of our political history has seen in every instance,
where measures have been introduced by other
parties, which were, in their nature, adapted to confer lasting benefits upon the Nation at large, the
Democratic leaders have uniformly thrown their influence against them. Facts, on the other hand, con-
clusively show that measures—such as cheap postage,
free homes, the National Banking system, return to
Specie payments, etc.—which the Democracy strenuously opposed, have proved themselves not to be
merely theoretical, but thoroughly practical in their

good results, we thus find the political organization that has been the most clamorous in promises of devotion to the special interests of the "poor man," has done him the least good.

Dividends Compared.—These, so-called, friends of the "poor man," prejudice the wage-earners by asserting that manufacturers secure for themselves nearly all the profits. To obtain the truth of this assertion, we must ascertain the value of the two classes of capital invested, and, also, the proportionate incomes from each. Suppose we estimate the value of the knowledge, skill, and muscle of a competent workman—that is his capital—at $10,000. He gets, when he works, a salary of, say, $1,000, $1,500 or $2,000 a year; that would be 10, 15, or 20 per cent. on his capital. Wages or dividends of workmen are graduated from the highest grade to the lowest, in proportion to the value of their skill and muscle when properly put forth.

Suppose the plant of a factory cost $500,000, that amount, alone, at 5 per cent. incurs a yearly expense of $25,000. In addition, are the taxes, the raw material, but more than all, the wages of the employés. These expenses must be met before the manufacturers can declare a dividend. Their income is variable, since it depends upon many contingencies, but they must, however, pay the wages of their workpeople. In view of these facts does not the capital invested by the employed pay in proportion a more certain and larger dividend than that of the employer?

XXXV.

PARTY DISCIPLINE.

Democratic Devotion.—The Democracy has always been under the control of comparatively few leaders—the great mass following implicitly. Sometimes a limited number will disagree with these leaders in respect to their measures or policy, but they are soon compelled to succumb. The thinking men, who thus dare differ, are brought to terms by a system of ostracism unknown in other political organizations. The latter gentlemen may differ in opinion from the party leaders or politicians, and as we have seen them again and again, even express their dissent in debate or by writing, yet, strange as it may seem, when the time comes the much greater number vote with the party. These daring leaders care very little for the opposite opinions expressed by this small number of the membership. In proof of this statement let us look at the question of the National finances; on this subject there are and have been more opinions at variance than on any other. Those of the Democracy engaged in purely financial business, such as bankers, brokers, and dealers in merchandise, were almost to a man in favor of the finances being based on specie payments, in order that the commerce of the country might be conducted on a solid basis, and be free from the fluctuations of value, which passed over from the times of the Rebellion. Yet ·their representatives in Congress voted to retard this resumption. Now comes the marvel; the gentlemen just mentioned, with scarcely an exception, supported these same men when re-nominated to Congress, notwithstanding they had voted, as these financiers thought, in a manner to injure the business of the whole country.

The demand of the leaders, that the members of the Democracy should vote the regular ticket, is by no means limited to the unintelligent of the party, it is well understood that flinching will not be tolerated on the day of election, even on the part of those who are well informed. The latter are subjected to a social ostracism of only a little higher grade. How a political organization could wield such power over its members, is a matter of astonishment to those who are self-respecting and unfamiliar with the drill and demand of the party leaders. The managers—often virtually self-constituted—of caucuses and conventions, announce principles and nominate candidates, and woe to the member who thinks for himself and dares vote independently. Hard-money Democrats, as they were termed, or those in favor of coming back to specie payments, were among the most thoughtful and intelligent of the party, yet, when that question was under discussion, they were expected at the dictation of the leaders to belie the principles which they be-

lieved to be the best for the country. Thus, in the
State of Ohio in 1879, the Democratic Convention
nominated for governor a famous Greenbacker or
Inflationist in spite of the protests of the hard
money men of the party. In consequence, much
discussion was elicited within the party itself. Said
Senator Thurman, one of the most influential Democrats of the State, in speaking of these hard money
men, and of the incongruity of the nomination:
" Undoubtedly, a great many Democrats in Ohio
think that General Ewing's financial views are un-
sound, but when the day of election comes they will
be found voting for him, and it is the votes which
count on that day—not opinions " (*N. Y. Tribune*,
Aug. 14, 1879). Evidently with this expectation
the nomination was made and hard money Democrats were relied upon to lay aside their convictions
of duty, their self-respecting manliness and vote,
merely for a partisan gain, in support of the prin.
ciples they abominated.

Contempt for Dissenters.—The truth is, the
leaders of the Democracy care very little for the
occasional dissent from their policy, by some of the
intelligent members, because the discussions thus
elicited are neither heard nor read by the great
majority of the voters in the party. The latter, it
is notoriously known, have not the general informa.
tion necessary to understand the bearings of many
important questions, a true statement of which seldom reaches them. This class of persons or voters,
from the nature of the case, very seldom change their
political relations; when once they commit them

selves they cling with the greatest tenacity to their party. This is specially true of certain portions of the foreign element, because captivated by the term Democrat, which to them is the direct opposite of the governments they have known in their old homes; they believe in the mere name itself, as if it had some mysterious influence.

These leaders assume that they will always have the support of that large class of foreigners who are in the habit of crowding into the cities and along the railways near the large towns, but they are far from being so confident of these who settle as farmers in the West and the Northwest. Under these circumstances the leaders treat with contempt those Democrats who have the rashness to differ in opinion from the manifestoes of the caucus, or reject the nomination of candidates in their conventions, because the number of malcontents is usually so small that they can easily spare them from the ranks, seeing they have sufficient supporters in this unwavering class. In fact, the leaders would rather not have these inquisitive gentlemen in the ranks at all; they want implicit obedience to caucus dictation. Indeed, these troublesome members—so few in number that their absence would scarcely be missed, and their influence over the ordinary crowd of voters not worth mentioning—are often advised to succumb or be put under the ban. Free and frank discussion of current political questions within the ranks of the Democracy itself would be injurious to the organization—hence absolute obedience is demanded of every member.

Control of the Ignorant.—By leaders we mean the politicians of the party; not those citizens who in theory may believe in its dogmas, but do not take an active interest in politics, or even in political questions, but wish honestly for the good of the country in its varied interests. The former class live by office and its incidental emoluments; they are the many who for their own ends bamboozle their followers. They take care that the mass of their supporters shall learn nothing on passing discussions on National subjects, except what they think proper to put before them. Let any intelligent person notice the statements made in certain newspapers in the cities and specially designed for the enlightenment of the mass of the Democracy, and he will be astonished at the bold assertions, the misrepresentations; and garbled extracts in relation to current opinions and facts, that are furnished as political food for these devotees. By this means certain voters of the party are marvellously held in hand; should one of them vote an opposition ticket, he loses caste at once among his fellows, especially is this true in respect to Irishmen, who are so tightly held in political shackles. If the investigation is carried to the county or rural papers of the party, the facts revealed would be equally interesting in the same line.

The mass of these voters, though uninitiated as to the schemes of their own politicians, mean well, but they are grossly deceived, and we would not say a word to wound their self-respect, but this systematic effort to keep them in political bondage, and oftentimes, as we have seen, induce them to vote against their own interests, *is a crime*, and for that reason we denounce it and its perpretrators.

As it now stands the unenlightened voters hold an important position of power between the intelligent voters of the two main political parties of the day—the Democratic and Republican. The latter from the progress that springs from the counsels of thinking and active men, does much for the " poor man" in advancing the industries of the land, and putting the business of the country on a firm basis, thus securing permanent good results and employment for those who work for wages. The leaders of the former have not so good a record; in their crude theories and legislation up to 1861, they brought distress upon the business of the country, about every ten or dozen years and in consequence turned the "poor man" out of employment. There has not been a time of great financial disturbance and prostration of the business of the Nation for twenty-five years preceding 1861, but can be traced directly or indirectly to the crude legislation of the Democracy. No student of our history need be surprised that within the last few years when they were in control of the lower House of Congress, they made efforts to accomplish legislation—for instance voting against resumption of Specie payment—on financial and on industrial affairs, which, if they had succeeded, would have been of great and manifold injury to the material progress of the entire country.

XXXVI.

RESUMPTION OF SPECIE PAYMENT.

Assumptions.—We have already seen the characteristic manœuvre of these leaders in claiming for themselves the credit of measures that proved beneficial to the country. They have also actually claimed the merit of bringing about specie payments in 1879, and that in the face of their most persistent efforts to prevent it. Since resumption has been a triumphant success, as seen in the increase of business and confidence in commercial circles, these leaders proclaim to their followers that specie payments would not have taken place had it not been for their support. Said one of their prominent political managers :—" It was due to the support of a Democratic Congress that Resumption was made possible;" and he adds: "the party has always been a hard money party, considered in general," (*N. Y. Tribune*, Aug. 22 or 23, 1879.) Had that gentleman forgotten that when the act of Resumption was passed it was opposed by every member of his party in Congress who voted on it; while at the same time the bill was passed, the Secretary of the Treasury was authorized to make the necessary arrangements ; all of which was as

strenuously opposed? This mere assumption by one
prominent leader would have little influence were
it not calculated to deceive the unenlightened,
meanwhile, the leaders, if the measures which they
opposed turn out well and become a blessing to the
land, do not hesitate in a quiet way to claim
them as their own. In truth, since resumption has
been a success and business has revived, they have
no alternative but to acknowledge they made a mistake.

Business would not have revived had it not been
for the confidence inspired by the knowledge that
the Secretary was accumulating coin in the Treasury
to meet the emergency on January 1, 1879. The
abundant crops aided the cause, but they would not
of themselves have been sufficient had there not been
proper management and careful preparation to meet
the demand on the Treasury. This foresight enabled the government to secure the advantages derived from the balance of trade being in our favor.
Could all this have been brought about if the leaders
of the Democracy, both in Congress and outside as
represented by their press, had been able to prevent
the Resumption Bill becoming a law or had been
able to repeal it?

As the business of the country has been improving
more and more since we came back to specie payments, and the prospect that a large amount of our
immense grain crops, and food in the form of dairy
products, beef and cattle, etc, will continue to be
sent abroad, the leaders are at a loss how to make

this unparalleled success available politically. They proclaim they were always in favor of honest or hard money "in general," but *not precisely* in favor of the manner in which the business of the Nation has at length reached a coin basis.

Our great skill and recent success in manufactures may be traced, in part, to the fact that they have not been so much disturbed as usual by the hostile feeling toward them manifested by the leaders of the Democracy who have again and again endeavored to tinker but ineffectually the tariff in the interest of "for revenue only." They appear to be anxious to secure a portion of the credit of this industrial prosperity; why not claim that had it not been for the Rebellion, brought on by the Southern wing of the Democracy and connived at by many of their leaders in the Free-Labor States, there would have been no necessity for the imposition of duties so heavy upon foreign imports in order to defray the expenses of the war—thus they themselves have indirectly occasioned the building up of our magnificent system of industrial pursuits.

Resumption.—The Resumption Act passed Congress in January 1875; it required the government to resume specie payments on Jan. 1, 1879—four years later. This act was voted against by every Democratic member in Congress; and thus it was literally a measure of the Republicans. Afterward the former party attaining a majority in the House of Representatives, passed a bill to repeal this law; but not having a like majority in the Senate, they failed, and two months before they had the requisite number in the latter, resumption had taken place. That the whole Democratic party, as such, was opposed to the resumption of specie payments, is evident from the following as found in the platform of their convention held in St. Louis (June 28, 1876): "we denounce the financial imbecility of that party [Republican] which, while annually professing to intend a speedy return to specie payments, has annually enacted fresh hindrances thereto. As such a hindrance we denounce the resumption clause of the Act of 1875, and we here demand its repeal." The Greenback party had previously (May 16, 1876) said in convention; "we demand the immediate and unconditional repeal of the specie resumption Act of 1875." As to the result, the day after the original Act was signed by President Grant, the premium on gold began to diminish, and thus continue till on Jan. 1, 1879 it vanished.

Retarding Resumption.—These leaders evidently retarded resumption for a time, by their continued attempts to interfere in various ways with the finances, thus lessening that confidence in business transactions so essential to commercial prosperity. Though the crops of the country were abundant, and our immense exports caused the balance of trade to be in our favor—one of the elements in the country's preparations for resumption—these facts seem not to have diminished the intense hostility of the Democratic leaders to the resumption of specie payments and the consequent revival of trade. It would seem that they thought their only hope in the success of the coming elections (in 1878–1880, was in the depression of the business of the country. Thus we may infer from the frequent assertions of Democratic newspapers and speakers that the country was going to 'uin, and that a change in the National administration was the only remedy. It is strange that these leaders did not recognize the fact that the business of the country had been gradually improving from the day that the premium on gold began to go down—this latter fact alone was an evidence of the improvement in mercantile affairs. During this period of four years the Democratic politicians were playing fast and loose with the inflationists or Greenback organization. Many of their members of Congress were in favor of hard money or specie payments, yet, strange as it seems to the independent and self-respecting these gentlemen voted in accordance with the dictation of the caucus of the majority in the House of Representatives. Here was a measure, which, according to the experience of the past, would be of great advantage to the business of the country, yet at the behest of the caucus, the majority of which were ex-Confederates, they voted against it.

How can we account for this persistent opposition to resumption of specie payments? First: could it be that—contrary to all experience—they believed resumption would be injurious to the prosperity of the country? or Second: did they, be-

believing resumption would be financially beneficial
to the people, vote against the measure and also to
repeal it, because if its principless were carried out,
it would redound to the popularity of their political opponents, who had proposed and enacted the
law;—for moreover it would go into effect nearly
two years before the presidential election in 1880.
In justice to their integrity as patriotic men, we
must assume they thus voted in accordance with the
belief that the resumption of specie payments would
be injurious to the financial interests of the people ;
but does that view commend their statesmanship?

Policy of Obstruction.—The leaders of the
Democracy have not had absolute control of the
National government since 1861, but in the meanwhile they have played the role of obstructionists.
As an organization—not all, but a majority of the
individuals composing it—they have from that time
forward, opposed all the great national movements,
political or industrial. The party organization, as
such, aided and abetted the Confederates in their
efforts to break up the Union, while multitudes of
its individual members were loyal to the core, and
entered the Union armies, and served the Nation in
other capacities—none were truer than they. The
party opposed the Homestead Bill which has been
fraught with blessings to millions of American citizens; in connection with this, they opposed the
grants of waste or unoccupied lands to aid in building railways from the Mississippi to the Pacific;
they opposed reconstruction, which secures to all

civil rights; they indirectly injured the public credit by their alliances with inflationists; they opposed the resumption of specie payments; they opposed every measure designed to prevent fraudulent voting; and in State legislation they have the credit of never of their own accord enacting a registry law, one of the most effective means to secure the purity of the ballot-box. Meanwhile, in every available form, they manifested hostility to the manufacturing interests of the country by endeavoring to introduce into practice theories of tariffs, which, when in force hitherto, had brought ruin upon our mechanical industries.

The Republican party is by no means perfect; yet one custom it deserves credit for, that is, when abuses have grown up among government officials or members of Congress belonging to it, the charges are investigated and the delinquents brought to trial: for example, the cases of those who were connected with the " Credit Mobilier " scheme, and the " Star Route " affair; while it is just as stringent in relation to its internal management : witness the short work it made of the " Boss " system. Every political organization is liable to be imposed upon by selfish and dishonest men, who connect themselves with it for the purpose of carrying out corrupt or selfish measures. But we judge of the organization itself by the manner in which it treats such delinquents.

XXXVII.

POLITICAL TRADING.

THE Democratic leaders have always been famous, but more especially during the last thirty years, for making alliances with political factions. An instance in point occurred in 1872, when their convention adopted as their candidate for the presidency, Horace Greeley, because he had been already nominated by a portion of the Republican party, known at the time as "Liberals." It is inconceivable how an honorable and self-respecting political organization could promise their support to a man, who for more than thirty years had thought it his duty to oppose the prominent measures and policy of that organization. He was never sparing in exposing what he characterized as their "shams;" especially was he inspired with a sort of holy indignation, to protest against the assumption, when they proclaimed themselves the special friends of the "poor man." In behalf of this same "poor man" Horace Greeley fought the Democratic leaders for years; for "Cheap Postage;" for "Free Homesteads" for the landless on the public domain; for protection to the industries of the people at large, as a guard against the low wages being established here, which were paid workmen in Europe; while holding up to view in scathing terms, their willingness to be the pliant tools of the aristocracy of slave-owners. Now behold! when a portion of the Republicans, dissatisfied with certain measures of the majority, chose to express their dissatisfaction by nominating for the presidency the most advanced Republican, the Democratic leaders, no doubt hoping to slip in, adopted the same candidate—Horace Greeley—their old political and triamphant enemy, for he had beaten them at every point. Such negation of manliness on the part of the leaders, of a great political organization never before occurred in our history. The vast unenlightened crowd, that vote the ticket right or wrong, did follow their leaders, but great numbers of the intelligent refused to stultify themselves by voting for their old, inveterate political opponent.

Coquetting with Factions.—Again: when the bill to resume specie payments was before Congress in 1875, we have seen the Democratic leaders opposing it at every point, but the Republicans, having a majority in both houses, passed the bill which was signed by President Grant. From that day the indications were that in four years the resumption would take place, as the Secretary of the Treasury was carrying out the provisions of the Act, as he had been authorized by law of Congress. Meanwhile the leaders were not idle; first they saw that the influence of the prospective resumption, was likely to be beneficial to the business interests of the country—did they fear that their political

opponents would get the credit of the improvement?
—for they became very anxious on the subject, and
proclaimed to the dear people, that the latter were
not doing all they could to promote resumption.
This phase of the subject went on for some time,
when by degrees the inflation or Greenback movement began to attract visionaries from both the
political parties. Now the idea seems to have occurred to these leaders, that if they would coquette
a little with this new faction they might attract
sufficient numbers in Congressional districts, that
were about evenly balanced, to succeed in the coming elections. They tried the experiment in Maine
(1878) and gained in some of the districts—and by
a peculiar arrangement in that State—a governor.
Thus being encouraged, they bid for the good will
of the Greenbackers throughout the Union, and at
the time having a majority in the House of Representatives, they *repealed the Resumption Bill* as far
as they could, but the repeal failed to pass the
Senate, the majority there being in favor of a return
to specie payments, and honest money. Thus they
were playing fast and loose with the inflationists;
time wore along and on Jan. 1, 1879 resumption took
place, two months before the Democrats obtained a
majority in the Senate.

In the State of Ohio, during the canvass for
governor (1879), we have seen these leaders nominate one of the extreme inflationists of the time,
a virtual repudiator, though he may not have so
deemed himself, adopting, for the most part the

principles of that party; while in Maine they continued the alliance of the year before, and in both States demanded that the hard money and National debt-paying members of the party, should vote this combination ticket—no questions asked. Meanwhile, in the canvass for governor in the State of New York, they proclaimed themselves in favor of hard-money; that State being much engaged in mercantile pursuits; the latter's newspapers, also, using the strongest terms in condemnation of the Green-back heresy, and against the repudiation of the National debt. Consistent with this policy, we often see the leaders meeting in State, or National Conventions, and so framing resolutions as to express opinions, it may be differing somewhat from the general sentiments of the party's ordinary manifestoes, but apparently calculated, for the time being to induce factions of other parties to vote their ticket.

XXXVIII

PROPHETS OF EVIL.

Raven Croaks.—It seems peculiarly unfortunate for a great political organization at any time to be so straitened as to rely for its success upon the misfortunes of the people. During the war of the Rebellion, the hopes of the disloyal leaders of the Democracy hung upon the reverses of the Union armies; and they chuckled over every defeat with which the latter met. Financial distress or disturbances were a welcome boon to those leaders, meanwhile, giving them an opportunity to ventilate their peculiar theories of what they themselves would do in the premises if they only had the power. Thus they stood ready to avail themselves of any failure of the crops or in business. In the presidential campaign of 1880 such failures were deemed essential to their success, if we may judge from the gloomy forebodings of their orators and newspapers of the period. But the failures did not come; meanwhile the country was gradually recovering from the crash of 1873, as the adoption of specie payments—so bitterly opposed by these leaders—had been making business more and more stable for a year and a half, by inspiring commercial confidence.

Futile Prophecies.—The Democratic party being in the majority in the House of Representatives, in which bills in relation to the finances must originate, its leaders, at the close of the first session of the XLVI Congress in 1880, for reasons known to themselves, refused to pass a bill to enable the Secretary of the Treasury [Mr. Windom] to refund the portion of the debt coming due within a few months, and before Congress would again meet. Could it be possible that the prophecy, so confidently made, of financial disturbances during that summer, were based on the non-passage of such bill?

The United States Treasury had about $200,000,000 available to meet an indebtedness of about $650,000,000 in bonds, soon to become due and to be redeemed in some way. The Secretary, thus left to his own resources, proposed to the creditors, as a business transaction, to change the bonds they held to a lower rate of interest and to run for a longer time. The creditors agreed to the arrangement; the success was complete, and by the operation $13,000,000 a year in interest were saved to the people. Had these leaders in Congress authorized the Secretary to refund that portion of the debt, they might have claimed a portion of the credit of saving these millions, instead they had only obtained the credit of being obstructionists in opposing the Secretary's common sense financial policy, which proved successful, as the business of the country experienced no disturbance because of the Treasury not being able to meet its obligations. The nominal Democrats—that is, Democratic in name but in practical financial matters, Republican —applauded the policy and the success of the Secretary.

Party Lines.—These leaders are prone to resort to means that are calculated to inspire distrust in the minds of the people. In the presidential canvass of 1876, their cry was simply the word " REFORM "—and that word, continually repeated, leaving to the imagination of their followers to conjure up what direful things needed " *reform.*" Again : in the case of the Electoral Commission (February 1877),—a compromise arrangement empowered in Congress *by Democrats and Republicans alike*—consisting of fifteen members of as intelligent, high and noble-minded men as were found in the Nation, and who spent weeks patiently and carefully, while under oath, in weighing the evidence bearing upon the point in issue, and who decided that the Republican candidate was duly elected President of the United States ; notwithstanding all this, when the covenanted arbitration was decided against them, the Democratic leaders at once raised the cry of the single word " *Fraud,*" repeated *ad infinitum.*

Fallacies.—The advocates of Free Trade and for-revenue-only in arguing against a protective or equalizing tariff, ignore the fact that the money raised by import duties goes to defray the current expenses of the national government, and thus benefit the people at large. This money does not come from extortion, but from the free will of those who purchase the foreign goods on which these duties are levied. They need not buy them, as to own such class of merchandise is not absolutely essential. This immense amount of property—worth about $1000,000,000 a year—which is imported and pays so large percentage of profit to the importer and the merchant, ought to pay in the form of duties its share of the general expenses of the government. It is a little singular that these zealous gentlemen never, in their writings or in their lectures, contrast the wages paid abroad for the same class of work with those paid here; neither do we ever hear them contrast the manner of living of foreign operatives in respect to their food and the houses they live in—all in consequence of the low wages they receive—and their general comfort with those of the American. Why should not the people whom they try to influence, have the truth in all its bearings put before them, that they may judge for themselves? On the other hand, would they transfer the profits of which they complain to the foreign manufacturer, and in consequence, either cut down the wages of our own workpeople or throw them out of employment? The dividends of the manufacturer and of the workmen —the latter called wages—are the outgrowth of the combination of capital and labor—the latter performed by our own workpeople for which they are paid on an average more than twice as much as their fellows in Europe. This, however, it seems, goes for nothing in comparison with the importance of sustaining certain theories. Why do these writers and lecturers never say a word on the advantages our own workpeople derive from having something to do, and at comparatively good wages? Why not explain to them the difference in wages paid in the United States and in Europe? Why do they not draw a comparison between the comforts of living which the American workmen enjoy when compared with those of their fellows in Europe? Political economists, who have made this subject a special study, estimate that *three-fourths* of the adult population of the United States, literally work for wages. If this estimate is correct it would follow that the latter and those whom they support are the mass of the people.

The Workmens' Answer.—On the other hand they tell those employed that in consequence of the present tariff they pay higher for what they purchase. The workmen reply : We prefer to have good wages and pay higher for what we buy, than to have low wages and pay less. We can practice economy in both cases, and we can certainly lay up more for a "rainy day" on high wages than on low, and in respect to what things we need, outside food and rent, we virtually buy nothing strictly foreign, except tea and coffee, and on these there is no duty, while home competition has brought all textile fabrics that we use in clothing, down to a reasonable price. Therefore, the intelligent workmen say to these gentlemen, " We do not thank you, though your intentions are kind, for your advocacy of theories, which, if put in practice, would certainly lower our wages or deprive us altogether of employment, and thus prevent our earning the means to purchase the goods you recommend, though they may be nominally as cheap as you say." These sentiments are in substance expressed again and again by intelligent and industrious mechanics.

The Benevolence of Manufacturers.—You would infer from the strong statements by the opponents of an equalizing or protective tariff against American manufacturers, that the latter were tyrants, avaricious and cruel, when in truth there is no class of men who have done more for the advancement of the children of these workmen than they by their munificent gifts to found institutions for education. Many of these proprietors learned in their own experience to sympathize with struggling virtue, as often seen among their own employees, and at the close of their career, and sometimes before, have taken measures by means of their benevolences to promote at large the interests of the workpeople. How different this is in principle from that we have learned of so many of the English manufacturers, who congratulate themselves on having paid their *poor tax*, and thus done their share in providing poorhouses for their worn out workpeople, male and female. Yet owing to the political influence of political demagogues working men are tempted to distrust their employers,

and in consequence take but little interest in the
latter's business or success.   In addition to the
rich manufacturers that have aided the cause of
education by munificent gifts, numbers might be
named who in proportion to their ability, have
afforded opportunities in a less public manner for
their workpeople to improve themselves, by means
of reading-rooms and lectures and facilities for
social intercourse.   In truth no class of wealthy
men is so liberal toward those of limited means.
Peter Cooper was a manufacturer, and so was
John F. Slater, who gave a million of dollars to aid
education in the south; and Mr. Williston the
founder of the Academy that bears his name, and
the bestower of many other similiar benevolences,
was a manufacturer.   Scores of such liberal American manufacturers could be named.

But in all these matters the Democratic policy
seems to be the fostering of public fear by predic-
tions of evil, and the stimulation of distrust between
the employer-class and the wage-class.

XXXIX.

FALSE PRETENCES.

Economy.—One of the tactics of Democratic leaders has been that of endeavoring to secure advantages as a party by means which sometimes appear like false pretences. A favorite mode of bamboozling the uninitiated is the systematic boast of economy in the administration of public expenses. This is often done by making insufficient appropriations to carry on the general government for the ensuing financial year. This year closes the 30th of June, but Congress will meet again in December, before the small appropriations thus made have been exhausted. Meantime these leaders have been proclaiming in their papers, speeches and platforms how many million dollars they have saved the people. The great mass of their followers seem never to become aware of the exact truth on the subject, as their papers are careful to reiterate from time to time how much these professed economists have cut down the extravagant appropriations of the other party. The unenlightened but faithful Democrat believes these statements most implicitly, and as a patriot votes the ticket in the next fall elections.

In due time Congress assembles, and after a

while, comes a report from the Departments, stating that the appropriations made when Congress was last in session, are about exhausted. These economical gentlemen at once bring in the necessary deficency bills, and pass them without a word —as meekly as unweaned lambs. The rank and file scarcely if ever hear of these deficiency bills, for they are not paraded from day to day and week to week in the party papers, though the latter's readers are not permitted to forget the millions asserted to have been saved the tax-ridden people by the insufficient appropriations just noted. This sort of economy has been practised every year, when fall elections were in prospect—can this be merely a coincidence?

An Illustration.—When the Democracy obtained control of the Lower House of Congress they proclaimed they would reform the government in relation to its expenses, and they cut down the appropriations for 1877, about fourteen million dollars, less than had been appropriated for 1876 by the previous Republican Congress. The following year they entered upon a crusade against the *army*, and what was known as the "*fast mail*," which was designed, especially, to facilitate the business of the country; they also caused the suspension of work for a time, on necessary *public buildings* by refusing sufficient funds to carry them on, the sum of these general reductions amounted to about $35,000,000. But when the deficiences were added in, "the appropriations of 1877 were $83,000,000 greater than those for 1876." Yet in the platform of their National Convention at Cincinnati (June 1880) they say: "we congratulate the country upon the honesty and thrift of a Democratic Congress, which has reduced the public expenditures *forty million dollars a year.*" But it is a singular fact in the face of this assertion, that when the deficiency bills for the five years (1876–1881) were added in the average yearly expenditure in the form of legitimate current expenses of the government was in round numbers $8,000,000, more than the last Republican appropriation in 1876, making in all $40,000,000. The increase of the pension list had much to do with this extra expense, and to meet it was necessary. But was it not a species of false pretense to make too small appropriations, and then eke out the necessary funds to carry on the government by quietly passing deficiency bills?

Warlike Patriotism.—Take an instance of another character. In 1862, the leaders of the Democracy took the ground that the war was not carried on vigorously enough to suit their patriotic and belligerent emotions. This was the lament just before the fall elections of that year. One unacquainted with the deep glow of patriotism that thrilled their bosoms, would have supposed the leaders were held by some invisible leash or they would have hastened to the field of battle, and scattered the rebel hordes like dust before a March wind. It was a little striking that these terrible censures could not be directed against the western

armies, as they had been advancing from point to
point, and made no retreats. It must have been
the slow movements of the Army of the Potomac, that
moved their indignation. This army was not a whit
inferior of itself to the victorious Western armies; it
had been drilled and drilled, but was, after a long
while, led into the swamps of the Chickohominy.
Here the results were as marked for their failure
as elsewhere, those of other armies had been for
success. The political canvass of this year glowed
all along the line of the loyal States with the un-
wonted zeal of the leaders of the Democracy to
prosecute the war to the knife. Two years afterward, these gentlemen nominated as their candidate for the Presidency the general who commanded
this army and to whom history attributes this, the
only failure of the war, and the one which they
had eagerly charged against the government! The
belligerent furor was specially rampant in the State
of New York. There a Democratic Governor was
elected—many thousands, allured by these protes-
ations of patriotic zeal contrary to their custom,
voting that ticket. This governor, the following
year July 1863, met the rioters face to face in the
city Hall Park of New York city—their hands
stained with the blood of innocent persons—but
instead of denouncing their murders, robberies and
house-burnings and other violations of law, the
governor called them his *friends*, and told them
he had sent his adjutant to Washington to have the
draft stopped. The inference was that the National

government was wrong in demanding men to prosecute the war, and the rioters were right in refusing
to allow it. But the Supreme Court of the United
States decided otherwise. Similar instances of
these false pretences can be found in almost every
" election year."

Another Election Cry.—When President Harrison died, (1841), the Whig Congress granted his
widow one year's presidential salary, $25,000. This
was done " out of consideration of his expenses in
removing to the seat of government, and the limited
means which he had left behind." Though in office
the greater part of his life, according to Thomas H.
Benton, " his salaries had passed away in charities
and in hospitalities—the poor man's friend, he himself died poor." Yet this act, so commendable in
itself, was paraded with a great clamor throughout
the land by the Democratic leaders and their country papers, as one of unwarrantable extravagence
on the part of Congress in their voting away the
public money. In consequence of this clamor the
party was successful in the next election. It adds
zest to this hue and cry about economy to know
that it was made by the leaders and managers " who
had actually robbed, plundered and stolen, during
the previous ten years, more than $60,000,000 of
the people's money." (Democracy, by Norcross,
pp. 205-208.)

XL.

CHANGE OF BASE.

It is remarkable in how many instances, during the last twenty or more years, the leaders of the Democracy have been forced to approve measures which were introduced by the Republicans, against strenuous Democratic opposition.

Abolition of Slavery.—The Democratic party organization—not all the members—encouraged the Southern wing in their efforts to break up the Union and perpetuate slavery, but since the end came in the destruction of that system, and in making the Union stronger than ever, they have come upon the ground originally held by their opponents, and hail with satisfaction the fact that we are no longer cramped in our energies by the influence of human bondage. This change of sentiment was by no means made at once, but at length they even recognized the vast importance of having the Nation's progress freed from the incubus of slavery. This is creditable to their good sense—though it comes somewhat late.

Paying the Debt.—The leaders of the Democracy in 1868 favored in their platform paying a certain portion of the Nation's debt in the then depreciated greenbacks; the Republicans the same

year came out in their platform unequivocally in
favor of paying the Nation's debt honestly in full,
and upon that ground they appealed to the intelligence and honesty of the people and were by them
sustained. The latter party looked upon any form
of virtual repudiation as dishonorable and a crime,
and as such condemned it under any form or name,
announcing that "all creditors at home and abroad"
should be paid, "not only according to the letter
but the spirit of the laws under which it was contracted." Now the Democratic leaders profess to
be in favor of paying the national debt, principal
and interest, since honesty seems to be popular.

The Amendments to the Constitution.—The
XVth Amendment to the Constitution of the United
States having passed Congress in due form came
before the legislature of New York for the latter's
ratification, which was given it. Afterward, when
another legislature had assembled, which had a
majority of Democratic members, the latter went
through the formal farce of voting to annul the
sanction given by the previous legislature. The
same spirit seemed to actuate these leaders throughout the land. But in 1872 the same leaders
pledged themselves in their platform " to maintain
the union of these States, emancipation, and en-
franchisement ['the civil rights of the freedmen']
and to oppose any reopening of the questions
settled by the XIII, XIV, and XV amendments to
the Constitution." This was accepting reconstruction, which they had bitterly opposed ; it had

now become a fixed fact, and popular. They had
come upon the ground which had been taken by
those statesmen who comprehended the necessity of
giving the colored man a chance to perform intelligently his duties as an enfranchised citizen. Four
years afterward (1876), to make it doubly sure,
they declared in their platform that "In the whole
country, we do affirm our devotion to the Constitution of the United States with its amendments
universally accepted as a *final settlement* of the controversies that had engendered civil war."

These leaders also opposed Reconstruction, except
on principles that would have been injurious to us
as a progressive Nation, that is, they wished Restoration in accordance with Andrew Johnson's policy,
and they were consistent when they connived at
and virtually encouraged the Ku Klux outrages in
order to neutralize the effects of reconstruction.
(*American People*, pp. 1033–44.) Why is it that
these gentlemen have accepted the measures introduced by their political opponents, and which at
the time they opposed with all their strength?
There can be but two reasons assigned; either they
have found that they were mistaken in their opposition and now see it, or because these measures in
consequence of their good influence have become
popular, and therefore better policy to accept them.
The one supposition shows that the statesmanship
of their opponents was the better and more comprehensive in its influence and beneficial in its
effects; the other that acquiescence is the better

policy in order to stand fair with the American people.

Final Approval of Measures.—It seems from the very first to have been the fate of the leaders of the Democracy to oppose measures which they were afterward compelled to accept because of their utility; for instance, in the earlier days, the policy of *neutrality*, and the Hamiltonian theory of managing the *finances*. In later times their opposition to the introduction of *cheap postage* is one of the most striking instances. The leaders of the Democracy, for the most part, have opposed the present *National banking* system, but those nominal Democrats, who are financiers and merchants, have come fully upon Republican ground on that subject. However, nothing definite can be predicted of the leaders on this policy so long as they continue to flirt with Greenbackers and Inflationists. On one political question they have not come on common ground with their opponents—the *Tariff*. No matter whether they say for "revenue alone " or "only for revenue," they mean their hostility to any system that equalizes the cost of production of foreign manufactured goods that in any form come in competition with those of our own make, or in other words, that affords protection to our mechanical industries, and thereby gives employment to those of our own people who work for wages. This is evident from the numbers in the party who are absolute Free Traders, and, also, may be inferred from the leaders coquetting with the latter organization. But here, too, they seem to lack the courage of their convictions, and are evidently afraid to commit themselves as a party to any definite policy. This is clear from the recent failure of the so-called "Morrison Tariff Bill," which the Free Trading section of the party tried to pass in Congress in the year 1884, and for which one-fifth of their members refused to vote.

It may illustrate the *progressive* views of the leaders of the Democracy on the subject of the tariff, to give extracts from the platforms of the last three of their National Conventions. In 1876 they demanded a tariff "only for revenue;" in 1880, "for revenue only;" and in 1884, " exclusively for public purposes." It is presumed the different meanings attached to each of the first two can be made plain, and also the reasons given for the change of base in adopting the third, " exclusively for public purposes." If the latter phrase differs essentially in meaning from the first two, that difference ought to be pointed out in order that the members of the party, outside the leader class, may be able to vote intelligently.

XLI.

ILLEGAL VOTING.

The Basic Principle. —In our government the final power rests in the hands of the people themselves, who express their will in choosing by ballot their executive officers and the representatives to their legislative bodies—both National and State. If these elections are kept pure the will of the people will be fully expressed, but if they are fraudulent, the result will be injurious to the purity of our legislative bodies. For this reason, among many others, all lovers of honesty and fairness in elections desire the people to have the opportunity of expressing their will by their votes. That *the voice of the majority should rule* is the keystone of our political arch; but how can this principle be carried out if dishonest men are permitted to cast more than one vote for each candidate at elections? To carefully guard the purity of the ballot-box is presumed to be the desire of every patriotic citizen; and to do otherwise is to merit the condemnation of every advocate of truth and honesty. Of the measures adopted to prevent this class of frauds, the most effective is to have the voters, under proper regulations, register their names and address, that, if necessary, their right to vote can be verified. It

seems strange that any portion of good citizens
should be opposed to a law designed to protect the
elective franchise from fraud.

Registry Law.—We are not aware—though
such a thing is not impossible—of a *single instance,*
either in the State Legislatures or in the National
Congress, when the leaders of the Democratic party
took the initiative in proposing laws to secure fair
and honest elections. On the contrary, we have
seen them in every instance playing the role of obstructionists to every measure that was introduced
by others to promote the purity of the ballot-box. In
what State have they of their own motion introduced
a *registry law,* in order to protect citizens entitled
to vote and prevent their wishes being neutralized
by fraud?

*[Since there may have been an instance in which
the leaders of the Democracy of their own motion
instituted a registry law we leave this blank in order
to insert an authenticated record of such fact when
it shall have been found.]*

Election Frauds.—There is no place in the
Union where the Democracy holds absolute sway
as in the good City of New York. Here are found
the classes—termed "dangerous"—by the police,

which adhere fervently to those who cater to their
vices and always vote in the interest of that political organization from which they expect to derive
the most benefits.   Out of such elements fraudulent
voters could be manufactured.   These are *notorious
facts*, and are not denied by good, intelligent and
respectable citizens of any creed, religious or political.   This accounts for the ease with which fraudulent voting could be carried out in that city.

Thus in 1868, when an election was to be held
for President and Congressmen with State officers,
it was determined by the Democracy to carry the
State at all hazards.   This was accomplished by
means of issuing naturalization papers to persons
not entitled to them.   Upon these forged papers
thousands upon thousands of fraudulent votes were
cast.   They had so large a surplus of these docu-
ments, that they were used by the same party for
other voters, in other cities and towns, and along
the railways of the State, and also, it was said, in
two neighboring States.   To make the matter still
more sure, a circular was sent from the city to the
inspectors of election belonging to the party, in
important districts throughout the State, requiring
them to telegraph immediately on the close of the
polls, to the headquarters of the Democratic Campaign Committee in the City of New York, their
estimate of the number of votes cast in their districts by the respective parties.   They were enjoined
to be thus prompt, before the telegraph would be
used in transmitting the real returns.   This circular

had attached as signature of the committee's chairman the name of a gentleman well known and
who has since been highly honored by the Democracy as their peculiar representative in the cause of
" Reform."[1] Some length of time elapsed after the
returns from the remainder of the State were in,
when the inspectors of election in New York made
their returns, and lo! the Democratic voters had
been so numerous in the city that the party was
overwhelmingly successful in electing both their
National and State tickets! There were circumstances connected with previous elections in the
State which made it evident that tremendous frauds
had been systematically committed. This fact was
clearly demonstrated by the investigation of a committee appointed by Congress for the purpose.
(*Report of Select Committee on Alleged Election
Frauds in New York.*) Had the present law been
so amended as to require the applicant to receive
his naturalization papers, not less than six months
before he was entitled to vote, would these wholesale frauds have occurred?

The Remedy.—The people throughout the whole
land were astounded. They were interested in this
election far beyond what they would have been if
the effect had been limited to the state offices
alone; they were not willing that Congressmen
and Presidents should be elected by fraud in any
State. The scheme had been devised by master
minds, and effectually carried out, yet, as sometimes occurs, they went too far, and attracted uni-

[1] Samuel J. Tilden.

versal attention. The crime was too dangerous to be overlooked, and thoughtful and patriotic men demanded of Congress protection from frauds in the elections for National offices. In consequence, Congress, after full investigation and debate, made the dishonest proceedings just mentioned, the occasion of passing a law to prevent similar frauds in the States, when elections are held for choosing Electors for President, or the Representatives of the people in the Lower House. This was in accordance with the Constitution of the United States, article I, sect. 4, as decided by the Supreme Court.

This law (*American People*, p. 1053,) cannot be objected to by those who wish honest elections. It provides for a registry of the legal voters; what true or honest patriot could object to that? It provides for inspectors of election to be appointed *from different political parties*—if the inspectors are honest and fair, this ought to prevent illegal voting, and if they are not honest and fair, they can prevent fraud by watching each other. Where can there possibly be an objection to this arrangement if honest elections are desired?

The law has worked well in preventing fraud, and has the sanction of those who wish the people to have a fair expression of their preferences when they vote for their representatives in Congress or for President. What possible motive could there be to repeal this law on the part of any political organization, especially if they wished fair elections. It applies only to cities and towns of a certain number of inhabitants—20,000 or more—and for the reason well known, that in these there are more facilities for carrying out schemes of illegal voting than in rural districts, where the voters are comparatively few, and well known to each other.

Opposed by the Democrats.—The propriety of this law must be obvious to reflecting minds, as Congressmen in their official duties have an equal right to vote on all the interests that pertain to the *whole people* of the Union, and therefore the *whole people* have a right to demand that these representatives should be elected by the free and fair choice of their *own constituents in their own several districts.* However, when the law was before Congress it was bitterly opposed by the Democratic members on the ground that it "interfered with the rights of the States." This was the old presumption under a new phase, which means that the Nation—the entire people—has no right to protect itself from fraudulent voters in any single State. When the bill was under discussion, its opponents proclaimed with nervous anxiety their willingness that elections should be free and fair, but when an amendment was offered forbidding persons coming to the polls armed with deadly weapons "*for the purpose of intimidating voters*"—thus even in its wording rendering the accusation or indictment liable to fail by means of a simple denial of the motive on the part of the accused—the Democratic Senators to a man voted against the amendment, and it failed. (*Congressional Record*, 1879.) May not the solution of this extraordinary vote be found in the fact that, to a certain extent, the custom of carrying deadly weapons to the polls prevails in the once slave-owning States? (*Report of Senate Committee on Outrages, etc.—Teller, Chairman.*)

The record shows that in all of our legislative discussions concerning illegal voting the Democratic party, *for some reason or other*, has invariably found reasons to object to every law framed for the protection of the ballot box ; and has equally *found it impracticable to propose any other* law for that purpose. The two facts bear their own comment.

XLII.

CENTRALIZATION.

Meaning of the Term.—The objection made to what is termed centralization, or the assertion that the national government at Washington has too much power, is only a modern phase of the old theory of State or Sovereignty Rights. The strict application of this doctrine would deprive the Nation of the power to sustain itself against those who might wish to violate its integrity. Under the presumption that the government has too much power these theorists would not permit it to protect the rights of the whole people; for instance, as noted in the last chapter, in guarding against fraud in the elections for Congressmen and Presidential Electors. The National government—both legislative and executive—is preëminently the representative and agent of the *whole people* of the Union, and to it emphatically belongs the duty of protecting them in every section of the land. The charge of Centralization is often specious and, it would seem, only used to cover an ulterior purpose; for instance the law to prevent fraudulent voting for Congressmen and Presidential Electors (1870) was opposed in Congress on the ground that it was

giving too much power to the National government
or leading to Centralization. But the Constitution
of the United States says in respect to elections for
Representatives in the Lower House: "Congress
may at any time by law make or alter such regulation." (Article I, Section 4.) But it is remarkable that these leaders did not interpose this objection when they wished to affiliate with the Green-
back-inflationists who would authorize the national
government as a *central power* to issue Greenbacks
without restriction or call them in, if the government wished to influence the money market. Still
more strange is the opposition made by our Democratic friends to the National government's aiding
in part, public schools in the States, and *pro rata*
to their illiteracy, on the ground that it leads to
Centralization. Thus the education of the young,
especially, in the recent slave-labor States must be
postponed and held subordinate to a mere theory.

A Strong Government.—What is meant by a
strong National government, is one that under the
constitution and laws would be able—for illustration—to protect its citizens in all the States in their
rights; among others the right of free speech and
honest voting; that is; be strong enough to protect its own integrity in the security and purity of
elections for the Nation's own officers, and enforce
the right for the citizen to migrate from one state
to another, and there enjoy the protection of the
government in his privileges as a citizen of the
whole Nation.

It may not be out of place to give an extract from a recent decision of the U. S. Supreme Court on the question of guarding the purity of elections, it says: "That a government whose essential character is republican, whose executive head, and legislative body are both elective, whose most numerous and powerful branch of the Legislature is elected by the people directly, has no power by appropriate laws to secure this election from the influence of violence, of corruption and of fraud, is a proposition so startling as to arrest attention and demand the gravest consideration. If this Government is anything more than a mere aggregation of delegated agents of other States and Governments, each of which is superior to the General Government, it must have the power to protect the elections on which its existence depends from violence and corruption." Again, in respect to the theory of the strict constructionists that there must be in so many words an *express* power etc., delegated to Congress, the court says: "It destroys at one blow in construing the constitution of the United States, the doctrine universally applied to all instruments of writing, that what is *implied* is as much a part of the instrument as what is *expressed*."

XLIII.

FINANCIAL COMPARISONS.

The Balance of Trade.—Having resumed specie payments, to make permanent this solid foundation for business transactions, the National government must be able to pay the interest on the funded debt, and defray its current expenses. To aid in this important result, it will be to the Nation's advantage to have the balance of trade in its favor, in order to avoid paying the difference in gold. With the aid of manufactured articles sent abroad in addition to our agricultural products, we can make our exports of equal or more money value than our imports. We have never before exported such immense quantities of our industrial products of various kinds, which hitherto we have made to supply but partially our own wants. The time was when we were satisfied with meeting these wants only, but since the Centennial Exposition we have had higher aspirations, even to send abroad our manufactured goods and compete with the rest of the world.

The American people were encouraged to do this because the majority of the goods made by themselves compared favorably at that Exposition with those of foreign make, while in respect to those for practical use, such as ingenious machinery and all kinds of labor-saving tools in various combinations, they were unquestionably the farthest advanced of all the exhibitors. They were never before in a position so favorable to compete with European nations in manufacturing, as then for the first time they had availed themselves of the skill acquired during *fifteen years* of consecutive protected labor and experiment. The following statement and estimate may give some idea of our industrial progress. We learn from the census that in 1860, the value of our manufactures was $1,800,000,000; in 1870, $3,400,000,000; and in 1880, $5,300,000,000. It may also be noted that during this same period our exports and imports, and the value of our agricultural products have increased enormously if not in an equal ratio. In addition a census report states that since 1860 prices have been reduced from 25 to 30 per cent, while about one half of the production is American. We once paid England $100 per ton for steel rails, but since American manufactories have grown up we purchase them at about $40 per ton, and in an exceptional case not long since, a lot was sold for $34 per ton. Before 1861 our mechanical industries were never free for more than four or five years at a time from injudicious intermeddling, such as changing the tariff from one basis to another, or making the attempt from time to time. This uncertainty had an injurious effect upon the mannfacturing industries of the land, as capitalists were timid in investing to much extent in such enterprises. On the other hand the certainty of no change in this respect for a number of years, has had much to do with our present vast industrial advance, as well as the application of labor-saving machinery, the most of which is of American invention or ingenious improvements on foreign ones. We can now in some respects compete with the world in skill and machinery but not in *low wages*.

Our Bonds and Exports.—Another good result from the balance of trade with foreign countries being in our favor is to change the ownership of many of our bonds held abroad, as they are frequently sent back to pay the difference, and instead of the interest on them being paid to foreign holders it is paid to our own people, and of course goes into the circulating medium of the country.

Care ought to be taken by appropriate measures to keep the balance of trade in our favor. It is not to be expected that failures of the crops in Europe will continue to last, and thus afford from year to year so large an outlet for our surplus grain. This deficiency may in part be supplied by our exporting the products of our mechanical industries. But the latter cannot be accomplished if these industries are materially injured by adverse legislation. It would seem as if the *special friends* of the workingman hoped to benefit him by lowering the duties on imports, and thus interfere with the amount of his wages by diminishing them,

and "compensate" him by reducing the tax on tobacco—a more or less useless luxury, and on whiskey—the working man's special curse.

Fancy Financiering.—We can judge of the
merits of a system only by its results. It seems that
much of the revenue collected in the Democratic
days of Jackson and Van Buren found great difficulties in reaching the United States Treasury; it
somehow stuck by the way, even more than it did
during the preceding Whig administration of John
Quincy Adams, (1825–1829), in which $885,374
all told, failed to reach the Treasury. In Andrew
Jackson's eight years, (1829–1837), $3,761,112 be-
came entangled in the pockets of the collectors and
their subordinates; no wonder honest old Hickory,
horrified at the result, said to Daniel Webster that
"he had always sought honest men for the offices,
but nearly all turned out thieves as soon as they
obtained full possession of their places." (*History
of Democracy* by Norcross, p. 216). Mr. Van
Buren has not left on record an account of his
emotions when he learned of the immense difficulties
his officers had in forwarding their collections to
the Treasury during his administration of *four*
years, (1837–1841), as $3,343,792 failed to reach it;
this was nearly as much as lost its way during
Jackson's *eight* years of rule.

The Loss on the $1,000.—Another form of com-
parison may be interesting to the reader. In
Adams's administration $2.75 on the $1,000 lost
their way; in Jackson's $7.52 on the same amount;

while in Van Buren's $11.71 on the $1,000 never
reached the Treasury. This period covered *sixteen
years*. Let us now, in connection with it, examine
another period, but of *twenty-one years*. In 1862,
under Republican administration, and collection of
vastly greater sums, this loss on the $1,000 was no-
tably less than it had been in the previous administration—Mr. Buchanan's—when it had been the custom, it is said, in making estimates of the public expenses to allow for an average of $14 on the thousand
to lose its way to the Treasury. Notwithstanding
the immense disbursements at the time—sometimes
at the rate of a million dollars a day—the loss on the
$1,000 continued to diminish from year to year, till
in Andrew Johnson's administration it fell to $1.65
on the thousand, and in General Grant's administration to $0.26; and still lower under President
Hayes.

The Contrast.—However, the most remarkable
contrast has been in the Internal Revenue Department, where, during seven years, ending June 30,
1883, $893,384,437 had been collected, and *not one
dollar* became entangled by the way, but all safely
reached the Treasury. This vast amount was collected through the medium of 126 offices, and the
entire expense was not quite three and one-half per
cent. on the sum paid in (Commissioner Raum's
reports). There have no doubt been losses, though
to a limited extent when compared with the past, in
connection with import duties, as there are so many
secret facilities for the dishonest importer to cheat

the Treasury by means of double invoices, (p. 119), or by undervaluations.

Successful Financiering.—The close of President Buchanan's administration, March 3, 1861, left the financial condition of the National Government in a sad state. The country had enjoyed a period of *thirteen years* of peace, yet, strange to say, under the system of financiering then in vogue, the Nation was saddled with a debt of $87,700,000, and its credit was so low that it could not borrow money in the markets of Europe at its offered rate of six per cent., while the regular price was as low as three and a half and three. It was at this time, and under such state of affairs, that the control of the National Government passed into the hands of the Republican party. The latter soon had to contend with a rebellion and to provide the funds to defray the expenses of crushing it and saving the Nation's life. The detail of the manner in which our finances were managed to accomplish this result and to provide for the debt thereby incurred, is too long to be fully introduced in this connection and we can give only a summary. Congress, in addition to increasing the rate of the tariff and imposing a tax on incomes and domestic manufactures, authorized the Secretary of the Treasury to issue United States notes—since known as "Greenbacks"—and bonds of various denominations from thousands of dollars down to fifty, and in which loyal people invested their earnings, as a pledge of their patriotism and of their faith in the ultimate success of the cause.

Diminishing the Debt.—In four years time, when the Rebellion collapsed in 1865, the National debt had increased to $2,756,431,571; which was left over after the current taxes and import duties paid in during that period had been expended, together with the immense sums privately contributed by the loyal people in the Free-Labor States. This vast debt had to be grappled with ; and since then the government has paid (up to Dec. 1, 1883) $1,783,967,355 an average of about $70,000,000 a year. The original debt was at unusual high rates of interest, ranging from 7.3-10ths to 5 per cent, but the Treasury, under the management of successive Republican secretaries, brought this down as soon as possible to four and a half, four, and even to three per cent, saving an immense amount in interest alone, so that during eighteen years in the diminishing of the debt and in the reduction of the rate of interest, a very great amount of the burden of the original debt has been removed. Experienced financiers say that this has been done under wise and honest management; but our friends, the Democratic leaders, say under "rascals," who ought to be turned out for the benefit of the "dear people."

The Interest for Each Individual.—In 1865 the annual interest charge on the whole debt was $4.29 for each individual of the Nation, but it has since been going down--by diminishing the debt itself as well as by lowering the rate of interest—till now (1891) it is on an average of about *thirty-six cents.* The latter result has been accomplished mainly by reducing the rate of interest on the bonds; not arbitrarily, but by a fair and open mercantile transaction, in which, when its bonds became due, the government, through the Secretaries of the Treasury, proposed to its creditors to pay them in full, or, if the latter preferred, to reissue the bonds at a lower rate of interest, but to run for a longer term; the exchange was made to the satisfaction of both parties. The political organization that has been in control of the National government since March 4, 1861, has dealt fairly with its creditors and has invariably repudiated repudiation, even in its most insidious forms.

A Republican Congress—XLVIIth, 2d session, 1883—made an effort to curtail the internal revenue $30,000,000, and to adjust the tariff so as to diminish its income $40,000,000. It was found, however, July 1, 1884, that the reduction of the former was only $19,000,000 and that of the latter only $23,000,000. The estimates had been in error, but on the safe side, as the material progress of the country had been so much greater than anticipated. Meanwhile, the net reduction of the Nation's debt for the financial year ending June 30, 1884, was $101,000,000, and also the ordinary expenses of the government for the same year were diminished $5,000,000, and the interest on the debt to the same amount. The net debt of the United States on July 1, 1884, was $1,450,050,285.80.

XLIV

CIVIL SERVICE REFORM.

Begun by Republicans.—The agitation in respect to the Reform of the Civil Service began in President Grant's administration ; the examinations of candidates as to their qualifications were instituted, and certain rules adopted. In accordance with the spirit of this movement, President Hayes issued an order (June 22, 1877), that was designed to be applicable to every department of the Civil Service. He says: "No officer should be required or permitted to take part in the management of political organizations, caucuses, conventions, or election campaigns. No assessment for political purposes on officers or subordinates should be allowed." After a few years of experiment, the general results arrived at have been embodied in a law. The latter was passed in the second session of the XLVIIth Congress (1883), and was in the main drawn by Mr. Dorman B. Eaton, a Republican, and also well known as an efficient member of an association whose object for years has been to promote this reform ; but as a matter of fact, it was presented in the United States' Senate by Senator Pendleton of Ohio, a Democrat, whose views were in sympathy with the movement. Since this

agitation began, and the law having gone into effect
the influence has been most excellent on the service. The government officials may see proper to
make changes among those whom they employ;
these changes are sometimes attributed, but very
often unjustly, to favoritism or political influence.
Still, as long as the service is well managed, as we
have just seen, those who take the trouble to understand the workings of the system will not complain,
any more than the stockholders of a manufacturing
company would find fault with its officers, who
may make changes among those whom they employ, but, at the same time, so manage the affairs of
the company as to pay good dividends. In this
case the American people are the stockholders. It
is hoped that under the regulations thus instituted, the National as well as State governments
may be able to employ subordinate officers who will
perform their duties efficiently, and that such appointments will be made on the score of merit and
not at the instance of politicians and office-brokers.

This law also enjoins an important regulation in
respect to the individual habits of the official thus
appointed; Section 8 announces: "That no person
habitually using intoxicating beverages to excess
shall be appointed to, or retained in any office, appointment, or employment to which the provisions
of this act are practicable." In accordance, likewise, with the spirit of this same law, President
Arthur (Jan. 1883) issued the following Rules:

Rule first—No person in Civil Service shall use

his office, his official authority or influence, either to coerce the political action of any person or body, or to interfere with any election.

Rule second—No person in the public service shall for that reason be under any obligation to contribute to any political fund or render any political service, and he will not be removed or otherwise prejudiced for refusing to do so.

Democratic View of it.—Since the close of the Rebellion, while for nearly thirty years the Republicans have been kept in office by the people, the leaders of the Democracy have manifested an unusual interest in talking about Civil Service Reform, though previous to that time this reform had not received their special attention. The passage of Senator Pendleton's Civil Service Bill in Congress marked an era in the progress of this movement, and the friends of good government rejoiced. But, for some unexplained reason, since that time the practical zeal of its Democratic friends, so ardent in words, has flagged considerably. The mutterings of disapprobation of Senator Pendleton's course in certain Democratic newspapers was the first intimation of this change of sentiment, which presently culminated in the refusal of the Democratic majority in the Ohio Legislature to re-elect him to the United States' Senate. Thus Mr. Pendleton, because of his sincerity, has been virtually consigned to a political Nirvāna. Numerous papers—organs of the party—within the State and out of it, have attributed his rejection to his zeal in the cause of Civil Service Reform.

The Good Results.—The theory of Civil Service Reform as held by its advocates is that subordinate employes of the Government, such as clerks in the departments, Custom Houses, Post-Offices, etc., when appointed in accordance with the requirements of the law, if found efficient, should be retained, while the rules (p. 311), if complied with, preclude their taking active part in politics, or becoming, as since defined, "offensive partisans." The advantage of appointing to office competent men, is self-evident, and the genuine friends of that measure of reform hope, in time, to rid the Nation of what is known as the "spoils system," which hitherto has had so injurious an effect upon political morals.

XLV.

THE LIQUOR INTEREST.

Its Power.—As, in the times previous to the Rebellion, Slavery held the balance of power in all National questions, so to-day, in its various forms, the Liquor Interest aims at holding the same kind of power between the two great political parties within the States. This active force in elections—either State or National—is not, by any means, to be despised. It includes in its ample fold all the wholesale dealers, who control millions of money; the keepers of drinking saloons; the distillers and brewers, and great numbers of those who raise the grains from which whiskey and beer are made; the keepers of gambling establishments, and all those who in divers ways cater to the vices of the community. To these, likewise, must be added the *foreign wine* interest; this includes the importers and dealers with but few exceptions. It is well known that beer is less injurious than whiskey when used to excess; in consequence, not so many are opposed to it as a beverage: yet its makers and venders, are *equally strenuous* in opposing any reform tending toward temperance in the use of either. This whole power is a unit in opposing any political organization that dares move in the direction of a temperance reform, however moderate, and liquor dealers finding the Democracy the acknowledged stronghold of their interest throughout the Union, act consistently, when they ally themselves with it, and become its right arm. This combined liquor power is by no means unconscious of its influence in elections, be they of State Legislatures or of Municipal Officers; it has not yet had the opportunity to try its strength directly on National questions, which pertain to its own special interests, but not less than if the latter were at issue, does it adhere in National politics to its party friends and advocates in local strifes. This interest, conscious of its power, is felt almost everywhere, hence it is courted by unscrupulous politicians, and consequently its demands are made with an arrogance that is astounding.

In an election (Nov. 6, 1883), New York City furnished more than thirty candidates for municipal or state officers, who were personally identified with that interest as keepers or ex-keepers of drinking saloons, etc. (*The N. Y. Telegram*, Nov. 8, 1883.)

This liquor influence permeates, more than is even suspected, much less known, the private life of the community; corrupting habits and morals and bringing sorrow and disgrace upon families, by catering to the vice of intemperance and its concomitant evils. The indications are that this power will henceforth exert an influence in controlling elections, both State and National, almost as great as slavery did in former days. As an element, it is much more diffused than the spirit of slavery, for that never came north of Mason and Dixon's line, except as a sycophant; but the liquor interest ignores State lines, and cannot be sectional, but what is still more dangerous to the Nation, it is all-pervading.

Its Political Allegiance.—If we judge from certain recent State elections, we are authorized to infer that while a portion of the Democracy differ on the Tariff question, on that of liquor they are as decided as the Hibernian rumseller, who declared he did not "*loike sumptuous laws at all, at all.*"

What estimate ought we to make of the patriotism shown by those who directly or indirectly encourage any business that must, from the nature of the case, have a deleterious influence upon the morals and the industries of the community at large? Take for illustration this subject of Temperance; why is it that the Democratic party contains nearly all those who make their living by selling intoxicating drinks? We have seen that, in its very origin, a hundred years ago, in the form of "Clubs," it had the countenance of the disorderly classes, and in its ranks to-day it has about the same ratio of the kindred elements of society. The liquor dealers, because of "aid and comfort" given them by this party, have become arrogant in their demands, and assume the *right, as individuals*, to sell intoxicating drinks to the injury of the whole

community. This assumed privilege they unblush
ingly demand, and come before the people with an
injured and demure aspect, as if they were the bene-
factors rather than the wrongers of their fellow-
citizens. They think "the world is governed too
much;" and they virtually demand for *their business*
as much protection and encouragement as if they
were engaged in making and selling sewing-ma-
chines.

Secular Day of Rest.—It is of immense importance to the success of the liquor traffic that it
should not be interfered with on Sunday; that day
being established by law as *one of rest* from secular
employments, their customers, being at leisure,
would the more likely patronize the saloons. These
dealers are not specially influenced by the fact that
the day is deemed sacred—because believed to be
instituted by divine authority—by the vast majority
of native Americans, and also by great numbers, if
not the majority of our fellow-citizens of foreign
birth; but they ought to understand that the laws
enacted in relation to the Sabbath, or day of rest,
*treat it only in its secular character, and not in re-
spect to its religious observance*, and thus that observance is not made a religious question. This is in
accordance with the principle that the State does
not legislate on religion, but for the good of the
whole people, and that those who, in accordance
with their rights as citizens, demand a quiet
day to attend worship, shall not be interfered
with; and as so many disturbances on Sunday are

caused by drunkenness, it is consistent that the law
should restrain those who make their living by promoting that form of vice.

Political Organizations on the Question.—
The question of Temperance has hitherto been confined to the action of State laws, as well as to municipal, but it is of national importance, and must become one of the great questions of the future. The
essential feature of the question will be, shall the
Nation be temperate or not ; shall those whose business has the effect of corrupting the morals, and
injuring the material interests of the people, be permitted to do so with impunity? This question will
be discussed and acted upon until the conscience of
the majority of the whole people will become satisfied on the expediency of the traffic and its moral
influence.

Let education, intellectual and moral, go hand in
hand with temperance and industry, and we may
avoid the rock of pauperism on which the English
" ruling classes" have stranded millions of the work-
ing-people of the kingdom. Let us carefully secure
the present rising generation in respect to these two
points—temperance and industry—and their moral
self-respect, thus perpetuated, will guard coming
generations from the degradation of intemperance
and pauperism. We cannot begin this work too
soon, for the American people do not wish to try
the experiment of going as near as possible to the
line of "starvation wages," with those whom they
employ, neither do they expect to influence their

posterity to be temperate if they permit their youth to be corrupted by the liquor-sellers.

We find, at the present time, one political organization mainly in favor of aiding the people to become and remain temperate: the other political organization we would not charge with designedly promoting intemperance; but is it not virtually doing so by encouraging and sustaining the rumsellers in their nefarious work, and thus aiding indirectly in debauching the community? The former is willing, and in the main urgent, that the question should be discussed and acted upon in some manner that will restrain, if not remove, the evil; whether it be by amendments to State constitutions, or by enforcing existing laws on the subject. But above all, the people should be so enlightened as to act intelligently; and it is a convincing proof of the assertions of this monogram concerning the Democratic party and its successive opponents, that no one in the land needs to be told *which* political party it is that favors the immoral and destructive liquor interest.

The Young Men.—The indications are that within a few years the question of temperance will become National; this may be inferred from the political action taken in so many states, which is designed to restrain the traffic in intoxicating liquors. These measures have been introduced in different forms, in some cases the Legislatures have granted individual counties what is known as "local option," in which the citizens by their own votes can regulate or prohibit the sale of such liquors within their own bounds; others attempt to secure the end in view by constitutional provisions. Compared with the past, the times seem unusually propitious for the people throughout the Union to take hold of this question, after the Presidential election in 1892, as we have seen, after much discussion, the leading subjects of our internal policy, such as the tariff, the banking system etc., have been so arranged that they will, in all probability, thus remain without radical changes for a long time.

The evils of intemperance within the last few years have been increasing more than usual, and to this fact the attention of the people has been directed. The cause is National and the measures for its restraint or removal must also be National in their extent. The evils accompanying rum-selling—its results, direct and indirect, such as drunkenness and idleness, and often gambling and its attendant vices, and nine-tenths of the crime of the community—make an appeal to the conscience of the entire people to remove the main cause. These terrible causes are not sectional, for they are found more or less in every portion of the Union, and there is no reason why the whole people should not go hand in hand in their suppression. Why should not the benevolent everywhere unite to rescue those poor unfortunate drunkards from their dire adversary the rumseller and his friends? The political conflict will be severe and may continue for years, but, at last, when the evils

of intemperance are more fully unfolded, the people
will see and feel their own responsibility in the
matter, and will rise in their majesty and crush them
out. They will not let the question rest *until the
conscience of the Nation is satisfied*, either in having
the traffic sufficiently restrained or entirely abolished.

The Question of the Future.—The political
questions of the past few years have had special
reference to material prosperity and industrial interests; that phase will still continue, but to this the
question of temperance will most assuredly be super-
added, because of its vast importance to the well-
being of society, and its good effect on future generations. Therefore, in no period of our history has
the responsibility of voters in a strictly moral sense
been greater than it is now and will be in the near
future. Just here our young men must take a decided stand, intelligently and morally. In *dead issues*
they have no interest except in their history; but here
is a *living issue*, whose influence is limited only by
time—if even by that—and with it the young men
must grapple. In respect to political organizations
the lines are quite clearly drawn. The one, as such,
is in favor of judicious measures that will remove the
evil of intemperance from the land; the leaders of
the other appear to be opposed to the enforcement
of laws or measures, that would attain that object,
under the pretense that they are "sumptuary," and
moreover that they interfere with the inherent rights
of the individual. That means but little check upon
the traffic, except in the way of license, and with

scarcely any restraint based upon its evils to society, as that would interfere with *their interpretation* of individual liberty, and the aphorism that "the world is governed too much." These facts are so notorious that it seems unnecessary to quote here in proof from general platforms of the party or from speeches and letters of its leaders, to illustrate their general tone on this subject.

We shall, however, obtain a truer exposition of the views of the Democracy on the temperance question in the platforms of their State Conventions than from the sentiments they put forth in their National Convention every fourth year. The reason is obvious; there is more diversity of opinion in the whole Nation than in individual States, hence in the National platforms it is essential to arrange statements in such manner that they can be interpreted in different ways, or in other words, to conceal when expedient and to reveal when necessary. If one will look over the platforms adopted in their State Conventions in 1882, he will find in eighteen of these that *five* express themselves in favor of no restraint being placed on the sale of intoxicating liquors ; *three* express themselves obscurely; *one* is alarmed at the spread of intemperance ; *nine* give no expression on the subject ; *not one* distinctly declares in favor of temperance.

In the State of New York the Democratic candidate for Secretary of State (1883)—whose private and public character was unimpeachable—was defeated by the liquor-dealers, because some years ago he dared vote in favor of temperance, and they avowedly combined against him and openly announced the reason. This they had a right to do, and the result showed their power, and also showed that the Democracy has *some* principles it dare avow and act upon.

The same year, in an election in the State of Ohio the Democratic leaders depended for success on the liquor interest, and on that ground they succeeded. At a previous session, the Republican Legislature, in order to restrain the increasing vice of intemperance in that State, passed an ordinance —known as the Scott law, from the name of the member who introduced it—on licensing the sale of intoxicating drinks ; the object being, by imposing a high license, as far as possible to secure a class of liquor-sellers who would not cater so much to the unfortunate victims of the degrading vice of drunkenness. The enactment of this law was a boon to these leaders, as it afforded them an occasion for descanting on the abstract principles of " civil liberty " and "sumptuary laws," and all that. In Iowa a similar influence was exerted and on virtually the same ground, but it was not so successful. In the State of Indiana an amendment was proposed to the State Constitution on the subject of restraining intemperance, and the same party's leaders opposed it vehemently at every step ; their most influential ex-United States Senator taking the ground, and clearly implying, that inter-

ference with the rumseller was a violation of
" certain inalienable rights," which were not to be
tampered with unless " for the purpose of securing
civil liberty."

This is the record. Self-respecting young men in
entering upon their career as citizens, will decide
for themselves in respect to their duty in the prem
ises.

Using Factions.—The leaders of the Democracy are proverbially shrewd in availing themselves of factions that may exist among their opponents, and in various ways leading the former to play
into their hands. The more simple-minded these
factionists are, the more susceptible are they of being
utilized. For illustration : the Prohibitionists ran
a presidential candidate in 1884 ; the leaders of
the movement—though posing as Christian temperance men—knew that nearly all their voters
would come from the Republican party, the only
political organization that ever passed a law re-
stricting the liquor traffic. In New York State
they polled more than 25,000 votes, and thus managed by a plurality of 1,047 to elect a President,
the representative of the Democracy which had in
its platform of that year a plank indorsing the
liquor interest, saying, " We oppose sumptuary laws
which vex the citizen and interfere with individual
liberty." In their platforms of 1888 and 1892 the
party also adopted the same plank.

XLVI

YOUNG MEN'S RESPONSIBILITY.

A Necessary Choice.—There can be no more interesting class of voters in our Nation, than the young men, who are from year to year coming of age, and assuming the responsibilities and privileges of citizenship. It is highly important that they should stand right in politics as well as in morals; and that their influence as voters should be thrown on the side of the Nation's *material prosperity* and its *pure morality*. As there will always be different opinions and parties as to the policy of the Nation, every young man should consider it is his duty as a citizen to identify himself with the one which he deems the most progressive, from a Statesman's point of view, and which exerts the best influence; never failing to remember that it is his moral and patriotic duty to inform himself, at least, so far as to be able to vote intelligently.

Every young man of ordinary education and reading must judge for himself, concerning each political organization, whether it holds views of policy which are likely to promote the Nation's best interests—both industrial and moral—and if he is of correct moral principles he will vote in accordance with his convictions. In addition, the various questions that come up in respect to the affairs of the country at large, or of the State, the young man should as a matter of conscientious duty study carefully in order to vote intelligently. This much, at least, his own self-respect requires, that he never at any time be a mere partisan—voting "the ticket, right or wrong."

Correct Principles Important.—When our intelligent young men are governed by high-toned and morally correct principles, shameless partisanship will receive a check, and the office of the demagogue become a sinecure. The latter succeeds only when he leads ignorant men, and this class ought not to be numerous in these days of common schools and means of information on all subjects pertaining to the progress of the Nation. Let the young man study the probable effects of proposed measures in the light of the past; he may be able to trace to their source the influences that have made the Nation hitherto prosperous, and almost with certainty divine what would be the effects of honesty and industry upon its future progress.

We would say to every young man on entering upon his duties as a citizen : "Never vote for others to carry out measures for which you would not give your individual support as a legislator. Never be led to do for the sake of partisanship, what you would not do for the good of the whole community. Remember as a principle of correct action, the responsibility of the intelligent voter should equal that of those elected to office. Questions of morals are often mingled in the issues of the day. Especially beware of any political association, whose influence is such that the immoral classes and those who cater to their vices find within its folds a welcome."

It is well for young men to start right as citizens, and not to identify themselves with measures and parties that in their more mature judgment they would be likely to repudiate as mistakes or moral wrongs. They can ask themselves which political organization—as there will always be parties—has the brightest record; which has done the most to promote the material interests of the Nation; which has labored the most to raise the plane of the general intelligence of the people; which one does *not* count on the votes of the vicious classes? Questions such as these, every young man should ask himself, when studying the points at issue, if he wishes to vote intelligently for what he deems the best interests of the country.

Voting Qualifications.—It is time the American people took higher ground in respect to the qualification of those who elect their executive officers and their legislators. Let them demand that, henceforth, no native-born young man on becoming of age, be permitted to vote *unless he can read and write;* and also let them require the same qualification of foreigners, who have ample time during the five years before they become naturalized, *to learn to read and write,* and if the latter neglect this duty, let them be disfranchised as well as the native-born.

The result would be that in less than a quarter of a
century, there would scarcely be an illiterate voter
in the entire Nation. In these days of common
schools, both these classes should be disfranchised
if they failed to comply with this reasonable qualification. And if young men or foreigners from
mental incapacity cannot learn thus much, let them
be refused the privilege on the score of imbecility—
for from the nature of the case they could not vote
intelligently. It is not difficult to foresee the effects
of such an education combined with moral and
correct principles, upon the future progress of the
country. This question looms up in importance,
when the number of illiterates who vote in the
Union is taken into the account, and that they are
so liable to be led astray by demagogues.

The Bright Illiterate.—It has been sometimes
said, that there are men, not knowing how to read
and write, who are more intelligent than others who
do, and are, therefore, more competent to vote intelligently. This is a fallacy, if designed as an
argument against the small amount of education
required, for where there is one such case there are
a hundred, perhaps, who do not rest satisfied with
the acquisition, of being able to read and write merely,
but pursue the advantage still further. Suppose
this statement may be occasionally true, still how
much better qualified would be *this bright illiterate*,
who has attained his knowledge perhaps from one
individual alone—for he must get it somewhere—
if he had been able to read, and having thus the

whole field of knowledge thrown open to him, he
could have studied both sides of the questions discussed, and consequently been more able to judge
for himself. The line must be drawn somewhere,
and certainly the most fair and simple, is *that of
being able to read and write*, which opens the way
to all the others. Make this a qualification, and you
enhance the dignity of the voter, a condition that
citizenship, must be obtained only through the *exertion* of the individual himself, rather than to depend on time to make the one twenty-one years of
age, or keep the other alive for five years, that he
may get his naturalization papers.

Helps to a Decision.—The wish is often expressed by numbers of the elderly gentlemen, who
have been prominent in the ranks of the Democracy,
that the young men entering upon their duties as
citizens should be enlisted in the cause of the party.
No one of these gentlemen has our respect more than
the venerable and kindly disposed Ex-Governor
Horatio Seymour, who has again and again advised
this course. Do these Nestors of the party expect
intelligent young men to enter upon a series of dead
issues? The leaders of the Democracy have been
holding a negative position for the last twenty years
or more—that is they have been in the habit of opposing measures, which because of their excellence
have since become the policy of the land, and have
the sanction of the great majority of the intelligent
classes among the people. We would aid our young
men to make the decision for themselves in view of

the following well known facts. The tariff, for illustration, has been adjusted to afford sufficient revenue and in the main, to promote our mechanical industries, meanwhile to give employment to those who depend upon their daily labor for their living; our National banking system, after a trial of thirty years, has been so satisfactory that it is to be continued with the sanction of our bankers, merchants and all those who are especially engaged in financial affairs, this class, also, includes Democrats—no matter what their theories may be as to abstract notions about Centralization, State Sovereignty, Strict Construction and all that—who, in all practical and financial matters are Republicans, and also in favor of specie payments, as a basis for moneyed transactions; the Civil Service reform has been so arranged that there appears to be no reason why its general principles cannot and will not be honestly carried out, according to the law. This question has been so long before the people, who have taken an unusual interest in the subject, that even if technical politicians of any party should attempt its evasion, they would be unable to succeed. Those who have studied the politics of the United States, are aware of the curse brought upon the land in the application of the "Jacksonian" policy of appointing men to office, not because of their fitness but as partisans. The people may well ask themselves, why may not the national government be managed in respect to economy and the appointments of *efficient subordinates,* on the same principles that

govern great corporations, such as the central railroads of New York or Pennsylvania? These corporations retain men as long as they properly perform
their duties, and they value at their true worth the
experience and aptitude acquired by their employees,
from the superintendents down to the brakemen.
With this arrangement the stockholders in the roads
are satisfied; and the people, the stockholders in the
National government, would be equally satisfied with
a similar efficiency in the " Civil Service " of the
country.

XLVII.

DEMOCRATIC SELF-DISTRUST.

Uncertainty of Principle and Action.—In writing the history of a political organization—so different from ordinary history—it is legitimate to notice what it does, and also what it attempts; because the latter is not without influence, especially if the attempts are in the direction of changing the laws in respect to financial or industrial matters. Though such efforts may not be successful, they have the effect of unsettling values, and throw a shadow of uncertainty over the business of the country, and this is more likely to be the result when the people are so well satisfied with the existing laws and regulations, that they do not even wish, much less petition Congress to make changes, but prefer to let well alone.

It is singular that for the last few years, when the Democracy gained an election, in consequence of which they could control National legislation, the whole mercantile and industrial community became anxious lest they would pass laws whose effect would injure the business interests of the country. The well known theories of many of their prominent leaders on the general subject of financial mat-

ters being at variance with the received principles
of experienced commercial men, manufacturers and
financiers, a mysterious influence pervades the public mind, and capitalists curtail their operations, or
hesitate to invest in enterprises that might be thus
affected. This uncertainty thus brought about,
meanwhile, injures no persons really so much as
those who work for wages, because they are less able
to bear the wrong.

Anxiety of the Leaders.—This distrust is not
the outgrowth of partisanship, for it often pervades
the minds of thousands and thousands of intelligent
gentlemen, who are theoretically professed Democrats, but on financial and industrial matters, are in
accordance with those of the Republican organizations. The more sagacious leaders of the Democracy are also worried, but for a different reason;
they are apprehensive lest by some maladroit legislation, their majority in Congress will become an
obstacle to the immediate *political success* of the
organization. One cause of this universal distrust
among the intelligent of both parties, is that the
Democratic leaders in Congress are so often hampered by pledges given to all sorts of theorists on
such subjects as the Tariff, Free Trade, or the National Banking system. Though the latter has been
found remarkably efficient for the last twenty or
more years in promoting mercantile exchanges
throughout the land, and at scarcely any expense,
yet the people have the impression that many of the
prominent leaders in the Congress (1884) are on

the alert to injure the system by indirect, if they cannot by direct, means.

Even the more considerate editors of their influential papers are ill at ease, when their party has control only of the Lower House of Congress, lest they "commit some blunder"—as they put it—that would jeopardize, *not the interests of the country,* but the success of the *party itself* in future elections. We would not by any means make a charge of such lack of patriotism, but really the leaders to whom we refer must have overlooked that phase of the subject, for they only mention the danger of failure that would accrue to party organization in future elections, especially the impending Presidential one in 1884. It is still more strange that this sentiment seems to be all-pervading, for even in the counsels given by the venerable *emeritus* leaders, who are not in active political life, all other considerations are deemed of secondary, if not tertiary importance, compared with that of the future political success of the organization.

The Warning Voices.—These venerable Nestors seem of late to have been more than usually imbued with the spirit of caution, which they have urged should be the ruling genius in the councils of the Forty-Eighth Congress, (1883–1885). They had evidently in mind its first session. The leaders in that body were implored again and again not to do anything rash in relation to the finances or the tariff; that is such as would awaken *suspicion* in the minds of the people. Said the venerable Democratic ex-

Senator Eaton of Connecticut; "A tariff for revenue only, lost us the Presidential election in 1880. A like platform, or even a doubt as to the disturbance of the tariff policy of the country would defeat us again. We cannot afford to adopt a policy that is offensive to Indiana, Ohio, Pennsylvania, New York, New Jersey and my own State, Connecticut." Does the admonition thus given impliedly indicate that the impending Presidential canvass should be entered upon under false colors? But, says an Editor of a leading journal of the organization: "The Democratic party has made a tariff record which it cannot escape. The question is, Shall the party run away, pursued by the Republicans, or shall it stand its ground, unfurl its flag, and fight for its convictions?" When the Forty-Eighth Congress elected for Speaker an out and out Free-Trader, said another influential paper of the same party. "The Democratic majority of the House of Representatives, have definitely planted themselves upon the doctrine of Free-Trade, and have declared their hostility to *every form*, degree and kind of tariff protection toward American industry." This choice of a speaker is looked upon by this same paper as "*a blunder*," as such position taken by the House might interfere with the party's success in the next Presidential election!

Another influential Democratic paper finds consolation in the fact that though the election of a Free-Trade Speaker is a misfortune, yet it hopes "Congress will act prudently." For what purpose?

For the good of the country? No;—but in order to secure success in 1884. Still another is quite worried, and thinks that the election of such a Speaker " can do no harm because the President and the Senate are Republicans! " This language sounds strange. Must the *united wisdom* of the great Democratic organization be thus hampered in doing what that wisdom would dictate, by a Republican President and Senate? But in this case the latter is looked upon as a *friendly obstruction* that saves the Democracy from its own leaders.

Though the majority in Congress at the request of the caucus rejected the advice of the ex-Senator, it so far compromised as to introduce the new Speaker to the country, not as an advocate of Free-Trade, which would be decidedly radical, but as a " Tariff Reformer," and consistent with this role, he announced his position, saying he was not in favor of " sudden and radical changes in the laws and regulations affecting the commercial interests of the people."

Is it not clear that the Democratic party is distrusted for the most part by its own wisest men?

XLVIII.

A COMPARISON.

Democratic Theories.—The question may be raised why the leaders of the Democracy do not have some available policy that would enlist the sympathies of the intelligent portion of the American people. It would seem that the only policy they can adopt, if any, is that of Opposition, as long as the people are so contented with their own present policy as represented by the Republican Legislation, which covers the whole theory of managing the finances, of deriving revenue, of promoting mechanical industries, and thereby giving employment to our workpeople, skilled or unskilled; and while they are equally interested in other subjects, such as fair and honest elections, and the promotion of education and temperance. In their present state of self-complacency on these points, it would seem difficult to change the sentiments of the American people to favor opposite theories, which by no means are original, but as far as they have been put in practice hitherto have ever proved failures; and the people are consistent with their convictions, when they are unwilling to re-adopt such theories and to run the risk of ruining their present industrial and financial condition.

The American people have prospered beyond compare; and yet they have never, except as experiments for a time, adopted the distinctive Democratic theories in relation to their financial measures or their industries. The ardent Democrat, as he reads the history concerning the application of so many of his party's distinctive theories, must be inclined with a feeling of disappointment to apologize for their failure to make a permanent impression upon the material progress of the land, or to exert influences that would tend to elevate the people intellectually and morally. To-day the danger seems to be that the organization will come under the control of leaders who are theoretical rather than practical in respect to the principles of political economy.

Republican Practice.—On the other hand the Republican organization has no apologies to make to *this generation*, as it has originated and carried forward measures of vast importance to the welfare of the people. It was forced by the Southern wing of the Democracy, when the latter fired on Fort Sumter, to take up arms to defend the integrity of the Union; it was forced by military necessity to free the slaves, and ever since it has labored to elevate them by establishing schools for their benefit. Having, in order to protect him in his rights, made the freedman a citizen, they have thus given him a chance to prepare himself to exercise intelligently the privilege of voting, which was given as a matter of expediency to enable him to protect himself, as it was in the form of hostile legislation that oppression for the time bore hard upon him. (*American People*, pp. 1037–1039.)

Neither need it fear the *censure of posterity*, as the measures it has introduced must, from their nature, redound to the great benefit of future generations : such as the dotting over of the vast territories of former unavailable lands with homesteads and farms, and threading the same regions with railroads,—measures that even now in their effects are adding immensely to the prosperity and happiness of the people at large. And this is only an earnest of what will be the result in the future. Of the same beneficent character is the establishment of public schools, for the first time, throughout the former slave-holding States, and the provision for educating both races, white and colored, and paving the way for their success in time to come in material prosperity, be it in cultivating the soil or in manufacturing industry. The most important of all, is this influence of education combined with pure morality, thus brought to bear upon the mass of the people, without regard to race or condition, either in the present or in former times.

In the same class of benefits are the measures of finance established in the organization of National Banks, whose notes are at par throughout the Union, because they are secured by United States bonds, and are equal to gold in value. Thus by means of these banks the merchant can do business anywhere in the Union, virtually without the expense of discounts, or one can travel all over the land without being subjected to inconveniences for want of funds that are current. In marked contrast is this with the Democratic system of State Banks, whose notes even if they were sound, were not at par, outside their own State. In consequence the business of the country at that time (1836–1863) was enormously taxed in the form of discounts or exchange, when money was paid at distant points. Yet in the face of this, which is undeniable history, some of the Democratic leaders even now favor a return to the State system.

In point of fact, the Democratic theories have always been specious and outwardly attractive, especially to the unthinking; but in *practical statesmanship* their record is but a barren one.

XLIX.

DEMOCRATIC SUCCESS.

In the Presidential election of 1884 Grover Cleveland, of New York State, the candidate of the Democratic party, was elected, he having carried that State by a plurality of 1,047 votes over James G. Blaine, of Maine, the candidate of the Republican party, thus securing New York's thirty-six electoral votes. In that State there were cast in this election about 52,000 votes for Presidential candidates of other parties than the main two,—Prohibitionists, Labor party, etc.

A noticeable feature in the political situation at that time was the relative position of the two great parties on the tariff question. Under the existing tariff the accumulations of money in the U. S. Treasury were so great as to leave a surplus of more than a hundred millions of dollars annually. Thoughtful men of all parties recognized the danger of this as a temptation to extravagance, and even to fraudulent claims and iniquitous schemes of plunder. Both parties, therefore, denounced extravagant expenditure in their platforms and promised to revise the tariff, regulating its inequalities and reducing the surplus.

The Political Slogan.—Early in the canvass a New York City Democratic newspaper raised the cry, "Turn the rascals out!" meaning the Republicans. The persistent reiteration of this political slogan throughout the country by the press of the party may have influenced multitudes of well-meaning but unintelligent voters. The utter untruthfulness of this implication in respect to the financial dishonesty of the party in power was thoroughly proved by means of the action of the incoming Democratic administration itself. That action was proper; it was nothing more nor less than a comprehensive and thorough investigation, or auditing the account books of the Republican party for six administrations—twenty-four years. During this period had been collected moneys in various ways and from numerous sources—such as dues from the Custom Houses and the internal revenue, a war tax, levied at first upon numberless domestic articles, but of late years only upon tobacco and alcohol—and also the disbursement of these vast sums, the vouchers for which were in the archives of the various departments. These moneys exceeded by far the entire amount of funds collected and disbursed during the eighteen previous administrations, or the seventy-two years of the existence of the Nation. At the end of this elaborate investigation or auditing of the accounts there was found a deficiency of a few cents. Such was the verification of the integrity with which the financial affairs

of the national government had been administered
by the Republican party from March 4, 1861, to
March 4, 1885—an instance of faithfulness unequalled in our history. (See pp. 305-309).

The Financial Laws Remain.—The present
Democratic administration (1888) has been in existence three years and six months, to September
1st. The general laws under which it has governed were enacted by Congress in previous administrations. The law in relation to the management of the finances has not been changed, and
in consequence the latter have been conducted on
the usual basis. Sometimes the rulings of the
Secretaries of the Treasury have been different in
some respects from those of their predecessors,
but in the main they have not contravened the
spirit of the existent laws.

Tariff Revision Attempted.—The House of
Representatives of the 49th Congress, elected on
the same day with Mr. Cleveland, had a Democratic majority of 43. Its labors during eight
months comprised the enactment of the usual
laws, appropriations, etc., requisite to carry on
the Government, and the Presidential Succession
Act, and also for increasing the navy. It labored,
however, during the greater portion of its first
session to revise the existing tariff ; but the difference of opinion among the members of the
party itself was very great in respect to the leading principles to be applied in such revision.
Those known as favoring " free trade," or " a

tariff for revenue only," seemed to prevail—that
is, making the obtaining of revenue the *primary*
object of the tariff, thus subordinating to that
idea the feature of protecting and enlarging
American manufactures, which, as its friends
claim, results in keeping up the wages of the
American workpeople to a standard that will
promote their mental and moral elevation and
physical comfort. The latter characteristic of
the existing tariff had already been recognized
by that close observer of our Congressional
doings, the London *Times*, which, when speaking
of the measures introduced by Congress since
1861, says in its issue July 12, 1880, page 11 :
" *The object of their statesmen is not to secure the
largest amount of wealth* [*revenue.*] *but to keep up
by whatever means the standard of comfort among
the laboring classes.*"

The prominent feature of the tariff measure
discussed during the first session of the 49th Congress, known as the Morrison bill, was the " horizontal " idea (see pages 92–94), except that it did
not propose to reduce all duties to a uniform level,
but to reduce them all by a uniform rate, taking
off 20 per cent of every existing impost. It did
not pass the House, in consequence of the differ-
erence of opinion among the members of the
Democratic majority, and the almost solid opposition of the Republican minority. No special progress in the direction of revising the tariff or reducing the surplus was made during the second
session of the 49th Congress.

Congressional Votes Cast in Different Sections.—The platforms of both the leading parties (1884) agreed in the demand for honest elections—the Democrats saying : " We believe in a free ballot and a fair count;" the Republicans: "The perpetuity of our institutions rests upon the maintenance of a free ballot, an honest count, and correct returns." Throughout the Union, according to law, the number of inhabitants represented by each Congressman is the same. In 1884 it was, in round numbers, 151,000; but in the election of that year there was a discrepancy well worth noticing in this connection. The average number of votes cast for each member of Congress in the different sections was as follows: In the *twenty-two* original free-labor States it was 34,595; in the *five border* States it was 29,360; and in the *eleven* recent Confederate States it was 22,938.

Tariff Revision Again.—In the election (1886) for members of the Fiftieth Congress, the Democratic majority in the Lower House was reduced to *nineteen*, including all not belonging to the Republican party. In December, 1887, President Cleveland sent a message to the Congress, exclusively devoted to urging that body to make a prompt and wise revision of the tariff, in view of the rapidly-increasing surplus and the impossibility of properly using the money thus gathered upon imports. The response to this was a bill introduced by Mr. Roger Q. Mills, of Texas, and the first session of the Fiftieth Congress has been mainly devoted to discussing this measure. In the Mills bill, however, the *horizontal* feature has been dropped, though the friends of the present protective tariff think that the effect of the bill will be, in another form, virtually to remove the protective quality of the existing law, by diminishing, without what they consider to be proper discrimination, the rates of import duties, thus curtailing the revenue; and in addition, by the free admission of certain classes of raw material, which we can produce in great part ourselves— such as wool. The Republican members of Congress claim that, while the tariff should be revised, it should be done by its friends, and in the interest of our own manufacturing industries, placing a high rate upon foreign importations; while they would diminish the surplus revenue by taking off the internal tax on tobacco and on alcohol used in the arts.

Action Under Previous Laws.—In the Democratic platform adopted at St. Louis (1888) much merit is claimed for the Cleveland administration because of its reclaiming lands that were forfeited by certain railway companies, in consequence of the failure of the latter to fulfil their contracts for the completion of these roads. These forfeitures were made in accordance with the laws on the subject which were enacted by Congress previous to March 4, 1885. Neither the Forty-ninth nor the Fiftieth Congress passed any law on the subject, and the Cleveland administration is entitled to the credit of doing what was clearly its duty, in carrying out the provisions of a law already being enforced.

Civil Service Reform.—This reform was commended in the platforms (1884) of both the leading parties. While originally introduced into Congress by a Democratic Senator (p. 310), the Republicans had taken the initiative in this reform during General Grant's administration, when a commission was appointed to consider and report on the subject ; and under President Hayes the orders and rules were issued (1877). The general principles of the latter were embodied finally in a law enacted by Congress and signed by President Arthur in 1883 (see pp. 310–313). The reader is referred to the record of Mr. Cleveland's administration for the evidence of the manner in which have been carried out the announced principles, genuine spirit and purpose of the civil service laws, and of the rules laid down by the commissioners, in connection, finally, with the orders of the President himself in regard to their enforcement, extension to new departments, etc. As a basis for removal from office was utilized the charge of "offensive partisanship." The sole interpreters of this indefinite phrase were the President and his subordinates. Within two years and a half from March 4, 1885, of the 56,134 persons who at that date held United States offices, 42,992 were removed and their places filled by others.

L.

FROM MARCH 4, 1889, TO APRIL, 1896.

In the Presidential election in 1888 Benjamin Harrison, of Indiana, was the Republican candidate, and Grover Cleveland, of New York, was renominated by the Democrats. Harrison was elected, and took office on March, 1889.

The American people were unusually interested in the celebration of the centennial anniversary of the first inauguration of George Washington as President of the United States. This being at the close of the first hundred years of the nation's life, added zest to the ceremonies, and elicited in the minds of the people, universally, a strong national sentiment of union and of patriotism. The occasion was properly observed throughout the nation, but special interest was centred in New York, because in that city the original inauguration took place. President Harrison and his Cabinet, and great numbers of prominent citizens, attended and participated in the services, which lasted for three days (" *Four Hundred Years,*" etc., pp. 1134–1138).

The Legacies.—The Cleveland administration left as legacies to its successor several negotiations, which it had had for some time under discussion, but was unable to finish. One, the "Samoan affair," was in a very unsatisfactory condition; the parties specially interested were Germany, England, and the United States. Negotiations were promptly commenced, and under the skilful management of Mr. James G. Blaine, the Secretary of State, the administration secured satisfactory adjustment of the then existing difficulties.

The framing of a more effective extradition treaty with Canada was in progress, but also left unfinished. This, too, was concluded, its main features being the addition of a large number of offences for committing which persons could be mutually extradited. This law has in effect materially diminished the size of the American colony within the bounds of our northern neighbor. The Behring Sea controversy was also among the legacies. The entire subject in dispute between Great Britain and the United States, was transferred for settlement to a court of arbitration. That court in due time gave its decision, in which both parties acquiesced.

The McKinley Bill. — The most important measure of the Harrison administration was the enactment, in 1890, of what is known as the McKinley Tariff or Bill; thus named from the chairman of the Committee of Ways and Means, which reported this bill to the House of Representatives. Under the recent and present circumstances a brief sketch of this financial measure is proper, in order that the intelligent among the American people should have a succinct and clear view of the salient points of this tariff legislation, which has become a landmark in our financial history.

Let it be specially borne in mind, that the LIst Congress, which enacted this bill, contained an unusual number of members who had made the revenue affairs of the nation a subject of special study. These statesmen had been for years, and during trying periods, careful observers of the practical workings of the financial policy of the Government, and in moulding which policy many of them had personally taken a part. This tariff was the legitimate outgrowth of the original bill of 1861-62, and of a series of amendments, which were respectively introduced, in order to adapt the measure to the changing conditions in the course of *twenty-eight* eventful years. The majority of this Congress used common-sense, observation, and experience in framing this tariff, which passed the House May 21, and the Senate September 10, 1890, and was promptly signed by President Harrison, who from the beginning had kept himself intelligently in touch with the principles contained in the bill. It went into effect on the 6th of October the same year.

The Cost of Production.—This bill, more than any previous one, was framed on the basis of the cost of production of the competing articles of foreign manufacture. Since the item of wages comes in as the principal factor of *such cost*, it was essential to obtain authentic data, on that point, in order to institute a fair comparison of the wages paid abroad with those paid in the United States.

To secure this important data, upon which the schedules of our tariffs ought to be based, President Hayes's administration (March 4, 1877–81) instructed the United States consuls in Europe to take note, among other matters, of the wages paid operatives at the respective ports where they were stationed. The information thus secured was deemed most valuable, and in consequence the custom still prevails. Statistics of wages are easily obtained and appear to be unusually reliable. These reports made known the startling fact that the average amount of wages paid in the United States for similar service was more than double that paid in Great Britain ; about two-thirds more than in France, Belgium, and Denmark, while we paid three times as much as was paid in Italy, Spain, and Germany, and four times as much as in the Netherlands.

These remarkable facts, revealed from time to time by the reports of the consuls, stimulated investigation in another direction, and Congress, in 1882, authorized President Arthur to appoint a commission of nine members, gentlemen selected from civil life, and "who were recognized as men of great intelligence on these general subjects." The commission was to investigate the numerous questions pertaining " to the establishment of a judicious tariff, or the revision of the existing tariff, upon a scale of justice to all interests."

This commission, by means of sub-committees, spent a number of months in visiting manufacturing and commercial districts throughout the Union, and in taking testimony relevant to the subjects in hand. The commission made its report to the XLVIIth Congress, at its second session, December 4, 1882. This elaborate production covered the entire field of tariff revision. To the report was also appended a bill, which embodied the views of the commission. This bill, after some minor modifications, Congress passed, March 3, 1883. This tariff was the outgrowth of years of study and experiment ; it also utilized to the fullest extent the information received at that time from the two sources mentioned above, in respect to the *amount of wages* paid abroad and in the United States. In consequence, it was *more perfect* than any of its predecessors in its adaptation to the requirements of the numerous industries of the entire Nation.

The Salient Points of a Tariff.—It is expedient to put on record a concise account of the *salient points* of the McKinley Bill, since it will be often referred to as of financial and political importance. The tariff of 1890 was the legitimate outgrowth of the acquired experience of nearly thirty years (1861–1890), during which period, by means of judicious amendments suggested by the exigencies of the times, the original measure was adjusted again and again to the necessities of the National Treasury, and likewise so as to encourage the industries of the people. No tariff, taken as a whole, can be *absolutely perfect* in all respects, owing to the changes that are continually going on in the industrial and financial world. If judged by the good effects which it produced in its brief existence, the tariff of 1890 was the most judicious and symmetrical of any one ever passed by the Committee of Ways and Means and passed by Congress. It combined the best elements of that of 1883, and, also, appropriate measures to accomplish what ought to be an essential object in every tariff of the United States—that is, *to secure sufficient revenue, and at the same time encourage our commercial, agricultural, and mechanical industries, and thereby give remunerative employment to those who work for wages—about three-fourths of our adult population.* It was also truly national in its provisions, as by them every industry in every section of the land was carefully and impartially encouraged.

Schemes to Deceive.—This bill went into effect October 6, 1890, and on the 8th of the following month was to be held an election for members of the LIId Congress. On this occasion was concocted and utilized by certain leaders and their allies the most successful and unwarranted scheme ever known in ordinary business, for the purpose of deceiving that innocent victim—the American public, especially in the large cities. Importers, and certain merchants in collusion with them, at once instructed their salesmen to mark up the prices of their merchandise, and to give as a reason for the enhanced price the "high rates of the McKinley Bill." Another class of merchants, we are happy to mention, did not enter into the scheme. This mark-

ing up was sometimes done even in respect to articles that were on the free list, as well as those on
which the tariff had *not* been changed at all, for
instance, on gloves—we need not go into detail.
There was not an imported article in their stores
which had not come in under the previous tariff of
1883, and therefore there was no *honorable* reason
why their usual prices should be increased.

In accordance with the programme, these leaders
throughout the original free-labor States—it was not
necessary in the " Solid South "—commenced also a
series of gross and systematic misrepresentations of
the provisions of the bill, in every form available to
excite prejudice against it, and thereby secure votes
for Congressmen who were Democratic, or virtually
free trade.   Owing to the limited time since its enactment, the real provisions of the bill could not be
made known to the general public.   These tricky
measures continued till the day of election, and as
a result of such falsehoods, scattered far and near,
the Democracy secured an unprecedented majority
in the House of Representatives.   When the election was over, the high prices ere long resumed their
normal condition.   Meanwhile the beneficial character of the tariff of 1890 soon began to manifest
itself in the impulse that it gave to the industries
of the Nation, and to business in general.

Mineral Resources.—We have room for only
two illustrations on this subject, the one showing
the stimulating influence of the tariff of 1890 upon
one phase of our industries, the other the depressing

effect upon the same of a *mere threat* to repeal the
former measure, and substitute instead a tariff, so
called, "for revenue only." The facts in both instances are unimpeachable, and of necessity im-
partial in their presentation. The one : the output
in the year 1892 of the minerals of the United
States was valued at $688,616,954—the largest ever
known ; being more than 30½ million dollars greater
than that of 1891. The output of the same minerals in the year 1893 was valued at $609,821,670,
thus showing a decline of value in one year of $78,-
794,284 (*Mineral Resources of the U. S. for the
Calendar Years* 1892-93, pp. 1, 12).

The other : the depressing effect upon the above
phase of the industries of the American people
does not compare in its pecuniary magnitude with
the losses sustained from the same cause in the
other industries of the land, both of capital and
what would have been the earnings of the workpeople thus thrown out of employment. Their
sufferings cannot be reckoned in dollar and cent
values ; their deposits in savings banks were in
time used up, and they and their families often reduced to want and the mortification of receiving
charity. And for what? Why, forsooth! to put in
practice the theories of unpractical men.

Free Sugar.—One provision of the tariff of
1890 was of great importance to the people at large
—that of admitting sugar free of duty. This benefi-
cient measure reached every household in the land.
The revenue derived from the duty previously im-

posed upon sugar amounted annually to about $50,000,000. This duty or tax the consumers paid, because the sugar producer *fixed his own price*, to which was added the duty. The American people were unable to raise sufficient sugar to supply their own wants ; if they could have done so, they could also have fixed their own price in accordance with the *cost of production*, and to that price the foreign competitor would have to conform when entering the American market. The foreigner could not increase that price, though he might lower it.

In connection with this provision of the bill was that of giving a bounty of *two cents* a pound to the producers of domestic sugar, in lieu of the protection afforded them by the then existing duty upon the foreign article. The policy of paying this bounty, if carried out, would be far-reaching in beneficial results. It is very reasonable to suppose that in time, by these means, we would learn how to supply our own sugar from our own soil, as France and Germany have done within recent years. We have four sources of supply, while the latter two countries have only *one*—the sugar-beet. *First* we have the sugar-cane, which flourishes all around the region bordering on the Gulf of Mexico. This is a vast territory of fertile lands waiting to be brought more extensively under cultivation of the sugar-cane. The *second* source is the sugar-beet, which grows finely on the Atlantic slope and in the valley of the Mississippi, and luxuriantly in California. " Recent experiments, facts, and figures demonstrate the

peculiar advantages of the so-called arid region
[when irrigated] for the growth and maturity of
a beet rich in saccharine matter " (" *Beet Culture in
Colorado* "). The *third* source is the sorghum, which
affords a fair quantity of saccharine matter, and can
be successfully cultivated in the middle portion of
the Union. To these may be added the sugar-maple.
France and Germany have within a half century
been so cultivating the beet and extracting its sugar
that they are able to supply their own wants and
even have a surplus to export.

Democratic leaders have always been deficient in
comprehensive views that pertain to the promotion
of our national industries. And it was with zest
their majority in the Lower House in the first Session
of the LIIId Congress voted to repeal the law giving a bounty on sugar produced from our own soil.
It is estimated that at that very time fifty million
dollars were invested by sugar-planters in the enterprise, and in which were employed many thousands
of workpeople (*see* pp. 161, 266, 267, *for similar instances of votes to repeal*).

That the benefits derived from this free sugar
were appreciated by the wage-earners and the great
mass of the American people is proved by the tremendous increase of its importation under the conditions of Reciprocity. The well-to-do and the rich
never stinted themselves in the use of this essential
article of food when it came in under the tariff of
about $2\frac{3}{8}$ cents a pound, but those of *limited
means did*, and as soon as it came in free of duty

the increase in its consumption became enormous
(*N. Y. Tribune*, August 24, 1894, p. 1, 6th column).
For instance : the quantity of sugar imported in
1892, according to the report of the custom-houses,
if entered at the old rate of duty, would have
amounted in revenue to about $75,000,000. From
this sum substract, say, $12,000,000 paid in boun-
ties and you have $63,000,000 clear gain accruing
to the people themselves as individuals.

But here come those eminent and self-proclaimed
friends of "the poor man," who exclaim that the
money is taken from the treasury of the United
States. The answer to that assertion is, that the
money expended in these bounties is paid back to
the Nation many times over in consequence of the
treaties of reciprocity with several nations, by
which the outlet to American products of various
kinds was greatly enhanced and its foreign trade
increased. Let one instance of many that could be
given suffice. Previous to a reciprocity treaty concluded with Spain the duty on American flour in
the market of Cuba was $4.62 a barrel ; the treaty
reduced it to 90 cents ; in consequence, until its repeal by the present Democratic administration, the
American farmer supplied nearly all the flour used in
Cuba. Altogether the increase of our exports to that
island alone was *seventy per cent.* There were a number of such treaties concluded with several countries
from which we had imported their products, such
as rubber, gutta-percha, and sugar, free of duty, but
in accordance with these treaties these countries re-

moved or greatly reduced their tariff on American products of various kinds, such as provisions and certain manufactures. These reciprocity treaties, about twenty in number, were the direct outgrowth of a provision of the McKinley Bill.

The Prohibition.—The McKinley Bill—which no other had ever done—took high ground against impure literature. It forbid the importation of any obscene book, pamphlet, picture, or any article whatever that is suggestive of an immoral action or nature. It imposed a penalty for the crime—"All such articles shall be proceeded against, seized and forfeited by due course of law."

A Judicious Enactment.—It was persistently charged by Democratic leaders and Free-traders that American manufacturers were at a disadvantage when they exported their products in which material that had paid duty had been used. To obviate that difficulty and charge, a provision was made in the bill for refunding *ninety-nine per cent.* of the duty paid on a foreign material which had been used in the manufacture of an article, when the latter was put upon a foreign market.

Shoddy.—In order to prevent adulteration in the manufacture of woollen cloths, the tariff of 1890 imposed a duty of *thirty cents* per pound on *shoddy or woollen waste*—the old rate was *ten*—which could be used for adulteration in the making of such cloths. The Wilson, or rather Gorman, tariff (1894) reduced this duty one-half; that is, to *fifteen cents* per pound. What was the patriotic

motive for this change? Was it to induce the
American manufacturer, under the specious plea of
cheapness, to adulterate woollen cloths for the benefit of wage-earners or those of limited means?

Industries Transferred—Tin-plate.— Under
the provisions of the tariff of 1890, and the reasonable prospect that it would remain in force for
years, a number of foreigners transferred their factories to the United States. This movement gave
additional employment to great numbers of American work-people, but it came to an end in 1893.
For similar reasons several new industries were introduced into the country; among these was that
of making tin-plate. According to the official report on the progress of this new industry, on June
30, 1893, there were in the Union *thirty-five* mills
engaged in the manufacture of tin-plate, and which
were employing several thousand workmen. Yet is
it to be credited that the Democratic majority in
the House of Representatives of the LIId Congress
passed, about that very time, a bill to repeal the
tariff on tin-plate, and thus break up that industry!
(*See also* p. 266 for a similar action.)

According to *The Metal Worker* there were (1895)
in operation 28 tin-plate mills that rolled their
own black plates. "There [were] in the aggregate
155 mills completed or building, of which 110 were
in active work. These mills employ some 15,000
hands." The block-tin used in this manufacture
comes in free of duty.

Workingmen Misled.—It seems almost incredi-

ble that persistent misrepresentations of the leading provisions of the bill, and the slanderous im-
pugning the motives of those who framed it, should
have misled even those workmen who were specially
benefited by it, they being employed in factories
on articles that were thus protected against foreign
competition. For example, in a manufacturing
town in Connecticut, it is said, about 800 workmen
thus employed voted for the Democracy in 1892,
and when expostulated with, and warned that if the
latter were successful their wages would be cut
down in order to meet the competition abroad,
they sneered at the suggestion, saying "they
would keep up their wages by means of their trade-
unions, and, moreover, they wished a *change* anyway."
They did not then take into consideration the pos-
sibility of shut-downs, which came, when, owing to
the general depression of business, orders fell off
entirely. Meanwhile the Democratic leaders and
their free-trade allies were promising *very high
prices* for the products of the farmers, and *very
cheap* foreign goods for those who worked for
wages. The votes of these 800 workmen in Novem-
ber of 1894 gave clear evidence that they wished
another change.

Appropriations. — The LIst Congress was
charged by the leaders of the Democracy with being
extravagant in the amounts of its appropriations.
The Republicans when in control of the House of
Representatives, wherein appropriations legally originate, have made them in good faith and never for

the sake of political effect, hence they designate the amounts that were called for by the careful estimates for the financial year. On the contrary, when the Democrats were in control of the Lower House, they have uniformly (*see* pp. 282–284), especially if a presidential canvass was impending, made appropriations that were notoriously inadequate in their amounts. Then they go to the country on this fictitious economy, urging the unenlightened rank and file to witness how saving they have been of the money of the dear people.

The LIst Congress was thus hampered, as it had to make up an unusually large deficiency left over from the previous one (Democratic), in addition to the regular appropriations. From the surplus in hand it took sufficient to pay honest debts which had been neglected for years. It thus refunded to the loyal States $13,000,000, that being the amount of a direct tax paid by them to aid the Government during the war to save the Union. It also paid the "French spoliation claims," which had been due for a number of years—$1,304,095. The Harrison administration paid off $365,493,170 of the national debt, and thus saved to the people an annual interest of more than $11,000,000. This was done as a matter of business, as it was found cheaper for the Government to buy certain bonds that were not yet due and pay the premium on them than to let them remain unpaid and draw interest.

On March 4, 1893, there was sufficient money remaining in the Treasury to meet the current expenses of the Government for a length of time, but the threats made of radically changing the entire financial system of the country which had been so successful for thirty years, caused universal distrust. This feeling so depressed every form of industry and general business that in consequence the ordinary revenues fell off, and the money in the Treasury being nearly exhausted, the Government was compelled to resort to loans in order to defray its current expenses—an extraordinary transition from an overflowing Treasury to a deficiency.

Contrasts.—Under the tariff of 1890, during the last two years of Mr. Harrison's administration, " all our industries were active, exports and imports were the largest ever known, . . . prices were good, foreign capital was coming into the country by hundreds of millions every year "—not *borrowed*, but for investment. In consequence of threats to destroy the existing financial and industrial system of the nation, and finally the enactment of the Wilson-Gorman tariff, every mechanical industry in the Union was depressed—wages lowered or ceased altogether, while general business was paralyzed—all this within two years succeeding the 4th of March, 1893. Again, " during Mr. Harrison's administration our total foreign trade was $1,258,657,086, more than during Mr. Cleveland's *first* term " (*American Economist*, May number, 1885, p. 276). In both Congresses of this *first* term persistent efforts were continually made to change the then existing tariff, with the natural result of disturbing and retarding the progress of the industrial and commercial interests of the nation.

The exports of the last year of Mr. Harrison's administration under the McKinley Bill were $834,323,641 ; the exports of the year 1894, under the Wilson-Gorman Bill, were $196,186,065, while in the latter the *imports* were enormous, especially of textile fabrics of every class, which our work-people ought to and could make themselves. Mr. Harrison's administration paid $365,493,170 of the public debt. On the contrary, according to the Government's own showing, Mr. Cleveland's has thus far paid *nothing*, while within two years and a few months the national debt has been greatly increased.

Votes for Congressmen.—The following facts may properly attract the attention of the American people. The number of constituents that each Congressman represents in the Lower House is the same throughout the Union. The present number, being based upon the census of 1890, is 173,901. How, then, can we account for the discrepancies in the average number of the votes cast for each Congressman in the different sections of the Union? Taking as a basis the number of votes polled in the presidential election in 1892, we find the average number of votes for each Congressman in the twenty-six Northern States to be 40,337 ; in the four border ones, 32,713, and in the eleven Confederate, 19,543.

Democratic Principles.—Certain leaders are continually eulogizing what they term "Democratic principles." The question is suggested, What are they? Within the last thirty years or more these leaders have not even enunciated a comprehensive policy or principle in the application of which the American people have been or could be benefited, or with which they were satisfied. While these leaders, as Confederates in the South and Copperheads in the North, were trying to break up the Union, the Republicans and *loyal Democrats* were battling against them, and in the end frustrated their plans. Meanwhile the latter were originating and putting in practice principles that in their application were promoting the welfare of the people at large. They introduced honest financial measures that secured the confidence of the business portion of the community, meanwhile cherishing the manufacturing and other industries and developing the natural resources of the entire land. These financial measures, based on a solid foundation, broad and deep, enabled the Government to meet as far as possible the expenses of the war then in progress, and at its close to at once commence paying off the debt thus imposed. The American people have been complimented justly when characterized by intelligent European statesmen as a debt-paying nation.

Upon examination these Democratic principles appear to be mostly of the dog-and-manger variety. For illustration, on several occasions, when having a majority in the Lower House, that majority, at the dictation of the leaders, attempted to repeal measures which have proved themselves to be of inesti-

mable value to the whole country (*see* pp. 266--
269, 358). Critics should not, however, be too
severe, for what can these leaders do? The
naughty Republicans for about thirty years have
monopolized all the principles or policies—the
financial, the industrial, and commercial—which in
their application have brought in their train the
blessings of prosperity. In consequence, these leaders, in order to keep their organization in hand
before the eyes of its *unenlightened* members, are
compelled to play the *rôle* of *obstructionists*.

Cost of Production — Raw Material.

The
Democratic majority in both Houses of the LIIId
Congress (March 4, 1893–1895) manifested extreme
hostility to the prominent features of the tariff of
1890, and which it finally superseded by enacting
what is known *as* the Wilson or Gorman Bill. The
contrasts between the McKinley Tariff Bill and that
of the Gorman-Wilson are well worth noticing. The
one was based on the relative *cost* of production,
taking as a criterion the amount of wages paid
abroad as compared with that paid in the United
States for similar work ; the other is based virtually
on the *cost* of the raw material. The former, in order
to protect our work people, put a duty corresponding to the wages paid to employées on foreign manufactured articles that came in competition with our
own. The framers of the latter intimated they
would do something of the same kind, but that they
failed to carry out such intimation is clearly proved
by the universal depression of our manufacturing

interests, which began as soon as their tariff went into effect. The McKinley Bill imposed a corresponding high rate of duty on the most elaborately textile fabrics, such as velvets, woollen cloths, laces, and such like, and on all classes of luxuries ; for instance, on costly wines, etc.—that is, on high-priced articles which those of limited means *never* purchase. It also admitted free of duty the raw material for our factories which we could not produce ourselves ; among which were unwrought silk, rubber, gutta-percha, block-tin, and other articles ; but upon the raw materials that we could produce ourselves, for obvious reasons, a duty was imposed, as on iron-ore, coal, and wool. Then again, it looked after the comforts derived from the poor man's table by bringing in free of duty tea, coffee, chocolate, sugar, and the spices of the tropics. (For sugar *see* p. 355.)

On the contrary, the Gorman-Wilson Bill appears to have been based more on the *cheapness* of the raw material than on the *cost of production.* The labor, according to statistics, put upon the manufactured articles costs from 85 to 90 per cent. of the entire expense, while the raw material—from an iron ship to a sewing-machine—in value is not more than two or three per cent. of the entire cost. For illustration, what is the value in the vein of the iron-ore from which the iron ship is made ? or what the value in the mine of the coal which smelts that iron-ore ? or of the trees as they stand in the forest from which the wood-work is made ? The value of all these is enhanced alone by the labor of preparing them for practical use. The basic value of any raw material should, therefore, be reckoned its worth when in a primitive state, while its subsequent value is the outcome of the labor put upon it.

It is evident that the McKinley tariff, based on the comparative *cost of production*, is more especially in the interest of the greater number—our wage-earners, three-fourths of our adult population—while it is equally clear that the Gorman-Wilson Bill, being based on the *cheapness* of the raw material, is more especially in the interest of the manufacturer. That the main basis upon which the latter bill was designed to be placed—namely, the *cheapness* of the raw material—we are compelled to infer, because of the strenuous efforts that were made, pre-eminently by Mr. Cleveland, to have iron-ore, coal, and wool come in free of duty. The three articles of raw material thus mentioned we can produce, but they are very liable to be injured in their value and production by foreign competition.

In respect to wool, it was made free of duty by the Gorman-Wilson Bill. What has been the effect? Only that the wool industry of the United States, estimated in value at about $100,000,000, has been depreciated at least one-half. Again, what has been gained by that measure? The answer is, that a gentleman's suit of the finest quality, if its cloth were of American manufacture, and made from foreign merino wool of the highest grade and free of duty, the suit would be one dollar and ten cents *cheaper* than if the duty imposed by the McKinley Bill had been paid on the raw wool.

Where is the line to be drawn, by those who proclaim that *protection is unconstitutional*, between a duty that is " protective " and one that is " for revenue only ? " Every duty, however small on a competing manufactured article, in the nature of the case must be to *that extent* protective. It follows from this that a duty " for revenue only " can be imposed upon those foreign-made articles alone which we cannot produce, and therefore such cannot come in competition with ours. According to this view of the subject, to be consistent, we must admit free of duty every foreign manufactured article that competes with our own.

The Surplus—The Deficiency.—From 1866 onward to the second administration of Mr. Cleveland the National Government had always a surplus year by year after paying its current expenses. Such was the case for *twenty-eight* years till 1894. During this period the yearly average surplus was $68,429,828, including the four years of Mr. Cleveland's first term. That term was an earnest of his second, inasmuch as at its beginning great anxiety pervaded business circles, lest the policy of the Democratic party would injure all the industries of the land. In consequence of this ominous uncertainty, in the first financial year of his administration the surplus fell off $40,929,854. The people became assured, however, that the Senate would stand firm in resisting the changes proposed in the Morrison tariff, as well as any future measure that might have a similar effect upon their industries. As soon as this position of that body became known, an impulse was given to business, and as an evidence of that fact the surplus of the second financial year (1886) of his administration was $30,492,817 more than that of the previous one. This surplus increased each year to the end of Mr. Cleveland's term, in consequence of the indications being so promising that the people would restore the Republicans to power, and thus the latter's financial policy, which since 1862 had so grandly promoted the interests of the nation, would be continued.

During Mr. Cleveland's second (1893–1897) term, thus far, as Democratic financial theories have had full sway, instead of a surplus there has been a continuous deficiency, amounting in all at this date (April 1, 1896) to $117,883,782. Thus our proud and recognized distinction of being a *debt-paying* nation has degenerated into one running into debt year by year.

LI

IMPEDIMENTS REMOVED.

The Outlook.—We entered upon the second century of our national existence on March 4, 1889. Let us briefly notice the influences that will promote our material interests, and also those that will aid in elevating the American people to a still higher plane of intelligence and good morals, thus making more perfect their present Christianized civilization. What a number of impediments have been swept away, that during its first century hindered the Nation's progress in its widest and best sense! In consequence, the American people will henceforth be comparatively free and untrammeled in their onward progress, and meanwhile, by utilizing the noble institutions bequeathed them by the *first* century, will attain still grander results in the *second.* These results will include a continual advancement in the material things that pertain to the physical comfort of the people at large, and in a still more important sense elevating them to higher planes of intelligence and morals.

A unique and strenuous opponent to the genuine progress of the Nation in its first century, and which will be unknown in the second, was slavery. This system had a retarding influence in more senses than one : it was financially wasteful, the parent of untold wrongs, as manifested in its domestic evils, which penetrated the inner circle of the household. It was the enemy of universal education wherever it held sway. The slaveholders, the governing class in that section of the country, never established public schools, while in the free-labor States they were in existence more than two hundred years before the civil war. The ruling class designed as far as possible to keep the " poor white trash," as they contemptuously characterized the non-slaveholders, in ignorance. This was done on the assumption that their knowledge could be communicated to the slaves, who in consequence might become dissatisfied with their condition and foment insurrections, from which were prophesied massacres with all their attendant horrors.

The second century, in marked contrast, starts with public schools established throughout the entire Union, while the system is growing more and more in favor with the good, the intelligent, and progressive citizens. The public school is a promoter of material progress among all classes in the community ; and it extends still further in its influence in uniting in sympathy the different sections of the land by teaching all the youth the English language. Under such conditions the unfortunate illiterates will in due time disappear, and the American people, in theory at least, will become a nation of intelligent voters.

The Spoils System — Civil Service. — That most pernicious policy known as the spoils system, introduced by Andrew Jackson (1829) near the middle of the Nation's *first* century (see pp. 75-77), will, it is hoped, disappear in the early portion of its *second*. Measures have been taken to banish it forever from the politics of the Nation (*Four Hundred Years of American History*, pp. 1068, 1072) (see pp. 310-313), and whenever the reform contemplated in the Civil Service secures a complete triumph, national policies will thereafter be discussed on their merits alone. Writers and speakers on national topics will then be influenced by patriotic motives, and will not expect nor ask political preferment for doing their duty, except in an honorable and straightforward way, as when the offices in the gift of the people are conferred upon those alone whose fitness for the position they recognize.

The evil of the spoils system has had a degrading influence, especially upon the less intelligent, in giving them false views, as when they unconsciously deem patriotism and partisanship as of equal importance. This deceptive notion has hitherto prevailed to an extent among the followers of local leaders, who have dishonestly oftentimes promised, directly or indirectly, the same office to different persons in order to secure the latter's political favor. This demoralizing influence will receive its death blow when, on a *basis of merit alone*, appointments will be made to subordinate offices, such as clerkships, etc. The qualifications demanded as to knowledge will be that obtainable in the common schools or academies, but which education must be supplemented by practice, energy, and honesty. How much more dignified and self-respecting to hold such an appointment as the result of an examination than to secure it through the influence of a local political leader!

The Hopeful Prospect.—The system of Civil Service will become more perfect in its administration when the classes of public employees, that are now subjected to preliminary examinations and a limited probation before entering fully upon their duties, are appointed for a number of odd years, for instance, seven, nine, eleven, etc., as may be deemed best, the object being to overlap Presidential terms, and thus avoid the unseemly turmoil of office-seekers and their friends, so often seen immediately after the inauguration of a President.

The American people have an interest in their national affairs as conducted at Washington, and for that reason, why should not the classes of officials mentioned above be drawn from the several States in proportion to the number of their respective populations as ascertained by each census? Such an arrangement would enhance the existing goodwill of the people of every section of the Union.

Let these clerical or subordinate appointments be made or recommended by a commission instituted for the purpose of ascertaining the qualifications of the applicants. This policy would in time banish the absurd notion that the general government is somehow under obligation to appoint certain persons or their friends to these minor offices. If such appointees are efficient, why should not their tenures of office be judiciously extended, and thus the entire service be conducted on the business principles that prevail in the management of the great corporations of the country?

National Banks.—A prominent hinderance to the material progress of the Nation, during nearly *three-fourths* of its first century, was the frequent changes in the management of the financial measures of the National government, as well as in those of the respective States (see pp. 26–28, 80, 81, 199). This unsettled condition continued till the adoption of the present national banking system on January 1, 1863. Since then we have had no bad money. This system of banking, so comprehensive and national in its character, has passed over into the current century. In process of time no doubt there will be modifications which will adapt the system to contingencies that may hereafter arise, yet the grand and valuable feature, of being national in its practical utility, will be continued. As it is now, the notes of these banks are current throughout the Union and are redeemable at the United States Treasury. The immense advantages derived from these banks have been so great that in the future no other than a banking system adapted to the whole Union will be tolerated by intelligent people. The contrast between the two centuries, in respect to the benefits derived from their respective financial measures, is very remarkable.

Our Territory Ample.—The territory in the possession of the American people of the *second* century will be sufficient for their occupation and abundant, under the forms of agriculture that will prevail, to supply all their demands, since improvements in the cultivation of the soil will go forward and never retrogade. The moral tone and justice of the people will forbid unlawful efforts to acquire additional territory. In the days of the first century, in the interest of slavery, criminal filibustering expeditions against our weak neighbors on the south were carried on with the connivance and encouragement of the leading political party for nearly one-quarter of the first century. If territory is hereafter added to our domain it will be acquired honorably, and in accordance with the desire of the inhabitants themselves of such territory. The annexation will be made in good faith and for the mutual benefit of both the parties.

The Protégé.—Slavery, as long as it lasted, was apologized for, and, as we have seen, catered to by the Democratic party on every occasion of a national election. After it was blotted out the leaders looked round for a substitute, one that had within it elements to attract the same or similar classes which held sway in the Jacobin clubs in 1796 (pp. 11, 12), and whose votes the then leaders had learned to utilize. They chose the liquor interest (pp. 205, 314–318), whose adherents had uniformly voted to sustain the Democracy, and in return their business was connived at or protected by legal enactments. In the cities, with scarcely an exception, the rum-sellers and their customers, and the keepers of gambling saloons and their frequenters, together with those who kept various disorderly establishments, all voted the same ticket.

Up to 1884 this protégé of the Democracy had been only local in its influence, but now the sagacious and prominent leaders of the party, seeing its power, determined to utilize it as an ally in national elections. They recognized that by catering to its demands it could be made to hold the balance of power between the two prominent political parties. With this design the National Convention of the party, held in Chicago, July 10, 1884, endeavored to dignify the liquor interest as a national question by indorsing it in these words: "We oppose *sumptuary laws* which vex the citizen and interfere with individual liberty." This entire platform was afterward reaffirmed by their National Convention held in St. Louis, June 7, 1888, and then again by their convention held in Chicago, June 21, 1892. The Republican National Convention held in Chicago, June 21, 1888, adopted the following: "The first concern of all good government is the virtue and sobriety of the people. The Republican party cordially sympathizes with all wise and well-directed efforts for the promotion of temperance and morality." Their National Convention held in Minneapolis, June 7, 1892, adopted the same sentiment in similar language.

The reader will notice the consummate skill used in the *wording* of these indorsements of the liquor interest. The convention did not dare enunciate its true meaning in plain unequivocal terms, but shrewdly used the expression " sumptuary laws," as though that phrase would add dignity to the business of the rum-seller when thus introduced as a factor in our national politics. In consequence of these indorsements of a great national party, the special adherents of this direful business are more aggressive, and their demands more exacting, to-day, in the *third year* of the Nation's second century, than ever before. Every good and patriotic citizen cherishes the hope that, in the rapid progress of general intelligence and pure morality among the American people, this national curse will, early in our second century, be so restrained as to be stripped of its pernicious influence and perhaps virtually banished from the land.

Danger to the Public Schools.—There appears at present only one source of anxiety to thoughtful minds who attempt to interpret the signs of the times: that is, the danger which threatens our grand national system of public schools. The latter can be virtually destroyed by perverting the funds raised by taxation for their support to aid *sectarian* schools. If one sect obtains such aid, why may not another, and thus the whole system, now so universal and perfect, be broken up piecemeal? Certain ecclesiastics are credited with devising the scheme, and the probability is that a party which.

for the sake of votes, catered to slavery, and does now to the liquor interest, would not hesitate, for the same reason, to break up the public-school system, since it is continually found fault with by these ecclesiastics, and in such manner as to prejudice or mislead the unintelligent.

The Lien.—The liquor interest has a political lien on the Democratic party. Note an instance wherein its power was recognized and duly honored. In the presidential canvass of 1884, Mr. Cleveland's self-respect forbid his specially endorsing, in his letter of acceptance, the liquor plank in the party's platform of that year, and, also, the same influence induced him when again a candidate in 1888 to ignore the same. In the latter year, however, David B. Hill ran for the governorship of the State of New York, and because of his *notoriously* avowed principles in favor of the liquor traffic, he was ardently supported by the saloons and their sympathizers. Hill carried the State by about 15,000 plurality, while Mr. Cleveland lost it by about the same number. Then, in 1892, came the third candidacy of the latter. In his letter of acceptance in that year Mr. Cleveland laid aside his self-respect and most cordially endorsed the *liquor plank* of the Chicago platform. By thus sacrificing his better principles, he obtained the full vote of the saloon interest, which gave him the State of New York and secured his election.

LII

DEMOCRATIC THEORIES REJECTED.

How often we see men engaged in the business of
life, who are uniformly unsuccessful, and notwithstanding their incessant labor there seems to hang
over them a pall of misfortune. Though many may
say in respect to individuals, They have been unfortunate because they lacked judgment or business
capacity,—yet if they have been pure and honest in
their endeavors to succeed, they deserve sympathy
rather than carping criticism. Do we hold a sentiment as charitable toward a combination of individuals—a railroad company or a political organization? We assume the latter to be patriotic in its
motives, though it may be misguided, and charity
falls back upon the presumption that it did the best
it could, but unfortunately knew no better. This is
strikingly exemplified in the present instance, since
with *only two exceptions* the American people in the
end have rejected the application of every theory
of Democratic Statesmen in respect to the practical
workings of the measures which they advocated, but,
on the contrary, adopted the measures which they
opposed, especially those that had a favorable influence upon the industries of the land, and also those
that from their nature and purpose, were adapted

and designed to confer success, happiness and comfort upon the people at large.

In order to substantiate this statement, we purpose in closing this brief history to give a summary—from the first to the last—of the measures whose passage through Congress the leading men of the Democracy strenuously opposed, but which have since, because of their intrinsic merits, become popular among the intelligent portion of the American people, and are now the fixed policy of the Nation. We shall not omit to notice the *two measures* that were introduced by Democratic statesmen into Congress, and by means of their votes carried through, which are now also the law of the land.

SUMMARY.

1. One of the most important measures of George Washington's administration, was that of the United States government's assuming and maintaining **Neutrality** in respect to wars between other nations; this measure, though bitterly opposed by the Democracy of that day, has since become the fixed policy of the Nation. [p. 9, 14, of this monograph.]

2. The encouragement given by the first two Presidents to our foreign **Commerce** and its protection by a **Navy**, and afterward the policy of **Internal Improvements** by the National government, were opposed in theory by Jefferson, Monroe, and other leaders of the same school of Statesmen. [p. 29, 39, 46, 51.]

3. Democratic Statesmen—North and South—uniformly promoted **Slavery** till the people blotted it out. [pp. 122-124 ; 162-165.]

4. *In only two instances—from 1801 to 1861—did Democratic Statesmen enact measures that have become the policy of the Nation. The one when they reduced from fourteen years to five the time of residence required of an alien in order to become a cit-*

izen. [p. 36.] *The other when they instituted the* **Sub-Treasury** *for keeping the money of the United States.* [p. 98.]

5. **Cheap Postage,** that boon to the people, was opposed more or less for years and years by the leaders of the Democracy in Congress [pp. 113—116.] but was gradually effected by their political opponents.

6. The **Homestead Law**—in the application of which nearly 8,000,000 of Americans, in families of old and young, are to-day enjoying happy homes would have no existence if Democratic Statesmen had had their way. [pp. 182, 188, 189]

7. A little in advance of the progressive movements of these Free Homestead settlements, was the threading of the unoccupied territories by **Railways,** in order to bring the settlers of the fertile regions into communication with the older portions of the country. And the routes were made **Transcontinental** to transport the vast commerce of the Pacific Coast and of Asia beyond. Democratic Statesmen from first to last bitterly opposed the land grants by which these railroads were built. [pp. 191,196.]

8. From the first, Democratic Statesmen for the most part opposed any system of Banking that could facilitate mercantile exchanges between the States—such as the last two **United States Banks,** and the present **National Banking System.** [p. 80, 84, 199.]

9. The Democratic members of Congress from 1875

to 1879 opposed in every available mode the **Resumption of Specie Payments**—the solid basis of our present business prosperity. [p. 264, 266—269.]

10. The same class of Statesmen in Congress opposed at every step the present **Law to Prevent Fraudulent Voting** when members of Congress or Presidential Electors are to be chosen. [p. 292—295.]

11. More prominently from 1846 to 1861 the leaders of the Democracy discriminated in their **Tariff Measures** against rather than in favor of the mechanical industries of the land. Since then the Nation has rejected that policy. [pp. 53, 55, 93, 118, 146, 147.]

12. The position of the Democracy on the **Liquor Question** is so well defined that it need not be further specified [p. 314], except to quote from the platform of its National Convention held in Chicago, July 8, 1884, the following: " We oppose sumptuary laws which vex the citizen and interfere with individual liberty " [pp. 212, 316, 321, 323].

13. The Democratic National Convention held in 1888 in St. Louis, reaffirmed this plank, thus continuing the liquor question in National politics. The Convention held in Chicago, in 1892, did the same.

INDEX.

APPENDIX.

NATURAL RESOURCES OF THE UNITED STATES.

By J. HARRIS PATTON, M.A., Ph.D.

8vo, Cloth, $3.00.
Sent by mail on receipt of price, post-paid.

In announcing this work the publishers would state that the subject has never before been so fully presented, since hitherto only the precious metals, coal, iron, and petroleum, have received the attention of writers.

" In so far as the object is attainable within the scope of a single tolerably thick volume, it has been accomplished. The book affords a sufficiently comprehensive and clear account of the matters treated."—*New York Tribune.*

" A great value of the work lies in its readableness, adapting it to the wants of intelligent people, and furnishing them with an account of their country that should be read by all who feel a pride in the tremendous national wealth of the nation."—*Iron Age, Philadelphia.*

" The American people have also an invaluable source of wealth and comfort in the copious rainfall in the great valley, and in the modified climate of its northwest portion. Both of these advantages are traced to the respective influences of the Atlantic and Pacific equatorial ocean currents, and which benefits are estimated to be of more value to the United States than to Europe and Asia combined."—*American Economist.*

" The work is most complete, and the labor expended in its preparation must have been very great. The volume is not only invaluable as a book of reference, but interesting to the general reader."—*The Mail, Toronto, Ont.*

" Every statesman and every political student should have this book at his elbow."—*Boston Herald.*

D. APPLETON & CO., Publishers,
NEW YORK

www.ingramcontent.com/pod-product-compliance
Lightning Source LLC
Chambersburg PA
CBHW022257280326
41932CB00010B/889